# University Builder

Edgar Odell Lovett in 1911, as founding president of the Rice Institute.
*Courtesy, Woodson Research Center, Fondren Library, Rice University.*

*Inscribed for Peter Brown,*
*welcome to Rice.*

# UNIVERSITY
# BUILDER

## EDGAR ODELL LOVETT
## AND THE FOUNDING OF THE
# RICE INSTITUTE

## JOHN B. BOLES

*John B. Boles*

LOUISIANA STATE UNIVERSITY PRESS  BATON ROUGE, LOUISIANA

Published by Louisiana State University Press
Manufactured in the United States of America
First printing

Designer: Tammi deGeneres
Typeface: Sabon
Typesetter: G&S Typesetters, Inc.
Printer and binder: Thomson-Shore, Inc.

Library of Congress Cataloging-in-Publication Data
Boles, John B.
    University builder : Edgar Odell Lovett and the founding of the Rice Institute / John B.
Boles.
      p.   cm.
    Includes bibliographical references and index.
    ISBN-13: 978-0-8071-3275-3 (cloth : alk. paper)
      1. Lovett, Edgar Odell, 1871–1957.  2 Rice University—Presidents—Biography.
3. College presidents—Texas—Biography.   4. William M. Rice Institute—History.
I. Title.
    LD6053.B65   2007
    378.1′11—dc22
    [B]                                                                    2007004411

The Rice Institute seal is reprinted by the express permission of Rice University.
A subvention by the Rice Historical Society allowed publication of the gallery of
illustrations following page 80.

For
Nancy
David and Steffi
Matthew, Janica, and Parker

*The building of a great university is just like the living of a great life. Each calls for the intellect, energy, courage, and independence that characterize the other.*

*Edgar Odell Lovett,*
*Matriculation Address,*
*Rice Institute, 1917*

# CONTENTS

*Illustrations follow page 80.*

# FOREWORD

WHEN OUR FAMILY MOVED from the Boston area to Houston in 1985, we looked forward to the adventure of living in and learning about a new city. We were especially pleased at the way Houston welcomed newcomers. Even if native Houstonians always occupied a special niche, fresh arrivals were readily accepted and quickly absorbed into a city accustomed to vigorous expansion in and around the occasioned economic downturn. As I became fond of responding to friends and colleagues from the Northeast when they asked how I was adjusting to my new location, "Houston is a lot less provincial than Boston."

Of course, Rice University was also a new experience for us. But I had over the years become acquainted with high-quality American higher education. While Rice certainly has its distinctive qualities, it also has striking family resemblances with other leading colleges and universities, in particular with Princeton, where I had studied as an undergraduate.

There was a further reason that Rice felt quite familiar: I had an excellent tutor who guided me into its core values and traditions. His name is Edgar Odell Lovett, the university builder who is the subject of John Boles's excellent biography of the first president of Rice University. As this biography makes clear, "first president" is far too limited a characterization. Lovett, who was president of Rice from 1908 (four years before it opened) until 1946 (five years after he tendered his resignation), set the course that the university continues to follow today.

As for my tutorial from Lovett, it took the form of my reading with deep admiration what he had to say about his ambitious plans, his vision, for Rice. The tutorial began with the three-volume *Book of the Opening* that Lovett arranged to have published as the record of the inauguration of Rice in its first academic year, 1912. Catherine Hannah, a member of the search committee that convinced me to join the Rice community, gave me this rare and cherished set of volumes in the spring before I assumed my duties at Rice. She noted that I might find it helpful in understanding and appreciating Rice. What an understatement!

While the entire three-volume set is astonishing in its reach, the most remarkable address is Lovett's "The Meaning of the New Institution." In its printed form, Lovett's address comprises eighty-seven pages (not counting campus plans, photographs, reproductions of congratulatory citations from other universities, and other plates). It is extraordinary in its breadth and depth. It ranges across the history of education and research worldwide and also quite specifically in the United States. And it unambiguously expresses aspirations for Rice to be among the world's premier institutions of higher learning.

John Boles recounts how Lovett and Rice pursued that aspiration for the almost forty years of his presidency. He does not refrain from acknowledging the occasional lapse from what in retrospect he and others of us who are Rice partisans might view as a preferred course of action. But his account leaves no doubt that Lovett was a formidable leader who laid the foundation and shaped the prospective trajectory of a marvelous institution. I am delighted to recommend *University Builder: Edgar Odell Lovett and the Founding of the Rice Institute* to any and all readers. And on behalf of all of us who will be his grateful readers, I thank John Boles for telling a terrific story about an exceptional leader of an extraordinary institution.

GEORGE RUPP
President of Rice University, 1985–1993
President of Columbia University, 1993–2002
President of the International Rescue Committee, 2002–present

# PREFACE

IN PRACTICALLY ANY LISTING of the nation's outstanding academic institutions, Rice University ranks generally in the top twenty, one of only two or three southern universities to do so. Moreover, it is both the newest and the smallest university in the nation to merit such ranking. And it is located in a state that for many Americans is stereotyped as the antithesis of thoughtful scholarship and where the biggest is always equated with the best. Yet those in the know about higher education are fully aware that Rice University is an academic gem. How did this apparent paradox come to be—a small, carefully planned, intensely academic institution deep in the heart of Texas?

Perhaps more than with the case of any other university in the United States, Rice University is the outgrowth of the vision, direction, and leadership of one man, Edgar Odell Lovett. In some ways the history of the university whose development he oversaw seems to fit Texas stereotypes: the story begins with great wealth, a murder, then a sensational trial. But in Lovett's hands the university—only vaguely conceived by its benefactor, William Marsh Rice—acquired a character, an ethos, that has guided it from its opening in 1912 to the present. Lovett had two earned doctorates to go along with teaching experience at Johns Hopkins University, the University of Virginia, the University of Chicago, and Princeton University when he was chosen the founding president of the Rice Institute—still only a proposition on paper—and he immediately set forth on a round-the-globe trip to learn about best educational practices at the world's greatest universities. These were significant years in the evolution of the modern university, and Lovett was fully aware that in the past half century three important developments had occurred in American higher education. In the years just before the Civil War, natural science and engineering had begun to find a place in university curricula; in the next decade or two, university leaders tentatively at first then more confidently articulated a utilitarian purpose to higher education; and by the last two decades of the nineteenth century the most innovative universities—borrowing from recent European institutions—had begun to promote active research agendas, pioneering the role of universities in the expansion of knowledge. Lovett's conception of the university—which included these three significant developments—matured and expanded in the course of this trip, and he returned to Houston filled with ideals, ambition, and plans. The rest, as the cliché puts it, is history. And it is the history of that academic adventure, one so different from the story of all other southern academic institutions, that is the topic of this joint biography of Edgar Odell Lovett and the university he created.

UNIVERSITY BUILDER

# CHAPTER ONE

# DUAL BEGINNINGS

EDGAR ODELL LOVETT said or wrote very little about his parents or his childhood in the small northeastern Ohio town of Shreve, population 1,200, where he grew up. He once remarked that "I come of a race of teachers and preachers," but he said no more of that inheritance, except that his paternal grandfather "was widely read in our beautiful science [mathematics]." His mother's great-grandparents had immigrated from Alsace, France, in the early nineteenth century and settled in Wayne County, Ohio, where they became staunch "Northern Republicans." His father's parents, who had emigrated from Virginia to Ohio, remained determined "Southern Democrats." That little, and nothing more, was the substance of his autobiographical reflections. Edgar was born the first son of Zephaniah Lovett and Maria Elizabeth Speng Lovett on April 14, 1871; three years later his brother Guy D. completed the family. Zephaniah was a surveyor and lumber dealer, with no known proclivities for higher education. According to family tradition, Maria, a prize-winning quilter, was a severe taskmaster.

Young Edgar must have shown marked ability in mathematics at an early age, and, after a childhood infatuation with becoming a surveyor too, in his early teens he envisioned attending Ohio University to study engineering. But his devout parents had other thoughts. His Methodist father and his Lutheran mother each wanted him to attend a school of their denomination, so they compromised on a small church-affiliated college in nearby Bethany, West Virginia, in that tiny sliver of the state that protrudes northward between Pennsylvania and Ohio. Bethany College was a liberal arts college established by Alexander Campbell, the founder of the Christian Church (Disciples of Christ), and his "seminary of learning" had been duly chartered by the Commonwealth of Virginia in 1840 before there was a *West* Virginia. It had become co-educational in 1877, though women took a separate curriculum. Then as now it was beautifully sited amid the hills and forests of a small village, along Buffalo Creek, about a mile from Campbell's home, and several of its original buildings still stand exactly as young Lovett first saw them in the fall of 1886 when as a fifteen-year-old student he began his academic career. He had actually graduated from high school "with first honors" on May 28, 1885, but, as Lovett's father later wrote, his parents "on account of his delicate health kept him out of School one year." They may have really thought that at the age of fourteen he was simply too young to go away to college.

As with most small colleges at the time, Bethany provided no dormitories, and so Lovett roomed at one of several privately run boarding houses down the hill from the main collegiate building near the intersection of the road past Campbell's home and the road to Pittsburgh, some fifty miles to the northeast. Lovett worked his way through college with a job that involved picking up and delivering laundry to other students. During his sophomore year he became a "local" editor of the college's literary magazine, the *Bethany Collegian,* writing news of alumni and happenings both on campus and in the surrounding village, interspersed with witty sayings. By his senior year Lovett was editor-in-chief as well as business manager, although contaminated water had made him ill at the beginning of the year and for a short while he was unable to perform his editorial duties. Later in the year he received a telegram that his father was ill, so once again he had to forgo his editing responsibilities for a short while—he and his brother Guy, by then a freshman at Bethany, both returned home to be with their father.

Probably in his freshman year Edgar had also joined the Neotrophian Literary Society, founded in 1841 and possessing its own hall for student meetings and staged debates on various subjects of the day—an institution characteristic of collegiate life in the nineteenth century. Here on October 15, 1888, Lovett practiced his speaking skills with his first society declamation, entitled "The Singleness of Purpose," and although the text of the talk is lost, the title was eerily prescient of his later career. He would give his second oration on February 22, 1890, in celebration of George Washington's birthday, and on this occasion his title, "Born of the Ages," gives some hint of his message. Another student, describing the talk in an issue of the *Bethany Collegian,* reported that Lovett "clothed his thought in most beautiful figurative language," a style beloved at the time though it seems almost baroque today. Bethany had a chapter of the Beta Theta Pi fraternity, and Lovett was a member. Lovett also found time to play the violin. A fellow student remembered that he had composed a song for the Neotrophian Literary Society and fondly recalled Lovett accompanying the members' singing of it with "sweet strains" from his violin, while a brief notice in the *Collegian* for May 1889 mentioned Lovett's performing in a concert at the local Presbyterian church. Both public speaking and the enjoyment of music would characterize Lovett's future career.

Bethany College grew to slightly more than a hundred students while Lovett was enrolled, with a faculty of eleven, including the president emeritus. The academic program consisted of four separate tracks—a classical, scientific, ministerial, and ladies' curriculum—with only the classical track concluding with a bachelor of arts degree. The classical track, which Lovett took, had set courses in six categories: sacred history and moral philosophy; Greek language; Latin language and literature; mathematics and astronomy; natural science; and mental, moral, and political philosophy, along with belles lettres. The various categories of classes were offered by what were termed Schools. For example, under the auspices of the School of Sacred History and Moral Philosophy, students in the classical curriculum studied the Bible in English translation for at least two years, and the moral philosophy was "drawn from the Bible itself." Instruction in the School of the Greek Language began with a semester of basic grammar, followed over the next seven semesters by close reading of Xenophon, Homer, Pinder, Lucian, Plato, Sophocles, and Thucydides, concluding with lectures on Greek civilization. During his final two years Lovett served as a tutor in Greek. The Latin curriculum was similar, beginning with basic grammar and writing exercises, followed by readings in Caesar, Sallust, Cicero, Horace, Livy, Vigil, and Tacitus, finishing with lectures on Latin of the middle ages. Most of the language instruction utilized the recitation model, emphasizing basic translation. For the remainder of his life Lovett enjoyed reading the classics, and he would constantly mine these sources for quotations and illustrations to use in his public addresses.

The courses of the School of Mathematics and Astronomy swept from beginning algebra and plane geometry, through solid geometry, trigonometry, on to differential and integral calculus. Only in the senior year were there courses in mechanics and astronomy. Natural sciences were begun in the second year, and over the following six semesters students enrolled in physiology, zoology and botany, chemistry, geology, and, during the senior year, two semesters of physics. The School of Mental, Moral, and Political Philosophy offered courses only for a student's final two years. The junior year consisted mainly of rhetoric, with some attention to English literature. During the senior year attention was paid, in quick succession, to metaphysics, philosophy, physiological psychology, logic, moral philosophy, the U.S. Constitution, political economy, philology, the history of civilization, and, at the very end, Christian evidences. The faculty were teachers, not researchers who discovered new knowledge, and the students were expected to learn by drill and recitation, with the emphasis on memorization, not creativity. A science teacher might demonstrate something in a lab, but students did not themselves do laboratory work. Still, able, determined students—such as Lovett—gained from such a curriculum an admirable breadth of knowledge, although it was a curriculum that evoked the past rather than anticipated the future needs of an industrializing and urbanizing nation. Certainly Lovett benefited from the scope of his Bethany education, but his later graduate work, along with his teaching and travel, would transform his ideas of education.

Edgar Odell Lovett assuredly made the most of his opportunities at Bethany College, making the "Honor List" as the only student earning summa cum laude status, and he graduated with his B.A. in 1890 as class valedictorian. (Years later a former teacher told Lovett that he had been "an inspiration" to have in class.) His valedictory address, reprinted in full in the June 1890 issue of the *Bethany Collegian*, reveals only the fashion of his oratory—flowery, overwrought by today's standards, mainly a sentimental paean to dear old alma mater—and practically nothing of the quality of his mind or the direction of his career. Perhaps his ambition had not yet been kindled, for that fall he took what seems a cautious choice and accepted a position as "professor" of mathematics and natural sciences at another small college, West Kentucky College, founded in 1886 in Mayfield, Kentucky, and, like

Bethany College, under the auspices of the Christian Church. There for two years he taught primarily mathematics, but given the small size of the faculty and the breadth of Lovett's education, he also taught Greek. Nothing else is known of his career at West Kentucky College, but a notice in the local newspaper, the *Mayfield Monitor,* of May 25, 1892, about the upcoming "closing exercises" of the spring semester revealed that in the musical program, "Prof. Lovett" would be playing violin in a quartet consisting also of a pianist, a flutist, and an organist. Among the primarily student musicians and soloists was one of Lovett's students, Mary Ellen Hale, daughter of Major Henry Stevenson Hale, a prominent Mayfield banker, a former state senator, the current state treasurer, and one of the trustees of the college. Miss Hale was considered a beauty of more than local fame, and she would later be featured in a photographic spread on "Representative Kentucky Belles" in the June 28, 1896, issue of the *Louisville Courier-Journal,* the state's leading newspaper. Five years following their joint musical performance, Lovett—after earning two doctorates and joining the faculty of Princeton University—would return to Mayfield and on December 23, 1897, (in, according to the local newspaper, "one of the prettiest weddings ever seen in Mayfield") marry Mary, who had, in the interval, continued her musical training at the Cincinnati Conservatory of Music. They both would share a lifelong love of music, and it is tempting to imagine that the young professor (only twenty-one) and the coed fell in love while practicing for that graduation musicale—they had actually met in September 1890, Lovett's first month in Mayfield. (Incidentally, West Kentucky College closed in 1910, its two buildings becoming the Mayfield high school, so it is not the forerunner of today's Western Kentucky University in Bowling Green, Kentucky.)

During the spring semester of Edgar Odell Lovett's first year at West Kentucky College, another academic venture had an uncertain beginning a thousand miles to the southwest in the small Texas city of Houston. In 1839 a young, enterprising merchant from Massachusetts named William Marsh Rice had come to Houston after a short stay in the island port city of Galveston. Rice proved to have a genius for making money, and from his primary business as an import-export merchant to his

investments in land, railroads, hotels, and cottonseed oil mills, everything he touched seemed to prosper. He was already a wealthy man by
the outbreak of the Civil War—the 1859 credit rating of Rice by R. G.
Dun and Company, the predecessor of Dun & Bradstreet, characterized him as "One of the best men in the state, has ample means to pay
all his debts. Very rich and good for all purchases"—but Rice understood that the Union blockade would hamper his primary trade, so he
resolved to move his operations to Matamoros, Mexico, just across the
Rio Grande border and beyond the reach of the blockade. Hence William Marsh Rice continued to prosper even during the terrible carnage
of the Civil War that left so much of the South devastated. Shortly after the war Rice moved back to Houston, married a widow, Elizabeth
Baldwin Brown (his second wife), and, Houston being in the midst of a
yellow fever epidemic, the two left almost instantly for residence first in
New York City and later in nearby New Jersey.

The couple never resided again in Houston, though they occasionally
returned for social and family reasons, with Rice himself making more
frequent trips to oversee his various investments and businesses. Sometime in the late 1870s or early 1880s, Rice, who had dropped out of
school at age fifteen, became acquainted with Girard College in Philadelphia, which provided free boarding and education to white orphan
boys. For a time Rice considered establishing a similar home near his
farm in New Jersey, going so far as to draw up a will in 1882 leaving
money to establish the William M. Rice Orphans' Institute. About the
same time he came to learn something about the Cooper Institute in
New York City, which offered technical instruction to male students
and "instruction in the arts of design" to female students. Perhaps the
business careers of both Stephen Girard and Peter Cooper had caught
Rice's attention, and he may in some way have identified with them and
wanted to emulate their gifts to society. Obviously Rice was thinking
in the 1880s about not only what he would leave to posterity but about
the importance of education.

But there were real educational needs in Houston, the city where
Rice had made his fortune. On one of his periodical visits to the city,
perhaps as early as 1886 or 1887 but more likely in 1890, Rice met, as
he usually did, with one of his old friends, Cesar Maurice Lombardi,

who had immigrated to the United States from Switzerland and arrived in Houston in 1870, soon to become a prominent merchant and cotton factor. Lombardi served as president of the Houston school board, so he was fully aware of how abysmal the education facilities were in the city. His efforts to pressure the City Council for money to build a municipal high school had been summarily rebuffed on the grounds that "a High School was a highfaluting nonsense." Lombardi now turned to Rice and proposed that he provide funds to erect a public high school for the citizens of the city (implicitly meaning the white citizens) in which he had made his fortune. Rice was so preoccupied with business matters at the moment that he gave little thought to the request, but he asked Lombardi to send him some materials so that he could consider the issue more carefully back home in New York. No doubt Lombardi expected little to come of his request when Rice left. The following spring Rice returned to Houston, again on business, and another of his old friends, Emanuel Raphael, also a member of the Houston school board, talked to Rice about his funding a public high school building for Houston—almost surely Raphael and Lombardi had discussed the issue between themselves and developed a consistent rationale to lay before Rice. Such a high school could be his gift to posterity. Rice respected both men and had known them long and well. Raphael, whose father, Samuel Raphael, had migrated to Texas from England before the Civil War and served as rabbi at Congregation Beth Israel, was currently chief cashier of a major Houston bank and president of the Houston Electric Light and Power Company.

Again Rice turned down the proposal that he fund a high school, essentially saying to Raphael, as he had earlier to Lombardi, that he thought such a facility was the responsibility of the city of Houston itself. But he clearly had been pondering the educational needs of the city since his previous year's conversation with Lombardi, and probably drawing on what he knew of Girard College and the Cooper Union, Rice told Raphael that he wanted to establish a different kind of educational institution, one that featured lectures, instruction in various vocational endeavors, a public library, and several other useful functions. After further discussion, Rice requested that Raphael help him draft a proposal incorporating his wishes and asked him to serve as a trustee of the proposed institute along with Rice himself and five other prominent Houstonians: Rice's personal attorney, James A. Baker; Cesar M. Lombardi; Frederick Allyn Rice, the founder's brother; Alfred S. Richardson, a director (along with Rice himself) of the Houston and Texas Central Railway; and James E. McAshan, a young banker. These prominent businessmen were able, widely respected, progressive in their attitudes, and surprisingly cosmopolitan—indeed, two of them were from Europe, and Raphael was a leading Jewish layperson at a time when most American (and English) universities flagrantly discriminated against Jews.

Presumably the formal "Charter of Incorporation of the William Marsh Rice Institute for the Advancement of Literature, Science, and Art" was drawn up largely by Rice's lawyer, James A. (called Captain) Baker, and on May 13, 1891, the seven trustees signed the document, including a deed of indenture for $200,000 (an interest-bearing note) that Rice put up as earnest money toward the endowment. Rice insisted that nothing was to be done in terms of actually developing the planned institute until after his death—he would continue making money that would eventually benefit the endeavor. In fact, because Rice himself had little experience with academic institutions and the other six trustees were more accomplished as businessmen than as educators, the precise purpose of the newly chartered Rice Institute was frustratingly vague. No doubt the other trustees were just as glad nothing was to be done at present because it was not evident exactly what Rice intended. The charter did not mention the words *college* or *university*. The stated object was to be "the establishment and maintenance, in the City of Houston, Texas, of a Public Library, and the maintenance of an Institution for the Advancement of Literature, Science, Art, Philosophy and Letters; the establishment and maintenance of a Polytechnic school; for procuring and maintaining scientific collections; collections of chemical and philosophical apparatus, mechanical and artistic models, drawings, pictures and statues; and for cultivating other means of instruction for the white inhabitants of the City of Houston, and State of Texas." Moreover, this instruction was to be offered, at no charge, to both males and females. Was this then to be a vocational school? A polytechnic institute? Was it to be for instruction only and not for the discovery of new information? The trustees did not know, and William

Marsh Rice offered little clarification. (In a deed assigning property to the institute in 1892 he offhandedly referred to the charter as establishing a polytechnic school. Probably Rice himself had no higher aim than that.) The only thing certain was the $200,000 indenture secured to underwrite the endeavor that would come to fruition sometime in the indefinite future. And the institution was pledged to be nonpartisan and nonsectarian—completely independent.

By strange coincidence, the next year, Edgar Odell Lovett, in graduate school at the University of Virginia, happened to see a notice in a local newspaper of the incorporation of the Rice Institute and its financial underwriting. "On reading the announcement," he remembered years later, "I did what any university educator would have done in the circumstances. I threw the paper down and said to myself: 'Another case of misdirected effort in American education,' for here again it seemed to be proposed that the cultivation of the whole wide field of human knowledge should be committed to as many as two endowed professorships." A foolish effort, it seemed to him at the time, that would amount to little.

There is no indication of whether it was his teaching at West Kentucky College that ignited in young Lovett a strong desire to continue his formal education or whether that intention had developed during his student days at Bethany College and he simply first had to earn some money. Clearly most who knew him at Bethany expected great things of him. But whenever his ambition took root, he resigned after two years of teaching at West Kentucky and traveled east in the fall of 1892 to begin graduate work in astronomy at the University of Virginia in Charlottesville. For three years he held the rank of instructor in astronomy there and worked at the university's renowned Leander J. McCormick Observatory under the direction of astronomer Ormond Stone. Compared to Lovett's first two institutions, Virginia was a large and complex university. As later events would indicate, Lovett was greatly impressed by the architectural consistency of the lovely Thomas Jefferson–designed campus. In his final year there, enrollment had grown to 562 students, all male. Its library contained 54,000 volumes, so crowding the stacks that it was difficult to remove a volume. There was both a law school and a medical school, and the School of Theoretical and Practical Astronomy, established in 1882–1883 in anticipation of the completion of the observatory the next year, had the faculty and the equipment to offer instruction in the general principles of astronomy, the "theory of meridian and equatorial instruments, the methods of determining time, latitude, and longitude, right ascensions and declinations, the formation of star catalogues, the computation of orbits, and every other higher aspect of the science." The faculty members were expected to teach and conduct research as well, thereby adding "to the sum of general knowledge of the stars and of the laws that governed those heavenly bodies."

Lovett's coursework was not narrowly limited to astronomy, however. In his first session, 1892–1893, he took what was apparently a lecture course in astronomy taught by Stone and a similar-level course in mathematics taught by Professor Charles S. Venable (who was also both interested in and trained in astronomy). During Lovett's second session the following academic year he took the graduate courses Stone and Venable offered in their respective fields (including celestial mechanics, calculus, and analytical geometry) and a general course in applied mathematics (essentially mechanics) taught by Professor William M. Thornton of the School of Applied Mathematics (which in time became the School of Engineering). Lovett's third year of coursework was even more varied. Again he took a non-graduate course from Thornton, another graduate course in astronomy (apparently practical observational astronomy) from Stone, and a course in moral philosophy and ethics from Professor Noah K. Davis and one in natural philosophy from Professor Francis H. Smith (natural philosophy was essentially physics, not philosophy as understood today, with an emphasis on sound and light, electricity and magnetism, and laboratory work in experimental science). All in all, Lovett had fairly broad training in several scientific disciplines.

This new scientific environment exhilarated Lovett. His first professional paper was on his observations of comets, satellites, and double stars, but he soon moved more in the direction of mathematics, his scientific first love. His dissertation at Virginia, awarded in 1895, concerned "The Great Inequality of Jupiter and Saturn," and in published form it occupied a double number of the *American Astronomical Journal.* The topic had been suggested by the eminent mathematical astronomer George W. Hill, who, as director of the Nautical Almanac Office in Cambridge, Massachusetts, was engaged in an elaborate recomputation of all the orbital movements of the solar system and was particularly concerned with the complicated orbits of Jupiter and Saturn. On December 19, 1893, Hill, having heard of the mathematical skills of a certain astronomy graduate student at Virginia, wrote to Professor Stone, director of the McCormick Observatory there and founder of the *Annals of Mathematics,* suggesting the topic for Lovett. Hill recommended that Lovett, for his dissertation, consider working out "The Great Inequalities of Jupiter & Saturn," pointing out that all who had previously worked on the problem had failed, but "I should think Mr. Lovett would have no difficulty in pursuing it."

So young Lovett took this suggested topic and completed it with dispatch, finishing his work in time for his doctorate in 1895 (having already earned his M.A. along the way). In the midst of this academic regimen he found time to return to Shreve, Ohio, on November 23, 1894, to be named a Master Mason by the Garfield Lodge, No. 528, of Free and Accepted Masons, although he never appeared to be active in the brotherhood. A fellow student more than a quarter century later recalled Lovett at Virginia playing his violin to accompany the correspondent's clarinet. And somehow Lovett sustained a long-distance courtship with Mary Ellen Hale. Clearly he was, as a classmate recalled almost a half century later, "a man of great energy and vigor." His personal papers contain dozens of small notebooks whose pages are filled with careful ink-written notes and mathematical calculations, all in tiny, scrupulous script.

By now Lovett recognized that mathematics was his true calling, and in an era when the greatest universities were German, Lovett left Charlottesville to pursue further graduate training abroad. After a quick visit in June to Cleveland, where his parents now lived, and to Mayfield, Kentucky, to see Mary Ellen Hale again, he set out in the summer of 1895—crossing the Atlantic aboard the SS *Werkendam*—to attend the University of Leipzig, founded in 1409, among whose graduates was astronomer Tycho Brahe. Surely Lovett's mathematics professor at Virginia, Charles S. Venable, who had spent a sabbatical year in 1852 studying mathematics and astronomy in Berlin and Bonn, helped convince him that he should continue his mathematics education in Germany, perhaps even suggesting Leipzig. En route to Leipzig, the birthplace of Leibnitz, the co-inventor of differential and integral calculus in the seventeenth century, Lovett, by one of those incredible coincidences that often enliven history, met in Frankfurt another American graduate student, Lindsey Blayney, from Kentucky (and Lovett felt almost like a Kentuckian now, after his two years in Mayfield and his attachment to Mary and her large family there). The two Americans parted, Blayney to study at several European universities before earning his doctorate at Heidelberg in philology and comparative literature, and Lovett to Leipzig, where he officially enrolled on November 9, 1895. Years later they would be back together again in distant Texas.

Shortly after getting settled in Leipzig, a rich, booming, confident, and ambitious city with magnificent public buildings and townhouses and a population of about 400,000, Lovett penned a letter to Mary back in Mayfield, assuring her that "I am true to you" even though they were separated by thousands of miles. He shared with her his loneliness—"I know how your heart aches sometimes for don't I know how my own does. Do hope that you can write me every day as you thought you would." He attempted to justify his decision to come to Leipzig to earn a second doctorate. "I want you to be happy. That's what I want to live for. That as much as anything else brought me to Germany. The hope that it would put me in command of a position where I could make you happy. I mean to have no fears for I trust you. I wish we could be there together but I must be here and work."

At the University of Leipzig the great geometer Felix Klein had between 1880 and 1885 developed an eminent research center in mathematics. But illness and then depression afflicted Klein, and he left Leipzig in 1885 to go to the University of Göttingen, where he subsequently created a famous mathematics program. When Klein departed, university officials called another eminent mathematician, the creative geometer Sophus Lie of the University of Christiana in Christiania (renamed Oslo in 1924), Norway. Lie and Klein had met in Paris back in 1870 and had begun there a fruitful collaboration. So by the time Lovett arrived in Leipzig, the city of Bach, Mendelssohn, and Goethe, Klein had left for Göttingen, taking a number of students with him, but in the words of Lovett, "those who stayed to study under Lie got more." Just several years before, in 1892, the collaborative relationship and even friendship between Klein and Lie had completely broken down. Lie, however, did not find Leipzig to his liking; he was plagued with homesickness for his homeland, and he was apparently already suffering from the pernicious anemia that would eventually cause his death in 1899. A man who loved the outdoors, he sorely missed the forests and mountains of Norway. Nevertheless, in the 1890s Lie made Leipzig the leading attraction for Americans seeking further mathematical training, along with students from around the world. Almost twenty American students attended his lectures in the mid-1890s, and six, including Lovett, completed their doctorates under his supervision.

While Lovett was studying with Lie, Lie returned to Christiania for a portion of the spring semester of 1896, taking a group of his Leipzig students with him. Decades later Lovett would recall as "happy days" those weeks attending Professor Lie's lectures in Christiania. He remembered with especial fondness that on Saturday mornings Lie would come to the apartment Lovett shared with another graduate student, Karl Carda from Austria, and "urge us to spend the entire day walking in the beautiful environs of the city, concluding his exhortation by saying, 'Der Geist must auch schlafen!'" Lovett and Carda went to Lie's home for math tutorials. Lie would return permanently to Christiania in 1898 to a special chair created for him, but Lovett finished writing his second doctorate, in mathematics, at the University of Leipzig on July 4, 1896. Lie had been a spirited but informal teacher. Almost forty years later Lovett recalled in a speech having once asked Lie what he considered "the essential qualities of mind necessary" to being a great mathematician, and Lie had replied without hesitation: "energy, imagination, self-confidence, and self-criticism," an aphorism that Lovett had sought to apply to his own life.

The mathematics department at Leipzig then was housed in two buildings. One location, at Bruderstrasse 32, contained the model collection and a large lecture hall; the second location, at Ritterstrasse 24, inside what had once been the medieval city wall and less than a block from the impressive Nicholaikirche, contained reading rooms, seminar/ workshops, and the departmental library. During his first semester Lovett rented a room at Talstrasse 4, nearer the Ritterstrasse department, but in his second semester he moved to Ferdinand Rhodestrasse 21, more convenient to the Bruderstrasse facilities and only three blocks from the impressive new university library, with over 500,000 volumes, which had just moved into its handsome neoclassical building in 1891.

Because of the meticulous record keeping of Germany universities at the time, it is possible to reconstruct Lovett's career. During his first semester, October 15, 1895, through March 14, 1896, he—according to a curriculum vitae he later prepared—attended a lecture course in experimental physics, with emphasis on heat and electricity, from physics professor Gustaf Wiedermann; a course on optical instruments from astronomy professor Heinrich Bruns, director of the Leipzig observatory, who was also very interested in mathematics and geodesy; a course in differential equations and transformation theory from his mentor Sophus Lie; a course in differential and integral calculus from mathematician Adolph Mayer, a longtime friend of both Klein and Lie who had played a major role in attracting Lie to Leipzig; and a course in the theory of linear differential equations from a math lecturer, Georg Scheffers (a former Lie student himself). During Lovett's second semester, beginning April 15 and officially ending August 15, 1896, he completed another course in experimental physics, with emphasis on general physics, acoustics, and optics, with Wiedermann; a seminar on the theory of astronomical instruments taught by Bruns; a seminar on partial differential equations offered by Mayer; and a lecture course exploring the applications of differential and integral calculus to astronomy by Scheffers. Lie's seminar on geometry was offered in part in Christiania. The extremely studious Lovett finished writing his dissertation—entitled "The Theory of Perturbations and Lie's Theory of Contact Transformations"—on U.S. Independence Day, 1896, whereupon Lie recommended acceptance of Lovett's work with a grade of III (it seems that I's and II's were uncommon, so Lovett's grade was average) and permitted him to proceed to his oral examination. There Lie, Mayer, and Wiedermann examined him in mathematics and physics. In his oral exam, on

December 4, 1896, Lovett did somewhat better, earning a grade of II, hence passing with the honor of cum laude. His formal academic training was now complete.

It is unclear the extent to which Lovett entered into the style of student life characteristic of Germany university communities. In the spring of 1896, one of his former professors at Virginia (William H. Echols, an adjunct professor in the School of Applied Mathematics who became a lifelong friend) had written Lovett: "I hope you will during your stay in Germany cultivate a fine taste for beer—I do not know which I envy you the most—the beer or the mathematical opportunities." Long a popular student hangout in Leipzig was the Auerbachs Keller, the city's most famous tavern that had been founded in 1525 and immortalized in Goethe's *Faust* as the place where Mephistopheles tricked the local topers by disappearing into thin air. Lovett's mother's Lutheran faith would have accepted beer-drinking, but his father's Methodism would have frowned upon it, as did the Christian Church (Disciples of Christ) that Lovett had adopted as his denomination while at Bethany College. So despite the attractions of Auerbachs Keller, it is difficult to imagine Lovett spending a lot of time raising a stein in student song at a beer hall, for he seems to have concentrated relentlessly on mathematics, finishing in little over a year with honors. But he later indicated indirectly that at least on occasion he had enjoyed the German brewers' art when he jokingly mentioned to his former University of Virginia mentor in 1897 that he needed "a glass of—say lemonade to 'steady my legs'—for I'm not drinking beer in America."

The University of Leipzig at the time had approximately three thousand students, and during the 1890s more than fifty American students registered at Leipzig each semester, not counting auditors, but if Lovett met or befriended any of these fellow Americans, the record is silent. At Leipzig he did give up his favorite pastime, playing the violin, discovering amid the rigors of doing mathematics—at least at the pace of graduate school—that he "could no longer serve two masters." Accordingly, he "denied" himself the opportunity of developing further his skills on the violin and put it aside, never to take it up again seriously (he probably did not realize the finality of his decision at the time, although his love of listening to good music never waned). Surely he heard the famous Thomanerchor (boys' choir) sing Bach at the local Thomaskirche, where Bach himself had been the organist and choral conductor throughout the second quarter of the eighteenth century, but if so, he never mentioned it. The student Lovett concentrated on his math, winning the respect and affection of his teacher and his fellow students. He mentioned, with a disclaimer of modesty, to his former Virginia mentor in a letter on August 3, 1896, that "Six of us ate a farewell dinner the other day—German, Russian, Austrian, Frenchman, Norwegian, and American. The fellows voted that I had been Lie's favorite student of the year." (In 1908 Lovett's wife would visit the widow of Professor Lie in Stockholm, and following that pleasant visit Mary Lovett wrote to her young daughter that, according to Mrs. Lie, "her husband loved daddie better than any of his other students," and she too still had fond memories of him.)

In early 1897, his second Ph.D. in hand, with a dissertation on "Contact Formations and their Relations to Perturbations" in 187 meticulously handwritten pages, Lovett began his return to the United States, pausing only to attend a set of mathematics lectures at the University of Paris.* He had bought and was bringing back with him "a magnificent working library," which, he remarked, almost required that he return on "an emigrant ticket." But he also brought back for his fiancé a beautiful piece of jewelry—interlocking circles enclosing precious

---

* At the university then, as now, according to Jens Blecher, the current University of Leipzig archivist, the regulation said that one received the title of *doctor* at the moment one passed the last exam—for Lovett, that was December 4, 1896. Technically, however, when Lovett returned to the United States he had not yet received the formal certificate that officially marked the receipt of his doctorate because he failed to pay a mandatory graduation fee equivalent to about $1,800, a hefty fee (probably about double a student's annual living expenses) that often deterred students. He also did not completely fill out a required form, and he failed to submit a required curriculum vitae. In 1898, however, Lovett asked to be reinstated and paid the graduation fee (he had been teaching at Johns Hopkins University and the University of Virginia and now had the money); the Leipzig authorities gave him a reprieve on December 30 and officially awarded the degree. Lovett finally sent in a vitae on April 16, 1899, dotting the final *i* and crossing the final *t* on his student career at Leipzig. Procancellar (university official responsible for overseeing all formalities related to doctoral degrees) Karl Lamprecht, an eminent historian, signed the official university acceptance of Lovett's doctoral paperwork.

stones. He returned as well with a strong appreciation of European culture. No narrow provincialism could survive a year in Leipzig with its
rich traditions of music and scholarship, and Lovett came back to the
United States a convinced internationalist with cosmopolitan attitudes
that would mark his approach to education the remainder of his life.

Back in the United States in the spring of 1897—after a quick trip to
Mayfield, Kentucky, to see Mary—Lovett spent a part of the year as a
fellow in mathematics at Johns Hopkins University and simultaneously
was appointed a lecturer in mathematics at the University of Virginia,
with his schedule adjusted so he could teach at both institutions. He
commuted between the two by way of Washington, D.C., on a Baltimore and Ohio Railroad pass, which Professor Stone of the University
of Virginia had been able to procure for him through the good offices
of Senator Thomas S. Martin of Virginia. The Hopkins position did
not pay particularly well, but Lovett had dutifully accepted it because,
he wrote, Sophus Lie "prefers that I start there and he has taken such a
hold of me and done so much for me this year that I owe it to him to listen to his wishes in the matter." This proved to be a fortuitous appointment, for Johns Hopkins, founded in 1876 on the model of the German
research university, emphasized that teaching and research went hand
in hand, a principle that Lovett absorbed and promoted for the rest
of his life. He also valued the principle of the honor system and student self-government that he witnessed at Virginia, but as much as he
respected both institutions, neither position was permanent. So in the
late spring of that year he applied to several universities for a professorial appointment. One of Lovett's applications was to the University of
Minnesota, although he later turned down its offer (and the presidency
of Drake University, urged upon him by his former Greek professor and
by the former president of his undergraduate college) because Princeton
University tendered him an appointment as an instructor of mathematics. (Lovett would spend the summer term of 1897 teaching at the new
University of Chicago, founded in 1890 and opening classes in 1892
but already one of the nation's greatest universities—the model par excellence of the instant university.)

Lovett had sent a detailed letter to Professor Downey at Minnesota
outlining his qualifications, and Downey had in addition requested

recommendation letters from several of Lovett's former professors and others who knew him well. Once Downey understood that Lovett would not be coming to Minnesota because he had "something better offered," Downey did an unusual thing. Having decided that Lovett would "observe the Scriptural injunction, not to think of yourself more highly than you ought to think," Downey forwarded to Lovett his entire application folder, including Lovett's introductory letter and those of all his recommenders. In this one package, Downey provided a full contemporary assessment of Lovett as scholar, teacher, and man. Here was a portrait of Edgar Odell Lovett on the cusp of his career as an American academician.

Lovett, just a few days over age twenty-six when he wrote Downey on April 27, 1897, described himself as "over six feet tall; weigh 175 pounds; in splendid health; wear neither whiskers nor glasses [he might have added: hair, brown; eyes, blue]." (In an appendix to his letter he mentioned that he was a Mason, a member of a collegiate fraternity, "a believer in the religion of Christ," and a member of several mathematical societies.) Clearly the image is of a vigorous young man, no longer the blond snippet of a lad pictured in the Bethany yearbook in 1887. Then Lovett listed his various academic experiences and appointments from his undergraduate days at Bethany to his second doctorate at Leipzig. Following that, he listed his professional publications in a variety of prestigious journals such as the *American Astronomical Journal* and the *Annals of Math,* a total of ten either published or forthcoming, and a series of lectures on the "Geometry of Contact Transformations" already delivered at Johns Hopkins University and the University of Virginia and to be presented that summer at the University of Chicago. The following lectures, of course, were an outgrowth of his Leipzig dissertation. Then came an impressive list of works in progress. There could be little doubt that Lovett's career in mathematics was promising, though his work seems more descriptive than analytical or theoretical. He indicated as well that he could teach undergraduate courses in any field of math, along with graduate courses in several specialized areas.

Perhaps his next sentence suggests why Lovett was so appealing: he promised "to work heart and soul with you to build up one of the strongest departments in the country both pedagogically and scientifically."

Once he landed the job he wanted, Lovett intended to throw his whole being into the enterprise. He made clear that he was "in mathematics for the sake of the science and its use as a powerful educational implement," and he stated frankly that he was "in no hurry to settle and propose to be thoroughly satisfied that a place is the one for me and I the man for the place before I attach myself permanently anywhere." When an instructorship at Princeton was offered him shortly thereafter, Lovett withdrew his application from Minnesota, fully believing he had found his permanent academic home.

The recommendations from his former teachers and colleagues at the University of Virginia, West Kentucky College, and Bethany College spoke so effusively of his academic abilities and even more so of his personal qualities that they suggest the magnetism, even the charisma, Lovett already exhibited, and perhaps it was this feature that most determined the effectiveness of his future role in academic leadership. Astronomer Ormond Stone, his major professor at Virginia, called him "a *very* strong man, a skillful and inspiring teacher, a man of fine personal address." Professor R. S. Woodward of Columbia University described him as "dignified, courteous, and scholarly in bearing, . . . one of the most promising men available." Another faculty member at Virginia, J. M. Page, called him "an excellent teacher and a man of unspotted character." The Reverend A. McLean, currently the head of the Disciples of Christ Foreign Missionary Society but president of Bethany College during Lovett's student days, wrote warmly of his former student as "one of the most gifted men known to me. As a man he is all that any one could wish. . . . Dr. Lovett is a rare man." Lovett's next supervisor, H. H. Rumble, then a lawyer in Norfolk but formerly president of West Kentucky College, remembered that "a manly and dignified presence and bearing, social and intellectual traits of a high order combined with a genuine enthusiasm for his specialty, won for him the respect and confidence of his students and inspired them to their best efforts." Moreover, Rumble emphasized, Lovett was "a Christian gentleman of broad culture, and of high moral tone." But perhaps the most convincing recommendation was by another Virginia professor, William M. Thornton of the engineering department. According to Thornton, "Lovett is one of those rare young fellows of whom we speak with a certain reserve, for fear of seeming extravagant in eulogy. He is handsome, agreeable in manners and appearance, and of a genial temper. His character I believe to be irreproachable. His intelligence is of a high order, he has great industry, and is filled with ambition to make himself a great geometer. . . . In brief, he is a man whom I can commend to you frankly, fully, and without reserve, and you know how rare such men are."

What are we to make of such praise? Obviously recommendation letters always emphasize the positive and seldom use restrained language, but the similarity of these letters, and their emphasis on personal rather than primarily academic traits, do suggest that Lovett's personality, his character, his demeanor, his earnestness of purpose impressed everyone with whom he came in contact. (In 1948, for example, the widow of the Austrian graduate student Karl Carda, with whom Lovett had studied with Sophus Lie fifty years before, wrote Lovett recalling that her husband had often spoken affectionately of their coursework together more than fifty years before at Leipzig and Christiania. Lovett left a mark on people's memory.) Surely the strength of his character, his evident personal and intellectual trustworthiness, played a role in his later ability to inspire others to accept his vision for a new academic institution of great ambition planted in a seemingly raw and undeveloped part of the nation. To paraphrase a later famous characterization of Franklin D. Roosevelt, Lovett may not have been a mathematician of the absolutely front rank, but he had a first-rate temperament.

When Princeton called, Lovett gladly answered, moving there from Chicago (after a quick trip to Kentucky) in the fall of 1897, to be joined at the beginning of the new year by his new wife, whom he had married over the Christmas holidays. The young couple rented a home at 49 Prospect Avenue, just a short walk from the heart of the campus and several blocks from the commercial establishments along Nassau Street. Venerable Princeton had long possessed a beautiful campus, but in 1896 the board of trustees decided to adopt Collegiate Gothic as the preferred architectural style—connecting the university to the centuries-old academic traditions of Oxford and Cambridge—and for the next few decades one handsome Gothic structure after another went up, giving the university a consistent "look" that still characterizes the campus. Lovett watched the architectural transformation of the campus and was excited by the prospect of a long and productive career at this premier institution that had just the year before observed the sesquicentennial of its founding in 1746 with an elaborate, three-day celebration, an event he obviously studied in some detail and from which he drew inspiration. The proceedings of the Princeton celebration (it was at this moment that the College of New Jersey changed its name to Princeton University) were reprinted in 1898 in a handsome, oversized volume produced by the DeVenne Press of New York City, and Lovett obtained a copy. The large "memorial book" recapitulated the three celebratory days, listing the lectures by leading European scholars (including mathematician Felix Klein of Göttingen, whom Lovett had just missed at Leipzig) from Dublin, Utrecht, Edinburgh, Cambridge, and Leipzig. These had been followed by a succession of religious services, receptions, concerts, luncheons, and dinners, with a special poem written for the occasion by Henry van Dyke and a keynote address by Princeton's own Woodrow Wilson, "Princeton in the Nation's Service." The volume also reprinted hundreds of telegrams, letters, and certificates of congratulations from universities all over the world representing all the great centers of learning.

Simply reading this gilt-edged volume would have confirmed in Lovett's mind that he had won an appointment at the kind of university that could command his loyalty and support over a lifetime of scholarship. And he found persuasive Wilson's message that it was not learning for learning's sake but rather "the spirit of service" a university imparts in its graduates "that will give a college place in the public annals of the nation." Wilson was more skeptical of the value of science than was Lovett, and Wilson understood that most college graduates would not pursue careers in the academy. For that reason, according to Wilson, "the object of education is not merely to draw out the powers of the individual mind: it is rather its right object to draw all minds to a proper adjustment to the physical and social world in which they are to have their life and their development; to enlighten, strengthen and make fit. The business of the world is not individual success, but its own betterment, strengthening, and growth in spiritual insight." The duty of the college was emphatically not to "stand aloof from the practical world," but to train its graduates to make the world a better place.

Then and in subsequent years Lovett would have occasion to reflect on the purpose of higher education, and his sense that informed people should engage the world—so perfectly articulated for him by Woodrow Wilson—never left Lovett.

Little is known of the next few years in the life of the Lovett family; one letter, written by Lovett on February 1, 1898, inviting Mary's sister to visit them in Princeton, spoke of the young couple "as the two happiest people in the world." Lovett went on to say to his sister-in-law that he and Mary "haven't had a cross word yet and, what's more, we are not going to have any." In this letter and in several other very scattered references, Lovett indicated how warmly the Princeton family welcomed both Mary and him. After one year at Princeton Lovett was promoted to assistant professor of mathematics, "given charge of the mathematics of the Department of Civil Engineering in the School of Science," and awarded a substantial raise of $1,000. Justification for such a promotion was suggested in the Report on University Affairs presented to the trustees on June 13, 1898: "The Mathematics Department has been greatly strengthened by the addition of Dr. Lovett, who has proved himself to be a remarkably strong addition to the Faculty." Lovett after only a year had also demonstrated unusually effective teaching skills and for that reason was given oversight of the mathematics instruction of all the engineering students. While still a student in Germany Lovett had written that Sophus Lie had told another student that Lovett would be an "ausgezeichneter Lehrer" (excellent teacher), and Lovett commented that "I hope I shall not disappoint his expectations." Quite clearly he proved to be a natural teacher.

During his first year, his instructorship, Lovett had taught a highly specialized course, "Lie's Transformation Groups with Applications to Differential Equations and Geometry," obviously an outgrowth of his studies in Leipzig, but in the fall of 1898 he added a general undergraduate course in "Calculus and Elementary Differential Equations" along with a graduate course in "Partial Differential Equations." In the fall of 1899 he added another graduate course, "Linear Differential Equations" and, for the first time, a course offered through the Department of Astronomy entitled "Celestial Mechanics: Lectures and Collateral Reading." This was the first hint of an eventual shift in both his teaching and departmental responsibilities, a disciplinary shift for which his broad graduate training had amply prepared him. By his second year Lovett entered more directly into the life of the university, serving both on the Discipline Committee and on the Committee on Examination and Standards, a committee he would later chair.

By all indications the Lovetts were thriving in Princeton and enjoying their life together in the academic community. His and Mary's first child, Adelaide, was born on October 27, 1898, and in 1900, when Lovett was promoted to full professor, both wife and daughter went with him on a sabbatical year to Paris. They all fell in love with the City of Lights, and Adelaide even learned to speak French before English. Years later Lovett would say that if he could live in two places, Paris would be his second home. During this sabbatical year Lovett also traveled widely in Europe, inspecting university facilities and programs at the behest of the Princeton administration.

These early Princeton years were also very productive in terms of mathematics for the ambitious Lovett, who may have been working so hard that he worried some of his friends. From instructor to professor at Princeton in three years—clearly he was on what would be today described as the fast track. In May of that sabbatical year Lovett received a letter from a former professor at Virginia, W. H. Echols, who in a fatherly way wrote: "Let me give you here however one piece of advice, resulting from my own experience—remember that there are other things in life besides mathematics and with respect to which mathematics is insignificant—Do not let mathematics absorb the best part of you & your thought, or you may some day have cause to bitterly regret that perhaps even only in appearance you have neglected things that are nearer and dearer to you than *it* can ever be—." This may have been advice that was misdirected, or reflective more of Echols's experience than Lovett's, for there was at this period in his life never a hint of anything but domestic bliss. Or perhaps Lovett took this advice to heart and modified his work habits, because future family correspondence reveals him as a loving and endlessly patient husband and father.

Looking back at Lovett in 1900, with his full professorship in mathematics before his thirtieth birthday (and his first of many honorary doctorates awarded by Drake University two years before), his love of Princeton, his emerging friendship with government professor and university illuminary Woodrow Wilson, soon to be named Princeton's president, he seemed destined for a long and fruitful career there in the shadow of Nassau Hall. As he had written to his sister-in-law shortly after arriving at Princeton, "we are in the midst of splendid opportunities and thank Heaven for them."

William Marsh Rice's wife, Elizabeth Baldwin Rice, became quite ill in the winter of 1895, and Rice moved her back to Houston from New York in the spring of 1896, thinking she might do better in a warmer clime. But she continued to decline, suffering a series of small strokes. When the oppressive Houston summer seemed to make her health grow worse, Rice took her to Waukesha, Wisconsin, hoping the cooler weather would bring her relief. Yet she continued to sink, and after another, more severe stroke, she died on July 24, 1896. Subsequently Rice discovered that less than two months preceding her death, she had written a will—a complete surprise to him—in which she claimed ownership of half his estate and distributed it to a long list of relatives, friends, and Houston causes but not a cent to the William Marsh Rice Institute. In her will she claimed to be a legal resident of Texas, whose community property law gave her ownership of half of that portion of her husband's estate that he had acquired over the course of their marriage. Rice was flabbergasted to learn of this will and instantly suspected fraud on the part of her lawyer, Orren Thaddeus Holt. Rice began legal maneuvering to invalidate that will on the grounds that he and his wife had in fact been legal residents of New York, not Texas, and New York did not have the community property provision, hence protecting his estate from her power to dispose of any part of it. Holt responded in late 1898 by hiring another lawyer, Albert T. Patrick, then practicing in New York, to take depositions in New York City concerning the residency dispute, and in the process of doing so, Patrick became more aware of the size of Rice's estate. Soon a plot began to hatch in Patrick's mind, and he persuaded Rice's pliant young assistant, Charles A. Jones, to assist him.

No doubt it seemed foolproof to Patrick. Jones provided access to Rice's signature, and Patrick practiced until he could reproduce it exactly. Then Jones sent envelopes to Patrick from Rice's apartment to create a paper record of correspondence indicating a client-lawyer relationship. With that completed, Patrick drew up a fraudulent will (dated June 30, 1900) whereby Rice apparently gave his immense fortune primarily to Patrick, a succession of friends and dignitaries in Houston (apparently expecting them as a consequence to support the validity of this new will), and in effect leaving nothing to the Rice Institute. Patrick with his practiced hand signed the new will for the totally unaware Rice. All that remained to be done was to wait for the eighty-four-year-old Rice to die. But the plotters grew impatient because despite his infirmities (including an old knee injury that made walking difficult), Rice remained mentally sharp and determined to live to a very old age. His factotum, Jones, at the suggestion of Patrick, urged upon Rice a steady regimen of mercury pills, a form of laxative, and although they seemed to weaken Rice and drove him to try several unusual diets recommended by well-meaning friends, the indomitable Rice hung on to life. How long would Patrick and Jones have to wait?

Then on the second weekend of September, a devastating hurricane smashed into the island city of Galveston, Texas, killing at least six thousand people—the worst natural disaster in American history—and destroying most of the city's infrastructure. The damage was not restricted to the island, and even nearby Houston suffered roofs blown off and trees downed.* Among the structures on the mainland damaged was William Marsh Rice's Merchants and Planters Oil Company, effectively closing it down. When Rice got the news, he quickly wrote his business manager in Houston authorizing him to draw money as needed (up to $150,000) from Rice's account at his New York bank to put the mill back into operation. This authorization panicked Patrick, because he understood that the most fluid assets Rice possessed were the funds in the bank, and here they were being expended in Texas!

---

* The storm caused comparatively minor damage to Houston, however, and the city quickly recovered, while Galveston took years to rebuild. As a result, when in January 1901 the Texas oil age began with the famous Spindletop gusher in nearby Beaumont, Houston—not prostrate Galveston—quickly emerged as the oil center of the nation and began its growth into eventually the nation's fourth largest city.

Something had to be done before Rice remitted more of his monies to rebuild his damaged properties along the Gulf Coast. At this point, according to testimony Jones later provided, the decision was made to kill Rice by an overdose of chloroform applied by a wet towel placed over his nose and mouth while he was sleeping. Whether or not that was actually done, or was the real cause of his death, it is clear that on Sunday, September 23, 1900, William Marsh Rice died in his Madison Avenue apartment.

The next morning, before word of his death had spread, lawyer Patrick, with a check for $25,000 made out to him and supposedly signed by Rice, went to the bank to have it cashed. An alert cashier noticed that on the face of the check Patrick's first name was spelled Abert—in his nervousness or hurry Jones had misspelled the name—and Patrick, not noticing, had countersigned the check on the reverse with the correct Albert. This inconsistency bothered the careful cashier, who knew that Rice seldom let mistakes get by, and he insisted on conferring with the bank's chief clerk, Walter Wetherbee, who also knew Rice well. The mistake raising his suspicions too, he insisted on telephoning Rice's apartment and thereby learned that the wealthy merchant had died the previous day. Wetherbee promptly telegraphed Rice's personal lawyer in Texas, James A. Baker, confiding the banker's suspicions. The plot then unraveled. Baker quickly caught a train to New York, pressured the authorities to mount a vigorous investigation, the simple-minded Jones confessed, the Rice signature was proven in the courtroom to be forged, and, after a sensational trial, Jones was convicted on March 26, 1902, and sentenced to die, a sentence later commuted to life imprisonment in Sing Sing. The fortune of "Old Man Rice," as he was described in the yellow journalism of the day, was saved for his institute in Houston. A little more than a month before Patrick's conviction, the disputed will of Elizabeth Baldwin Rice had been settled out of court for $200,000. After all the accounting of Mr. Rice's properties had been totaled up, on April 29, 1904, Baker and the trustees of the Rice Institute found themselves in possession of assets totaling $4,631,259.08, one of largest endowments in the nation.

The remaining six trustees suddenly realized the significance of their fiduciary responsibility. In truth, they had even before Rice's death recognized that more funds would be available than they could have originally imagined. Between 1891 and his death, Rice had been slowly transferring assets to the institute: the Capitol Hotel in Houston; six-and-a-half acres on Louisiana Street also in downtown Houston as the supposed campus of the planned institute; 10,000 acres in Jones County, Texas; 47,000 acres of virgin timber land in western Louisiana; various secured notes owed to him. But Rice had instructed that nothing was to be done with regard to establishing the institute until after his death, so the growing endowment had not really required them to act. Now Rice was dead—what should be done? And as the size of the ultimate endowment became clear, that question grew in importance.

The trustees had made some preliminary inquiries: they had written to Girard College in 1892 to obtain a copy of its charter and several of its descriptive pamphlets. They hired a New York law firm in early 1901 to inquire of many colleges and universities about their acts of incorporation and business practices; they wrote to Purdue University inquiring of its programs. But after several years people began writing letters to the Houston newspapers raising questions about when and where would the proposed new institution be developed—what was the cause of the delay? In late 1904 the mayor of Houston appointed a three-person committee to call on the trustees and "ascertain . . . what progress has been made, and is being made towards carrying out the purpose of their trust . . . as the people of this city and State are deeply interested in the project." Clearly the trustees were now feeling the weight of their responsibilities and the pressure of time, and they were asking many people, including educators in the region, for advice. In late 1906 trustee Emanuel Raphael had made a trip to the East Coast to inspect a number of colleges, manual training schools, and art galleries, an experience he found so valuable that he recommended to the board on December 28, 1906, that each of them take a similar trip of reconnaissance. The board was engaged in a crash course to learn about higher education, including the leading institutions and the most respected academic leaders.

This research led them to send a carefully composed letter on January 10, 1907, to twenty-five "leading presidents and regents of various colleges in the United States," asking for advice as to whom they should hire as the "head" of the proposed institute. Emanuel Raphael acted as the leader of what would now be called the search committee. Perhaps because he had played a major role more than two decades before in seeking a new rabbi for Congregation Beth Israel, Raphael was assumed to have relevant experience in searching for an institutional leader. Back came names to consider and characteristics the trustees should look for in whomever they chose. For example, David Starr Jordan, president of Stanford University, wrote that they ought "to secure a young man of broad sympathies and broad education, who will have a knowledge of Applied Science and sympathy with the methods by which Engineering may be taught. At the same time, he ought to have an appreciation of the value of liberal education, and he should have personal qualities that would make him successful and acceptable to the people of your state." As the letters poured in from the presidents of Harvard, Columbia, Cornell, Massachusetts Institute of Technology (MIT), the University of Virginia, and even William Jennings Bryan, Grover Cleveland, and Theodore Roosevelt, the roster of nominees grew. William M. Rice, Jr., the founder's nephew and a Princeton graduate, had joined the trustees in 1899, and he suggested that the letter should also be sent to Woodrow Wilson, who in 1902 had become president of Princeton University.

This letter reveals the strategy of the board and the scale of opportunity it offered:

Dear Sir:

The William M. Rice Institute for the Advancement of Literature, Science, and Art is now being organized. It has an endowment of five million dollars, or more. It will be non-sectarian and non-political, free tuition to whites. It will be located here.

It is our desire to do the greatest good possible with the money at our command, and to cover the whole field as indicated in our title as rapidly as we can. We think it was the intention of the founder to give manual training, applied science and liberal arts preference in the organization. It is our desire to realize his wishes if possible and at the same time be affiliated with the school system of the country. In order to hasten our work, we need for the head of the institution the very best man to be had. We need a young man, a broad man, and we need him at once; and we are able to pay him such a salary as such distinguished services should command, and will be glad to do so if we can get the right man.

Our object in writing to you is to ascertain if you know of such a man, and if so advise us and place us in correspondence with him—such a man as you yourself would select.

Feeling that the importance of our work is its own excuse for this intrusion upon your time and attention, and requesting an early reply, we beg to remain,

Yours truly,
E. Raphael and J. E. McAshan, Committee of the Board of Trustees.

When Woodrow Wilson received this letter, he knew immediately whom he would recommend.

# CHAPTER TWO

# FAREWELL TO PRINCETON

THE TWENTIETH CENTURY dawned with Edgar Odell Lovett feeling on top of the world. In June of that year he was promoted to the rank of full professor of mathematics at Princeton University, with a substantial raise in pay, and that fall he and his wife began a glorious sabbatical year in Paris. Returning to New Jersey in 1901 after the Parisian sojourn, he was refreshed and eager to reenter the world of teaching and research. He discovered the Princeton social and academic life to be very pleasant indeed, and the community welcomed his wife and him graciously. He could easily imagine spending his entire scholarly career at Princeton. In 1900 the university had formally founded its Graduate College, which began operation in 1901. There had long been graduate work at Princeton, but the intent of the new college was to raise the prestige of the program, emphasize research, and begin the process of awarding graduate degrees. Lovett, of course, would have fully agreed with this development. Even more pleasing to Lovett, however, was the naming of Woodrow Wilson as president of Princeton on June 9, 1902. A phenomenally popular lecturer at the university, Wilson had long been thinking about ways to bring Princeton into the twentieth century by changing its curriculum and invigorating its teaching. He wanted to transform the university, which had been a leisurely idyll during which affluent students practiced their social graces, into a high-powered academic dynamo where students were challenged to think, to analyze, and to develop skills that could be translated into affecting the real world. Wilson entitled his inaugural address "Princeton For the Nation's Service," which represented a subtle revision of the ideas of his 1896 Sesquicentennial Address, "Princeton in the Nation's Service."

Within weeks of his October 25 formal inauguration as Princeton's president, Wilson began pushing his educational reforms. He called for a complete overhaul of how most of the teaching was done. Although

himself a gifted lecturer, Wilson knew that many students often slept
through lectures and then crammed via purchased lecture notes at the
end of the semester. He proposed to hire fifty young faculty—all with
their doctorates, all talented and energetic and committed to the life of
the mind—and have these so-called preceptors participate in the teaching. Wilson wanted to drop one of the lecture periods of the week and
substitute small (no more than five students) discussion classes led by
the preceptors. No longer could students coast along in the anonym-
ity of a large lecture class. They would instead be inspired to read, to
think, and to discuss. Hiring this many preceptors would increase the
faculty by a third and cost more than $2 million, but Wilson sold the
idea to the trustees and alumni by persuasively arguing that it would
literally revolutionize teaching and learning at Princeton. By 1904
Wilson was personally selecting the preceptors, who were appointed
as untenured assistant professors, and the program got under way in
the fall of 1905. The preceptors instantly infused energy and intellectual ferment into the campus, making Princeton the most academically
exciting campus in America. Dozens of brilliant young faculty came
to Princeton precisely because of the power of Wilson's ideas and his
visionary personality. He had a kind of steely resolve that commanded
the respect of many idealistic young scholars and made them desire to
hitch their careers to his rising star.

Wilson then quickly moved to advance his curricular reforms, reforms that were integral to his preceptorship program and reforms that
garnered quick and widespread support among the faculty and would
subsequently have much influence on colleges and universities across
the nation. Wilson sought a middle ground between the still common but old-fashioned rigid curriculum that allowed students practically no choice and the new elective system pioneered at Harvard (and
adopted at several other institutions) that offered students almost total
freedom—some thought too much—in choice of courses. The elective
system, after a flutter of popularity in the two decades before 1900,
had come under widespread criticism in the next few years. Wilson
wanted to reform the traditional curriculum but still channel students'
choices to an extent. He called for grouping the university's offerings
into twelve departments; students for the first two years would take a

broad variety of essentially introductory classes in different fields but at the end of the second year would choose to concentrate in one department (although one could change this department), adding related courses outside that department. In other words, students would choose and then pursue a discipline-related major, culminating in even more specialized and advanced work in the senior year, including a long research paper that counted as a course. By the spring of 1904 the Princeton faculty unanimously adopted these curricular changes. For Lovett, as for many other young faculty, there could be no more intellectually challenging campus in America than Wilson's Princeton, and Lovett greatly admired Wilson the man and the Princeton he was seeking to build. On March 14, 1903, Lovett had been the guest of honor of the Princeton Alumni Association of New England's annual dinner in Boston, and there he had spoken "with enthusiasm concerning Princeton's future, under the guidance of the new president."

Lovett's personal and professional life could not have been better in these heady days of reform at Princeton. After their return from Paris the Lovetts moved to a larger home at 79 Prospect Avenue. A son was born on January 8, 1902, Henry Malcolm, a happy addition to the Lovett family. Mary Hale Lovett's mother, after visiting the Lovett home, wrote to her daughter Annie back in Kentucky on July 25, 1902, proudly describing the Lovett domestic situation: "Mary is so beautiful and sweet, enjoys her home & children. Mr. Lovett takes such good care of her & the children—is an excellent husband & father. A *growing man,* whom this University is proud to have and to keep." By this time—and probably earlier—the Lovetts employed a domestic helper, an African American woman originally from Virginia who was a wonderful cook. Given her well-to-do upbringing in Kentucky, Mary no doubt simply assumed she would have such assistance about the home, especially now that she had two children to look after, and in fact having domestic help was common practice for people of their status throughout much of the nation.

Lovett was meanwhile presenting mathematics lectures and publishing papers, President Wilson named him chairman of the Committee on Examinations and Standings in October 1903, he was elected to honorary membership in Princeton's chapter of Phi Beta Kappa also in that year, and in 1904 he was admitted to membership in the American Philosophical Society—memberships he treasured throughout his life. In 1904 he was in correspondence with mathematicians and astronomers across the nation—Percival Lowell, for one, invited Lovett to visit him once more at his Flagstaff Observatory to again observe the planet Mars, whose so-called canals Lowell had been mapping for years. Lovett was a popular teacher and active in the life of the university in a variety of ways. For example, in 1904 he served as one of three faculty judges in a debate between Union College and Rutgers College on the topic "That England Should Abandon Her Free Trade Policy," bringing back memories, no doubt, of his debate society days at Bethany College. In March 1905 Wilson wrote Lovett that he, at the special request of the University of Virginia, was being sent as the official Princeton representative to the installation of Edwin A. Alderman as president of the University of Virginia, an assignment Lovett must have enjoyed. Several times the *Princeton Alumni Weekly* mentioned Lovett, along with one or two others, as representative of the distinguished faculty of the university. Several former students later wrote Lovett praising his teaching and mentoring. One added, "You probably never understood fully how much we undergraduates appreciated your spirit in spending so much of your time with us and in helping us with your good advice."

Then in early 1905 the eminent chairman of the astronomy department at Princeton since 1877, Charles Augustus Young, a pioneer in solar physics and astrophysics and author of a ground-breaking astronomy textbook, retired. On March 9, 1905, Lovett was named professor of astronomy to replace him. (Several years later Young would graciously write Lovett that "it was quite an element of comfort connected with my resignation, that I was to be succeeded by the person whom I desired to have in my place.") From near and far came fulsome letters of congratulations. Clerk of the Princeton faculty William M. Magie sent his good wishes and closed with the following: "I am especially glad of the new arrangement, because it ensures, at least I hope so, your staying at Princeton as one of us." Along with congratulations, the professorship of astronomy also brought a handsome house at 16 Prospect Avenue with an adjacent Observatory of Instruction, containing all the

apparatus necessary to teach and demonstrate the principles of astronomy to undergraduates (there was a research observatory on the other
side of the campus).

Within weeks of his appointment as professor of astronomy, the
Lovetts on March 25, 1905, welcomed a new daughter, Ellen Kennedy,
into their happy home. Edgar Odell Lovett could be forgiven a sense of
pride and contentment as he contemplated his situation in mid-1905.
But tragedy and disappointment often intrude when least expected. For
reasons that at this date are unclear (and family correspondence is extremely reticent on the point), Mary Hale Lovett became ill (probably
kidney stones) in the fall 1905,* and sometime afterward so did the
baby. On April 7, 1905, one of Lovett's professors at Virginia, W. H.
Echols, sent congratulations on learning of the new birth and said that
he was "so glad to learn that all is well, and that you are coming down
to be with us." That visit apparently never materialized. The retired
astronomer Charles Augustus Young wrote on September 5 of that year
that he was glad to hear that the Lovett family had gone to the Jersey
shore for a few days and hoped that "the sea-air will soon rehabili-
tate Mrs. Lovett." Apparently Mary Lovett's illness somehow affected
baby Ellen, because the infant died in August 1906. Family tradition
says that Ellen was lactose intolerant and could not metabolize milk
or milk products; consequently she suffered from terrible diarrhea and
basically died of dehydration. This condition occasionally arises shortly
after children are weaned from their mother's milk and their diet is
shifted to cow's milk and other foods to which they are inordinately
sensitive. One suspects that Mary Lovett's illness forced her to wean
the baby, perhaps prematurely, who then became fatally ill with what
is today called childhood diarrhea. By June 1906 Mary was already
convalescing (presumably from a physical ailment) in a private home in
West Philadelphia, supervised by a private nurse—the children had already been sent to Mayfield, Kentucky, to be with their maternal grandparents. Ellen died two months later, on August 21, apparently without

---

* She had also been quite ill in June 1895, when Lovett visited her in Kentucky immediately prior to going to Germany, and he had been relieved several weeks later to learn by
telegram that she had recovered. She would be plagued by illness throughout her life.

Mary having a chance to see her again. Mary understandably came to blame herself for Ellen's sickness and then death, and as a consequence, fell into a devastating depression. Several letters from colleagues to Lovett in the fall of 1906 referred to Mary's undergoing an unspecified operation and asked him to convey to her their best wishes.

The extant Lovett family correspondence, which is extensive, gives no hint of the cause of Ellen's death (it is never mentioned at the time) or the exact diagnosis of Mary's illness. Instead, for day after day through 1906 and much of 1907, Edgar Odell Lovett wrote patient, supportive, urgent, pleading, romantic letters to Mary. Mary, attended by a private nurse, Miriam Bowles, was moved from location to location—to Spruce Mountain House, to Buck Hill Falls, to Pocono Pines, to Atlantic City, finally to Mayfield, Kentucky—with the hope that a changed environment would speed her recovery. The consistent and overwhelming tone of Lovett's letters suggests that she was suffering from a depression so deep and dark that her life was almost without hope. Over and over again Edgar expressed his love, his hope that with her recovery they could renew the good times of before. He sent her books on birds and art, which he hoped she would enjoy. His letters were filled with words of endearment, with optimistic phrasing clearly intended to strengthen her resolve. "You have been nobly brave and I am certain that all things are working out right." "I am firm as ever in the belief that the old life, and better, is nearer to us every day." "You sent your love to me six weeks ago . . . Keep the old flame alive Mary. With me it burns deeper than ever." "Everybody asks after you and your health tenderly, and I am almost arrogant in the hopeful accounts I give them." "Keep your courage strong and be of good cheer my precious wife. We are going to get you well and you *are* coming back to be the star of my soul and the sun of my life. With my heart's deepest affection, Your devoted EO." "Come back to me, sweetheart, come back to me." "Bless your dear, dear heart, you just must take care of yourself and your spirits that we may have another whole generation of life together! Let's forget the hard year, and look only into the fair face of the future." "Your sweet spirit is over me as I write, and I can feel your hand on my shoulder, your breath on my cheek and your lips near. There's no sound to molest the secret communion but the soft and honeyed clicking of the little clock in its constant love-making to your girlish picture on my study mantel. . . . my heart leaps to the joyful memories of those early days when we first found each other and our souls rushed together in a bond." "Keep your courage up dear and try to revive the old love that was so real long years ago. You have not changed. It's all been a horrid dream—this one year—and like all dreams it is passing gradually out of your mind. Try to believe in all of us and in everybody." The letters so filled with hope and love came day after day from Lovett to Mary even as he was fully engaged in his work at Princeton, including several new projects. For months on end Mary never answered his letters, despite his pleas.

At times Lovett mentioned his near total exhaustion, consumed by work and worry about Mary and loneliness both for her and the children. (In late December a fellow astronomer, obviously worried about Lovett, wrote him to "Be always careful of your health. . . . Few are able to do good work in the higher branches of Astronomy, and much depends on *your* future activity. Take plenty of rest, and don't rush too much. You should have 40 years of activity yet ahead of you.") Included in Lovett's letters to Mary too were also poignant, romantic expressions of his sensual desires to be with her again that are so personal and heartfelt that even reading them at this long remove seems inappropriate. Not until near the end of 1907 did Mary Hale Lovett emerge from her devastating, remorseless illness and return as wife and mother to her two surviving children, Adelaide and Malcolm. The death of his daughter and the near loss of his beloved wife for almost two years clearly aged Edgar Odell Lovett, tempering his hitherto sunny disposition with a tinge of the tragic. Yet a stoical determination to do his duty, to see a job through no matter what, also emerged more strongly than ever before. Perhaps Lovett had learned to compartmentalize his mind, walling off the personal and emotional from the professional so that he could, despite his grief for the death of a child, the worry over an ill wife, and loneliness for children away in Kentucky, still pursue an active teaching and administrative life. W. R. Warren, an old friend from Bethany days and now an official of the Disciples of Christ, suggested as much when he wrote Lovett on August 22, 1906: "I am trusting that the equipose [*sic*] in which I found you last continues and that you are not attempting to bear the sorrows that are coming to you but absorbing your attention in doing the things required—the next thing every day." Among other things, Lovett had to develop a new repertoire of courses. He no longer taught math classes per se but instead offered coursework in such topics as "Elementary Astronomy," "Modern Theories of Celestial Mechanics," and "Theoretical Astronomy and the Calculation of Orbits." The breadth of his graduate training made this disciplinary shift possible.

Understandably, though, Lovett seemed more serious, graver, than ever before. On occasion the weight of his sorrows broke through in comments to Mary, times when Lovett with some justification may have engaged in bouts of self-pity. One day in late January 1907, writing from a hotel room in Manhattan, Lovett blurted out to her in a heartfelt letter: "I believe that I miss you more when I am away from home than when I'm jogging along at normal gait about my work at Princeton. You must hurry up and get well. I never can make this thing go without your help. I am trying hard to make it, but there are times when I want to sit down and cry my heart out. The year *has* been hard on you but there are times when I'm almost willing to admit that I have had the harder end of it."

Sometime in 1905, shortly after becoming head of the astronomy group within the faculty, Lovett had "barely mentioned" to President Wilson a proposal to equip a "Princeton Astronomical Expedition to South Africa." In November 1906 he wrote of the project again, arguing that if Princeton could establish a complete observatory in the southern hemisphere, it could do extraordinarily pioneering work in searching those comparatively unresearched skies. He believed that the result in a few years would be observations "with which every future student of the structure of the sky would have to reckon, real contributions to knowledge which would occupy a permanent place in the history of astronomy." No doubt Lovett had exhibited personal ambition in the past, but here for the first time he expressed great institutional ambition. He fully expected that if such an astronomical facility could be financed and erected, it would make Princeton's name glorious in the annals of science. Wilson clearly gave him the go-ahead, and as time permitted in 1906 and early 1907, Lovett traveled and made presentations on behalf of the project, seeking funds. In his papers are elaborate plans, detailing the personnel needed, the equipment desired, even endowed professorships, with a cost estimated to total almost half a million dollars. His correspondence to potential supporters indicates the scope of his activity, and letters to an ailing Mary occasionally mention his efforts, including a comment in April 1907 that "there seems to be a fighting chance that the expedition may get started this year but nothing is promised yet." No doubt by absorbing himself in work to achieve this bold, ambitious project for Princeton, Lovett found a measure of relief from his family concerns.

In the midst of Mary Lovett's illness, the university president Lovett so admired also fell stricken, at first physically, and then by the opposition of the enraged alumni of the university he was seeking to reform and revitalize. In the spring of 1906 neuritic pains in his left shoulder and leg had bothered Woodrow Wilson, and similar pains emerged in his right hand. Then suddenly one May morning he awoke only to discover that he could not see out of his left eye. This probably was the result of a minor stroke, a precursor to much more severe strokes years later, but it was diagnosed at the time as having been brought on by mental strain and overwork. After several months resting and recuperating in the English Lake Country, a region he dearly loved, Wilson was back at Princeton by the fall, hard at work and at the height of his popularity as Princeton president. Then in December he made a preliminary report to the trustees, a report he presented in full detail in June 1907 when the trustees met for the commencement exercises, that represented the beginning of the end of Wilson's honeymoon period at Princeton.

Wilson had long objected to the exclusive nature of the eating clubs at Princeton. Open only to juniors and seniors (and with room only for two-thirds of them), the clubs deprived freshmen and sophomores of the leadership and mentoring of upperclassmen, cultivated only the social skills of the students, and were tending to replace the university itself in the loyalty of their members. Wilson wanted to democratize the total student learning experience. He proposed replacing the elitist eating clubs with residential colleges arranged in quadrangles, each with their own commons and meeting rooms. These would be open to all students, democratically governed by the students themselves, with faculty masters and preceptors living and learning amid the undergrad-uates. Wilson saw the proposed residential college system as the cap-stone to his series of reforms that began with curricular change and the introduction of preceptors. But he immediately faced angry, intemper-ate, determined opposition from most of the alumni, who correctly saw their beloved eating clubs threatened. In the face of this opposition Wil-son stiffened, refused compromise, alienated even many of his earlier supporters by his intransigence, and by late October of that year met rejection by the trustees, a stunning and demoralizing defeat to Wilson and his strongest allies on the faculty.

Wilson, first incapacitated by illness and now thwarted by the united opposition of the alumni and trustees, no longer seemed an indomi-table force of nature. Another even more bitter fight was already brew-ing between Wilson and the Graduate College dean, Andrew F. West, over the location of the graduate college, and Wilson would lose that battle too, leading to his resignation from Princeton in the fall of 1910. Edgar Odell Lovett watched the slow downfall of his academic exem-plar during the exact months that his dear Mary suffered most griev-ously from her dark despair. To make things worse, fundraising for the South African expedition was not going as well as expected, leading Lovett to comment in June 1907 that "the expedition is in exceedingly hard lines." The former domestic happiness, the exciting promise of path-breaking research, the joyful expectations of long fulfilling years of teaching at Princeton may at times now have seemed only irrecover-able dreams from another era.

The search committee seeking a "head" of the Rice Institute had mailed out more than two dozen letters to the leaders of major universities on January 10, 1907, seeking nominations, and Woodrow Wilson must have received his copy several days later. Perhaps because he was at the moment so heavily involved with his proposal to do away with the eating clubs at Princeton, he neglected to act quickly on the request. Finally on March 11 he forwarded the letter to "My dear Professor Lovett," attaching a personal note saying: "Here is a letter which I wish you would read. I need not tell you that there is no man in the Princeton faculty I have more counted on to remain part of us, both in action and in inspiration, than yourself; but I feel bound, when a thing like this turns up, to present it to the man who seems to me best fitted, and let him say whether he wants to be considered or not. Apparently it might be made an opportunity to do a very great service to the South." * Lovett mentioned this possibility in a letter sent to the convalescing Mary postmarked March 13, confiding in her that "President Wilson told me yesterday of the opening he was wanting to make for me in the South, but fears he has waited too long. It would be a perfectly splendid opportunity and I shall tell you all about it when I come down. I do not expect anything to come of it," he cautioned her. "I am working on the other plan [the South African expedition] and am hopeful that something may come of that."

Lovett, obviously moved by Wilson's trust in him, replied to Wilson within a day or so, the copy of the letter being undated and the original not located in the Wilson papers.

My dear President Wilson:

I cannot tell you how hard it is for me to say to you that I shall be compelled to consider the matter of which you wrote if the opportunity presents itself. Your recommendation will mean a call, but I am not going to face the situation until it is upon me. In the meantime you must not question my loyalty—you will not—for you know what faith I have had in your plans for Princeton, you know with what loyal pride I have done my modest part in your administration, you know, too, how boisterously I have rejoiced over the things that you are bringing to pass in this place. I am deeply touched by your letter. For reasons that are sacred I broke into tears over it. I thank you for the expression of confidence and good-will which it contains, and with most affectionate regards, I beg to remain.

Faithfully yours,
Edgar Odell Lovett

* Wilson of course knew that when the prestigious Association of American Universities had been organized in 1900, only one of the fourteen founding institutions, Johns Hopkins, was located in the South—and of course Baltimore was only peripherally southern. Even in 1910, when Edwin E. Slosson famously identified the *Great American Universities* (New York, 1910), still only Hopkins hailed from the South.

The letter that Wilson subsequently wrote on behalf of Lovett to the Rice trustees is missing, but letters from others indicate that Wilson communicated his "unqualified endorsement." Lovett was understandably impatient to hear from the search committee, writing to his wife on March 20 and again the next day that he had "had no word from Texas yet." He assumed they would write Wilson first and, perhaps to lessen the blow of an anticipated refusal, he said that he expected to soon have the negative news and hence the matter off his mind. Still he was bound to admit to her, "it is going to be a disappointment but I am nerved up to it." Meanwhile back in Houston the trustees were busy considering names recommended to them, and on March 20 they voted to invite two Princetonians, engineering professor Howard McClenahan (who had been recommended by former U.S. president Grover Cleveland) and Edgar Odell Lovett, "the expense of such visits to be borne by the Institute." (Another candidate, A. Ross Hill of the University of Missouri, an early favorite, had withdrawn his name from consideration.) The next day Emanuel Raphael sent an invitation to Lovett (and McClenahan) to visit Houston, and on March 26 Lovett graciously accepted the invitation, writing Raphael that he would appear about April 10 "if that date will meet your convenience." Raphael quickly replied, saying that date was fine, enclosing a certified copy of the charter (vague as it was) of the Rice Institute, and he directed Lovett, upon arriving in Houston, to proceed directly to the Rice Hotel, where "you will find apartments ready for you." Later by telegram Lovett confirmed receipt of the charter and stated that he would arrive by train at midnight on April 10. On March 26 Lovett had also written Mary, "I wonder what the next thirty days will bring forth. They have asked me to come down as soon as possible. . . . Do not say anything about this to any one. . . . I am almost hoping that the opportunity will come."

A letter written the day Lovett was to arrive, April 10, by the chairman of the trustees, James A. Baker, to the president of a teachers' training institute in Huntsville, Texas, inadvertently reveals that the trustees, through thinking about the opportunity offered by the potential of the Rice Institute and the responsibility that immense potential placed on them, had educated themselves to a significant degree about university leadership. Writing to H. C. Pritchett, Baker said, "the trustees of The

William M. Rice Institute are trying to select a man for the executive and administrative head of the Institute. A man who will be to it what Prof. Harper was to Chicago University and Mr. Elliott [*sic*] to Harvard, etc." Baker, by singling these two out as exemplars, had chosen the two university presidents most historians of higher education would list as perhaps the greatest in nineteenth-century America. William Rainey Harper had been the founding president of the University of Chicago; he had recruited faculty, developed the curriculum, overseen construction, and made Chicago almost instantly a great university. Charles W. Eliot in his forty-year presidency of Harvard really created the modern Harvard, with an elective curriculum, strengthened entrance requirements, and the introduction of many new disciplines. Clearly Baker himself, and presumably the other trustees, had developed a quite sophisticated understanding of the leadership qualities they sought.

Lovett arrived in Houston as per schedule at midnight on April 10, and early the next morning, April 11, he took a long walk down Main Street. He was happy to discover the recently built Carnegie Library, judging that its existence relieved the proposed Rice Institute from having to immediately incur a major expense in meeting the provision of its charter to provide the city with a public library. Later in the day he was driven about the city to see several prospective sites for the institute-to-be, including the large lot on Louisiana Street near the center of the city; a site on the former Rice ranch much farther west, where the present-day city of Bellaire is located; a tract out along and on both sides of Main Street (including a golf course); and three other sites. Obviously the trustees already realized that the six-and-a half acres downtown was too small. That evening Lovett had a grueling interview with four of the six trustees (Lombardi then lived in Dallas and was absent, while William M. Rice, Jr., known then and now as Will Rice, was out of town).

Years later Lovett recalled that "I happen to have been in many an examination, but I think the one that night was the most trying ordeal I have as yet passed through." The trustees asked him question after question, many of which he subsequently said he had never thought about before, but Lovett must have given as good as he took. He offered a number of suggestions, for example, that the university should live out of its income alone, never touching its endowment; it should secure "an extensive site outside the city and on the side to which the industries would never come"; it should develop a comprehensive architectural plan before starting the first building; and "they ought to get Woodrow Wilson to do the job." Toward the end of the interview Lovett made an important point that shaped the future of the enterprise. Clearly he had read the charter carefully, and he noted that the title *institute* usually had a very restrictive connotation meaning normally either an eleemosynary institution for "defectives" or a narrow institute of technology. "So I told them," he recalled with certainty, "that I could not be a party for any such undertaking that would not assure as large a place for pure science as for applied science. It was an entering wedge away from technology and towards the university idea. I always have thought that it bore fruit in the future."

Lovett indicated that he was impressed by the perspicacity of the trustees, and he obviously impressed them, though Lovett did not realize for months how well his interview had gone. As trustee chair Baker later confided, Lovett had "youth, vigor, experience, and ambition." Consider what Lovett offered them. Here was a young man, only days short of his thirty-sixth birthday; a scholar with two doctorates, one from a prestigious German university, a long list of publications, and possessor of a full professorship at Princeton; he had taught and learned about university organization and leadership at Virginia, famous for its honor code; at Johns Hopkins, the first American research university; at Chicago, the instant university of world renown; and then at Princeton, under the leadership of Wilson the most innovative and progressive university in the nation; and this vigorous, cosmopolitan young scholar was currently engaged in developing an ambitious program to develop a major astronomy research center in the southern hemisphere. In addition, he was widely read and liberally educated, knowing literature in both classical and modern languages, and he enjoyed a wide correspondence with scholars in the United States and across Europe. On top of that, he was tall, handsome, well spoken, and had a winning personality while at the same time being obviously a man of substance and considered opinions.

Would such a man be willing to leave stately Princeton and come to a new, almost raw country to build up a university in a part of the nation not yet associated with major academic development? The trustees kept close counsel and continued for several months to interview other candidates and consider their prospects. On April 12, the day after his interview, Lovett dashed off a note to his wife, thanking her for her recent letter ("did me more good than I can tell, and if I have won this thing it is all due to that"). He reported that "the whole matter is still open and may not be decided for some time. I believe that I have a fighting chance." That night Lovett began the long train ride, via New Orleans, back to Mayfield, and thence to Princeton. Once there he waited, and waited. Over the next month his regular letters to Mary often indicated his eagerness to hear from the Rice trustees: "I had hoped to have a word both from you and from Texas in my mail." "I have no word from or about Texas." "Neither McC. nor myself has heard anything from Texas." "[Close friends] are much distressed because I have had no word from Texas." Sometime later that summer a much-improved Mary returned home, so Lovett's epistolary record of impatience ceased, but no doubt his nervous anticipation continued.

Throughout the summer months the Rice trustees interviewed, discussed candidates among themselves, and acted with great deliberation, fully cognizant that the munificence of the endowment gave their ultimate decision a momentousness they had little expected when first called to membership on the board. Finally at the board meeting on November 20, 1907, after another full discussion, Will Rice (who had yet to meet Lovett) made a motion, quickly seconded by Raphael, declaring "Edgar O. Lovett, of Princeton University," to be the choice of the board for the "educational head of the Institute." The vote was unanimous, including a letter from Lombardi, who could not be present, giving his vote for Lovett. The board then authorized Will Rice, the founder's nephew—perhaps that was why he was chosen to convey the message to Lovett—to travel to Princeton and call Lovett "to take charge." Rice was authorized to negotiate compensation and term of contract, with a salary limit of $7,500 per year and a maximum five-year contract. Rice approached the task obliquely, writing Lovett on December 3 that "I expect to be in New York on the 14th Inst. and would like to see you before returning home—Will you kindly wire me upon receipt of this letter stating if you will be at home on the 14th & oblige." Of course, Rice would be in New York City only because he was coming to present an offer to Lovett. Perhaps the letter was worded thus so that in case Lovett was no longer interested, or felt the terms offered were unacceptable, he would not feel that he had unduly inconvenienced Rice if he declined the offer.

How conflicted was Lovett about accepting the position offered? He had what could only be termed an ideal appointment at Princeton, with a spacious house; he still harbored hopes of completing an astronomical expedition to South Africa and erecting an observatory there. But opposition to Wilson had arisen among the alumni and some faculty and administrators, thwarting his most ambitious plans for reform. And now Lovett's last two years at Princeton were haunted by memories of a dying infant, months of painful separation from an ill wife, an often empty house that no longer seemed a home. Perhaps Lovett wanted a change of scene, a total break from the last few years, a chance to start over again both with a rapidly improving Mary and a fresh academic mission even bolder than a southern hemispheric observatory. Did he sense that administration and leadership—not the single-minded dedication to research necessary to attain real distinction in the field of astronomy that was already moving away from observation and mathematical description to theoretical astrophysics—were his signal strengths? Like many national educational leaders, Lovett no doubt also recognized the importance of improving educational opportunities in the South, and perhaps his marriage into a Kentucky family had even strengthened his consciousness of a duty to attempt—in President Wilson's words—"a very great service to the South." But Lovett never expressed any strong sense of regional identity. He likely saw improving educational opportunities in the South as true service to the nation. By what mental calculus integrating hope for domestic renewal, a strong educational ambition, a sense of duty, a perception of personal skills, and a recognition of great opportunity did Lovett conclude to make a dramatic move away from the familiar to the new terrain of Houston, Texas? However it was arrived at, the decision was made carefully—and not easily—with full consideration of all factors, and with an eye to practicalities.

Will Rice returned promptly to Houston after his Princeton conference with Lovett and on December 18, 1907, made a report to the eager Rice Institute trustees. Rice said he had tendered the offer to Lovett, offered him a salary of $6,000 annually, and when Lovett indicated that was simply insufficient, had raised the offer to $7,000 with a house. Lovett played his cards close to his vest, pointing out to Rice that he had "entered upon some new work [the South African venture] which he would like to carry on," and therefore could not say immediately if he would accept or not. Will Rice apparently did not push Lovett for a quick decision, gave no indication that he had tried to persuade Lovett to accept but merely had communicated the trustees' offer, and had finally suggested that Lovett take thirty days to consider the proffered position of head of the Rice Institute.

The more prescient of the trustees realized that they had to lobby, to court, Lovett, had to make him even better aware of the opportunity that awaited him in Houston and the leeway they were prepared to offer him in shaping the new institution. Trustee chair James A. Baker the very next day sent Lovett a long entreaty, clearly laying out all the reasons why Lovett should accept the position. The letter deserves to be read in full.

My Dear Mr. Lovett:

Mr. William M. Rice returned home yesterday and reported to the Trustees the substance of his recent interview with you in reference to becoming the educational head of the William M. Rice Institute, and I write now to express my disappointment in learning that you had not been able so far to give the Trustees a definite answer one way or the other, *and to urge upon you to cast your lot with us.* The Trustees have proceeded quite deliberately in making a selection of an educational head, and purposely so, because they realized that there was no more important step for them to take in the inception of the enterprise than to get a proper man to take the lead and blaze the way. They have talked to a great many persons in and out of Texas, all of whom were recommended by some one or more persons for the head of the Institute, but I want you to know, that the position has been offered to no one except you. With but one exception, I do not recall now that any one beside yourself has been seriously considered for the place. Your presence in Houston made a fine impression upon the Trustees; they like your manner, your frankness and candor and they believe your qualifications, to say nothing of your youth, eminently fits you for the place. We all realize that it is no small sacrifice to give up a position such as you have in Princeton; while this is true, yet I can assure you that in coming to Houston you and your family will find a warm welcome among generous and hospitable people, who will strive in every way to make you feel at home among them.

Our institution is well endowed—more so than any institution I know of in the South; the Trustees are practically without any experience in educational matters and they will be disposed to give you a very free hand. As a rule they are broad minded and liberal, and desire in establishing the new institution to lay its foundations broad and deep, and to employ at all times the best talent that can be had anywhere. The opportunity offered you is an unusual one, and however promising may be your prospects at Princeton, you ought to be slow in declining. Such an opportunity rarely comes to one so young in life.

Of course the question for you and your family is a serious one, but while you are considering it, I want you to know that you are the first choice of the Board of Trustees; that the offer has gone to you practically unsolicited, and we are all anxious that you should accept it and cast your lot with us.

Yours faithfully,
[signed James A. Baker].

Three days later the trustees' secretary, Emanuel Raphael, also wrote Lovett a long letter. After acknowledging that Will Rice was an old and close personal friend, "an able trustee and an all round splendid gentleman," Raphael admitted that he "lacks personal magnetism; and I fear that he did not put enough enthusiasm in his talks to you indicating that we wanted you, and we want you badly." Raphael then proceeded to rehearse the advantages of the offer, starting with the salary and the expectation that it would be increased over time; moreover, Lovett would be released from all teaching obligations in light of his expected administrative duties. "We are likewise agreed that your faculty should be high class men, nominated by yourself, because it is our express aim to make the Wm. M. Rice Institute a high class institution patterned— in great measure—after the Massachusetts School of Technology." He next described the trustees as relatively young, harmonious, and "free and untrammeled to make our institute as broad and as progressive as the heart of any ambitious educator could desire." Raphael then quoted back to Lovett words Lovett must have expressed during his April 11 interview. Knowing, Raphael wrote, that "we have *unanimously* selected you to lay the foundation, and be the leader of an institute that (to quote your own words), 'shall contribute powerfully to the sustaining sources of the life of the Nation—where by the Nation I mean the life, the thought, the conscience, the authority, of all the people of all the land,' can you imagine that any work appeals to you more powerfully than this great work in our Southland? I honestly think not." The trustees' secretary went on to characterize the people of Houston as "warm hearted, hospitable, cultured and refined," a good environment for Lovett and his family. Raphael closed almost prayerfully: "Heaven grant that your choice will fall in our direction."

If Lovett had been hesitant or even leaning toward rejection of the Rice position, these two strong letters may have changed the equation, for at a specially called meeting of the Rice board of trustees on December 28, Will Rice reported that he had received a letter from Lovett that "stated in substance" that he would accept the Rice offer, "provided that the salary was made $8,000 and a house." Moreover, Lovett said that if the terms were acceptable to the trustees, "he could be released from" his Princeton obligations before the end of the semester and could come to Houston about the first of March 1908. The board discussed Lovett's letter, found all the terms fully acceptable, and unanimously elected him to head the institute. Raphael quickly telegraphed the news to Lovett, and the next day, December 29, sent him a long confirmatory letter that made official his "election" as the "educational head of the said institute," at the salary desired and with a house provided, rent free. The salary would commence whenever Lovett could exit Princeton and begin his service in Houston. Raphael conveyed the trustees' pleasure with Lovett's acceptance and closed by saying that "I wish that I were close enough to you to shake you heartily by the hand and offer my congratulations and sincere wishes in person, but as this is impossible, please take the will for the deed. With renewed expressions of confidence and goodwill, in which the entire members of the Board of Trustees join."

All that remained was for Lovett to arrange his departure from Princeton, a departure that, no matter the sadness and frustration of the last two years he was leaving behind and the shining opportunity before him, was personally wrenching. He wrote Raphael on January 2, thanking him for the official letter (and for Raphael's personal letter of December 21). Lovett said that within two weeks he would send a formal acceptance; he had to delay "in order to meet certain formalities connected with the resignation of my position here."

> I have told you how long and deep my roots are here, and I need not tell you how hard I am finding the breaking of them [Mary had returned to be with Lovett, and surely her presence, and her support, helped him through the decision-making process]. I am trying to move in such a way as to retain the interest and influence of Princeton in our undertaking at Houston; the importance of this you of course recognize.
>
> On the other hand I want to assure you that I look forward to the work ahead with great joy, and I am almost arrogant in my hopefulness. I believe we are going to have the patience and the power to do the right thing, and by all the demons dancing in the Dog-star we will make the thing go. [After several lines missing in the extant letter comes a sentence fragment: "honour and glory to the city of Houston, a tower of strength to Texas, and a permanent source of inspiration to the whole South."]

The next day Lovett sent a carefully composed letter to President Wilson.

My dear President Wilson:

> It is with very great regret that I am writing to ask you to receive and present to the Trustees of the University my resignation of the professorship which I have had the honour to hold at Princeton. . . . I am making this request in order that I may be free to accept an administrative appointment which seems to offer unusual opportunity to translate into action the inspiration received here under your

leadership and the tutelage of those who have been associated with you in shaping the policy and directing the destiny of this institution.

I grew into Princeton from the Faculty side, but the best of the formative years of my life have been lived here, and I am leaving Princeton a Princeton man firmly believing that whatever training I may have achieved here can be devoted to the interests of the University in no better way than in an effort to bring to realization in another environment those spiritual and intellectual ideals and traditions which have made Princeton conspicuous in the Nation's service, and which, in terms of your far-reaching plans for the development of the University, are now making Princeton the most interesting educational center on the continent.

I have been trying to make this letter a formal one, and to keep my feelings out of it, but I am unwilling to bring it to a close without saying to you again that my roots here are long and deep; I cannot tell you how hard it is for me to break them.

With great respect and affectionate regards. . . .

Lovett no doubt did choose to see his departure as in no way a rejection of Princeton but rather as an opportunity to transplant the Princeton (and Wilsonian) academic ideals to another part of the nation, and this framing of his resignation may also have been to a degree an effort to reassure the beleaguered Wilson (his college system having been rejected several months before in such manner as to convince Wilson that some of his closest friends had betrayed him) that Lovett's departure did not signal a loss of trust in Wilson's plans for Princeton. Wilson replied to Lovett on January 14, reporting that he had read Lovett's resignation letter to the members of the Princeton board the previous week, and they voted to accept the resignation "with the greatest regret." Wilson continued that the board instructed him to convey to Lovett its "deep sense of the distinguished services you have rendered in the faculty and its very cordial hope that you would have the most abundant success in the new work which you are undertaking." Wilson added that these good wishes "were in no sense perfunctory, but sprung from the warmest feeling and from a real knowledge of your work and worth." (Almost exactly a year later, in his 1909 annual report to the Princeton trustees, Wilson summarized Lovett's career at Princeton and captured some of the qualities of the man that so strongly recommended him to the Rice trustees. Wilson sketched Lovett's quick rise through the faculty ranks to become the chair of astronomy. "He had grown in reputation and in mastery of his subject with singular rapidity," Wilson recalled, "carried forward by a most engaging eagerness in study and an irresistible impulse to learn and push inquiry to its limits; and yet he had shown himself fit for counsel also and a man whose disposition inclined him to the close companionships of academic life. When the trustees of Mr. Rice's bequest sought a man to take charge of the great institute of technical and liberal learning he had provided for in his will, it was hard to be generous and recommend Professor Lovett to their attention; but he has gone to his new work a thorough Princeton man, and it would indeed be churlish not to be willing to contribute our best men to the great educational work now so hopefully going forward in the South.") Clearly Lovett was leaving Princeton on exactly the terms he wished.

Now Lovett was free to give the Rice trustees his formal acceptance. In a letter to Raphael dated January 18, 1908, he graciously accepted the presidency of the William M. Rice Institute to which office the trustees "have done me the honour" to elect. "Will you not say to your colleagues on the Board," he continued,

> That with a deep sense of the obligation to service imposed by the donor's philanthropy and a firm faith in the determination of his Trustees to build for Houston, for Texas, the South, and the Nation, I pledge whatever strength or training I may have to the great task in which we hereby join hands and hearts, believing that in common counsel we are going to find the wisdom which shall issue in constructive ability to plan and executive courage to achieve the manifold possibilities of the splendid foundation on which we have the good fortune to build.

Lovett spoke of those attributes—"largeness of mind, strength of character, determined purpose, fire of genius, devoted loyalty"—out of which he hoped to craft a sense of institutional leadership on the part of the new university, and he looked forward to the day in the not distant future when "from its walls shall go forth a continuous column of men trained in the highest degree, equipped in the largest way for positions of trust in the public service, for commanding careers in the world's affairs"—a resoundingly Wilsonian goal.

Four days later, January 22, having read Lovett's formal letter, the Rice trustees "unanimously received" "the letter of acceptance of Dr. Lovett." The deed was done; the Rice Institute had a new president ready to turn the institution that until then had been but a dream on paper into a living, breathing reality. And Edgar Odell Lovett had found his life's work. Within the next few months letters poured in to him, congratulating him on his new mission and some wistfully regretting that his scientific career was effectively over.

During the following weeks Lovett prepared to move, tying up loose ends to activities at Princeton, thinking about moving his recently restored family, planning the next steps to take in Houston, and saying a long series of goodbyes and replying to well-wishers. The *Daily Princetonian* had noted his leaving with "personal regret," but the student newspaper wished him well: "May he carry the ideals and the spirit of Princeton with him and inculcate them in the great institution he is to build up." That was, of course, precisely Lovett's hope. At the end of February he again rode the train to Houston, arriving on February 29. At the next meeting of the board of trustees, on March 11, Lovett appeared for his first conference with them in his new capacity. Trustee chairman Baker formally welcomed him. Lovett then "outlined a rough sketch of the work of organizing the Institute as it appeared to him, at the present time." Probably at the instigation of Emanuel Raphael, who had found his late 1906 trip to eastern universities so valuable in forming a better idea of what might be accomplished in Houston, the board of trustees asked Lovett "to make a tour of observation and investigation of the best work done in the Universities and Technical Colleges, both in the United States and Europe." Accordingly the trustees asked him to submit, at their next meeting or as soon afterward as possible, a written plan of such a trip, with an estimate of how long it would take and how much it would cost, assuming he engaged a private secretary to assist him on the voyage of academic discovery. In the several days following the board meeting, Lovett was introduced to Mayor H. B. Rice (no relation to William Marsh Rice), took a trip on the mayor's yacht, the *Zeeland*, down the Buffalo Bayou, and was invited to attend a "smoker" held by the board of the Houston Business League. Lovett was entering on his duties as president, a substantial part of which would be reaching out to the community, and Lovett would prove to be unusually adept at such public relations. The board was also already considering acquiring a larger site for the campus than its downtown location, something it had been contemplating since at least 1905. Lovett had been supporting such an acquisition since his April 1907 visit, although he was not closely involved in the process. (At the June 24 board meeting, with Lovett present, it was mutually agreed that a site of from two hundred to three hundred acres was advisable, and Will Rice was authorized to begin negotiating with George Hermann for land on both sides of the extension of Main Street, with the desire that the matter could be settled early in the fall.)

Lovett returned to Princeton (he evidently still had some duties there until June), sending word back to the trustees in April that he wished to hire a recent Princeton graduate and Houston native, F. Carrington Weems, to be his private secretary largely for the upcoming trip, an appointment the board approved at its May meeting with an annual salary of $1,000. Lovett was working hard on the proposed itinerary, but there were powerful distractions. Lovett was still saying his goodbyes to Princeton colleagues, and on May 25 he, along with Professor Harry Augustus Garfield, who was leaving to become president of Williams College, were honored at a farewell banquet at the Princeton Club, where, after a stunningly elaborate dinner, toasts were offered by President Wilson and representatives of the board and faculty. Finally on June 4 Lovett wrote apologetically to Rice trustee Raphael, confessing that "I am going through the harrowing of leave-taking from a home hallowed by the deepest experience of my life. It is taking more of me than I anticipated and I beg the indulgence of the Board if I seem to be getting at the work of the Institute with less of singleness of purpose than I promised." Yet in the following paragraph Lovett listed seventeen nations, from Austria to Switzerland, with fifty-eight actual cities named to possibly visit. He understood that this extensive a trip would be excessive, so he offered a second list of cities as his tentative itinerary: Princeton, Boston, Montreal, Liverpool, Glasgow,

Edinburgh, Manchester, Birmingham, Cambridge, Oxford, London, Brussels, Paris, Bordeaux, Madrid, Athens, Rome, Turin, Milan, Zurich, Vienna, Munich, Prague, Leipzig, Berlin, Copenhagen, Christiania, Stockholm, St. Petersburg, Moscow, Tokyo, Yokahoma, San Francisco, Palo Alto, and ending up in Houston. On his own initiative he had extended the board's instructions and proposed journeying beyond Europe to include the Orient. He reported that past experience suggested that he could travel alone for between $4 and $5 a day in addition to railroad and Pullman fares. "I shall do the thing as economically as is consistent with the prosecution of the problem and the preservation of health. I shall not hesitate to spend time or money as the occasion may demand, but always with a view of making every dollar count for the Institute." He then suggested the kind of office equipment he would need (typewriter, stationery, notebooks, camera, and a large trunk to transport all this paraphernalia), along with the steamer passage for himself and Carrington Weems and a variety of minor expense items. He also thought he should bring with him two letters of credit for $500 each. Raphael duly communicated this letter to the board of trustees, and at their June 10 meeting they agreed to advance Lovett the sum of $1,625 to cover the trip.

Lovett planned to take his wife Mary along on the trip, at his own expense, and surely they were imagining this as almost a second honeymoon celebrating her restoration to good health. She was spending several weeks in Mayfield with her parents and the children, for Adelaide and Malcolm would be staying with their Kentucky grandparents. Carrington Weems, who had met Mary and the children during his student days, wrote her "to say that it is great to know that you are going with us, and that before long all three of us will be on the briny deep, and the work fairly underway." Lovett wrote her again on July 8, suggesting she should return to Princeton in a few days because they would be leaving soon, stopping first for a while in Boston and a day in Montreal before departing on July 24 from Quebec. They were preparing to circumnavigate the globe, from the New World to Europe to the Orient, inspecting university campuses and facilities, laboratories, and libraries; interviewing professors and university leaders; looking at architecture and building materials—developing, in short, an inspired idea of what might be accomplished in Houston for the Rice Institute. The resulting trip, intentionally planned to better develop the concept of the new university, would in its scope and duration be unprecedented in the history of American higher education.

# CHAPTER THREE

# THE GRAND TOUR

SOMETIME DURING THE LATE SPRING or early summer of 1908, as Edgar Odell Lovett was making final preparations to leave Princeton University and completing the plans for his upcoming round-the-world trip, his secretary, F. Carrington Weems, still in Houston, sent him an undated Houston newspaper clipping based on an interview with Lovett in which he had explained to the reporter the purposes of his forthcoming voyage. Here Lovett had laid out the entire rationale of his trip, summarized by the unnamed reporter as "searching among the universities of the two hemispheres for the educational and architectural ideas that will be incorporated in the new university to be planted in Houston." There would be nothing provincial in the conceptualization of the Rice Institute. Lovett was quite specific about his intentions. "I expect to inquire intimately into the workings of the various city colleges in England, because it is the problem of the city institution that we will have to meet here in Houston. University college in London, and the various institutions in Manchester, Liverpool, and Edinburgh ought to be able to furnish some valuable and interesting suggestions. Oxford and Cambridge I shall visit for their architecture." But it is important to realize that when Lovett spoke of the importance of the city colleges, he was not referring primarily to their urban locations.

For centuries Oxford and Cambridge, with their classical curricula and elitist traditions, had completely dominated higher education in England. Then beginning in the early nineteenth century, reformers, noting the rise of scientific and engineering universities and technical institutes in late-eighteenth-century Germany and France, began to push to modernize the offerings at Oxbridge and to advocate the development of new universities that were more democratic in their admission procedures and more focused on the educational and technological needs of both their local communities and business and in-

dustrial interests. Previously the two leading British universities had accepted students almost exclusively from private schools with upper-class
backgrounds. Educational statesmen like Viscount Haldane advocated
a series of new and different universities, which Haldane termed *civic
universities* and others called *redbrick* or *municipal universities*. These
new universities, located in rapidly growing, industrializing cities such
as Manchester and Liverpool, had curricula that combined training
and research in pure and applied science with traditional humanistic
studies, carefully tailored to fit the needs of their particular location.
Despite elitist objections, these new institutions quickly gained full university standing, developed innovative outreach or extension programs,
including lecture series to lay audiences, and represented a significant
democratization of higher education. Lovett understood that these new
institutions were more relevant to his task of creating a university from
scratch in Texas than the centuries-old and tradition-bound Oxford and
Cambridge.

Lovett also knew that universities in general had undergone great
changes in the nineteenth century. In addition to the rise of polytechnic
institutes and technical high schools (*Hochschulen* in Germany) that
emphasized practical or applied sciences and engineering, Germany
universities especially, beginning at Berlin, had come to put highest priority on discovering new knowledge, using the laboratory as a teaching
and research tool in the sciences and the research seminar in the humanistic disciplines. Students were accorded a great deal of freedom to
choose their own course of study, and faculty members were expected
to conduct research and publish. Universities began to construct large
libraries and well-equipped laboratories, and various research institutes sprang up in many European cities. Germany and France took the
lead in many of these developments, attracting able graduate students
from all over the world. Graduate studies—not undergraduate teaching
alone—began to be the hallmark of the greatest universities. In short,
the modern university was emerging, and Lovett wanted to study the
new institution in its most innovative form. One can imagine the questions on his mind. What is an ideal enrollment? How may the best faculty be identified and recruited? What is the proper balance between
research and teaching? What disciplines and fields should be covered?

How should students be housed, fed, and governed? What size campus and what kinds of facilities are advised? How should a university relate to the larger community? Lovett was open to new ideas but grounded in traditions that privileged both character and learning. His familiarity with Virginia, Johns Hopkins, Chicago, and Princeton meant that he already understood to a substantial degree how the most innovative educational practices might be adapted to an American locale.

Lovett of course intended to visit the full range of long-established universities and new technical institutes that had proliferated in Europe, with especial attention to academic developments in Paris, perhaps because he knew that city best. "I consider that the intellectual capital of the globe is in Paris," he commented to the Houston reporter, and he wanted to study carefully the history and evolution of the University of Paris, where residential college life had begun. From there he planned to travel to the various German universities, and thence to "Zurich, Vienna, and possibly St. Petersburg." Also indicating great interest in the physical design of the new university, Lovett said, "I may go over into Spain to study the architecture." Warming to that subject, Lovett continued: "We don't know many things definite about our plans for the college because we don't want to decide on any features of the institution until we are sure that they are best, but one thing is settled, and that is that a definite style of architecture will be settled upon and followed throughout in the construction of the buildings and in the construction of all future buildings. We have not decided what the architecture will be, what style will be selected—I will look out for this on the trip—but when it is determined, it will be strictly adhered to throughout and in all future expansion of the institute." More than on any other topic at this moment, Lovett was convinced of the importance of architectural consistency, disparaging most universities for their "conglomeration of styles." With his views to that extent already formed, the Lovett party prepared to sail to England. The two Lovett children, Adelaide and Malcolm, would be staying with their grandparents in Mayfield, which must by now have almost seemed like home to them. Throughout the trip their mother would periodically write to them, "My dear chicks" as she addressed them from Princeton shortly after leaving them in Kentucky and joining her husband for final trip preparations.

Edgar Odell Lovett, his wife Mary, and Lovett's private secretary, F. Carrington Weems—along with a substantial stack of sturdy, closely packed trunks—left Montreal on July 24, 1908, aboard the *Empress of Ireland*, a small steamer owned by the Canadian Pacific Line. Lovett had written Rice trustee chair James A. Baker in early July that the crossing would take six days and that their permanent foreign address would be in care of Brown, Shipley, & Co., 123 Pall Mall, S.W., London, England. Members of the Rice board could communicate with him via this address; also, early in his trip Lovett wrote a steady stream of letters to university officials and scholars setting up appointments, and his correspondents replied to this London address.

Lovett had purchased in advance two large bound volumes, with the institute's name embossed on the front cover, consisting of very thin paper for recording observations, with a carbon made of every page. The top page could be torn off (it was perforated), leaving a copy, with the original ready to be remitted to the trustees back in Houston. The pages were preprinted, with a line at the top for the date and sheet (page) number to be inserted, then a series of printed prompts: "appointments to-day with," the subjects discussed, the buildings visited, what their purpose was, their construction material; people met during the day, with the subjects discussed and remarks; a place for listing letters and telegrams sent and received; then a series of other entries, including at the bottom a place to itemize expenses. The next two pages were left blank for the recording of impressions and other information regarding the day's experiences. Even the first pages, with the blanks to fill in, were seldom completed in their entirety, with sometimes hardly more information than the places visited, but in total the two volumes provide a vivid and accurate record of their academic tour around the world. Lovett also wrote a series of long letters addressed to Emanuel Raphael, the secretary of the Rice trustees, and in these letters he much more fully described what he heard, saw, and learned. These letters, along with the daily record book, provide an ample portrait of the voyage of academic discovery.

The first notations were listed for August 1, 1908, immediately after arrival in Liverpool. Dr. Lovett had an appointment with Vice Chancellor A. H. H. Dale, professor of classics at the University of Liverpool. They visited three buildings, including a basic administration

facility and a physics laboratory, with Lovett noting that they were constructed of brick and stone, and he sent three letters to faculty persons
at Newcastle-on-Tyne, London, and Paris setting up appointments for
future interviews. Lovett was particularly impressed both by the public support in Liverpool for the university and by all the educational/
cultural opportunities it provided for the citizens of the city. Arrangements were made for Vice Chancellor Dale to send Lovett the rough
plans of the physics laboratory they had visited. Then at the bottom of
the page were listed the expenses of the day and the balance of moneys
on hand. In the blank pages for general impressions, Lovett reported
that in a lengthy conversation Dale had told him that "You will read no
more books, write no more papers, and take no more vacations" now
that he had become a university administrator. (In truth, though he may
not fully have realized it, Lovett's scholarly career as a mathematician/
astronomer was over. Instead he had accepted a new calling, the creation and nurturing of a new university.) Dale also advised that they
"should consider men and equipment rather than expensive buildings."
Dale talked about a number of issues, but he did not have names of
people to recommend for faculty at Rice. Lovett's next notation was for
August 3, although there were no appointments that day because it was
a bank holiday in England; he did, however, send three letters, including one back to Emanuel Raphael to give his first report. Lovett purchased a Baedeker guide to England to facilitate the remainder of their
travel there. The following day the Rice visitors again inspected various
university buildings, and Lovett sent out four more letters.

   On August 5 the group traveled by train to Glasgow, arriving the
next day. The schedule was much as before, inspecting buildings, writing letters to arrange future appointments, commenting on such things
as "excellent lighting and ventilation" in a laboratory. Professor John
Gordon Longbottom, essentially contradicting Chancellor Dale at Liverpool, strongly recommended "substantial buildings." Lovett noted
that he had received letters from a number of American universities informing him that the Rice Institute had been placed on their permanent
mailing lists to receive automatically the publications of the various
universities—no doubt this was in response to an earlier request from
Lovett. Several days later, still in Glasgow, Lovett listed twenty-one

American universities and colleges to which he sent letters acknowledging their expressions of good will and advice. He was doing everything he could to spread the name of the new institution. For most American universities, this meant sending them letters of announcement and an introductory pamphlet. For European universities, Lovett hoped in his travels to visit as many as possible and utilize these visits not only to inspect their facilities and perchance interview their leaders but also—and maybe especially—to alert them to the scope and aspirations of the new university being planned in faraway Texas.

En route to Edinburgh on August 10, Lovett filled up an entire page outlining the various professors and other teaching staff of the Rice Institute as he imagined them to be. This faculty list proved to be far more expansive than was possible in the beginning, but the plan suggests the directions of Lovett's thought at the time. Listed first was the professor of mathematics, really the chair of mathematics, and underneath him were a junior professor of pure mathematics and a junior professor of applied mathematics. Then Lovett envisioned four lecturers covering analysis, geometry, astronomy, and mechanics. Following were four instructors in pure and applied mathematics, and last, four fellows. Under similar format Lovett listed his at-the-moment complete idealized faculty roster. There would be a professor of physics and two junior professors, one of theoretical physics and the other of experimental physics. Four lecturers would offer instruction in electricity, thermodynamics, spectroscopy, and radiation phenomena. Four instructors would be provided for mathematical and experimental physics, and, as in mathematics proper, Lovett proposed four fellows.

There would be a professor of chemistry, along with two junior professors of organic and inorganic chemistry. Four lecturers would specialize in physical chemistry, electrochemistry, biochemistry, and chemical technology. The four instructors would offer courses in qualitative analysis, quantitative analysis, chemical synthesis, and mineralogy and metallurgy. As in the other sciences, there would be four fellows. Under the professor of biology would be a junior professor of biology and a junior professor of botany; four lecturers would be appointed in anatomy, physiology, histology, and biometrics. Four instructors would offer work in "forestry, agriculture, etc.," and again there were four fellows. Engineering would consist of one department, equal in size to each of the basic science departments. Lovett imagined a professor of engineering, followed by junior professors of mechanical engineering and chemical engineering. He listed four lecturers (in civil, mining, sanitary, and electrical engineering), four instructors (in geodesy, geology, graphics, and geography), and, as usual, four fellows.

Lovett planned for substantial offerings in the humanities as well. He listed a professor of philosophy, supported by a junior professor of logic and a junior professor of psychology. There would be, he proposed, four lecturers, one each in the history of philosophy, the history of scientific ideas, experimental psychology, and ethics. The four instructors would specialize in the philosophy, respectively, of Greece, England, France, and Germany. Then there would be four fellows. Under the direction of the professor of letters would be *three* junior professors, one of English, one of ancient literature, and one of modern literature. The four lecturers would offer courses in the literature of England, France, Germany, and Italy, and *six* instructors would offer work in English (two), French, German, Spanish, and Italian—all modern—languages. There would, moreover, be four fellows. The professor or chair of history would supervise a junior professor of ancient history and a junior professor of modern history. Four lecturers would be responsible for American history, international law, jurisprudence, and politics, while the four instructors would teach Texas history, South American history, economics, and sociology. Four fellows would continue their research and assist with the teaching. The professor of art would work with a junior professor of archaeology and a junior professor of architecture. Four lecturers would offer drawing, painting, sculpture, and music, while the four instructors would teach sketching, painting, engraving, and illustrating. Again there would be four fellows. And the last department probably to be developed would be the professor of the history of religion. This list proves more an index of Lovett's mind and his understanding of the various subfields of learning than it does a chart of the development of the Rice Institute. The number of faculty assumed—10 professors, 19 junior professors, 36 lecturers, 38 instructors, and 36 fellows—would not be reached at Rice until after World War II. The projected size of the faculty was a measure of Lovett's ambition for the university he was planning, one devoted to liberal and technical learning in the vocabulary of the era.

At the end of the day on August 11, in Edinburgh, Lovett recorded more observations. Drawing in part on what he had been seeing and hearing on the journey of exploration, he wrote that the university should "be prepared to *make science, teach science,* and *apply science.*" Because these ideals would be central to the mission of the Rice Institute as he saw it, Lovett elaborated on his meaning:

1. Make science (actual additions to knowledge, not only of facts, but of methods and processes, initiative and invention)
2. Teach science (To the public, to students young and old, and as the ground plan of the broadest training)
3. Apply science (Directly to the mechanic and industrial arts, and indirectly through inspiration to art and letters)
The work must be threefold:—Constructive in creating the new, educative in teaching the old, immediately utilitarian in application of new and old to the common good.

As these ruminations indicate, Lovett had moved a long way from the classical curriculum he had experienced at Bethany College. In his present understanding, clearly borrowed from what he had seen in Leipzig and at Virginia, Johns Hopkins, Chicago, and Princeton, and reinforced already on the present trip, universities did not simply pass on knowledge but, perhaps more important, created new knowledge through research and directed that research, at least partly, to practical ends. These emerging ideas would take physical shape as Lovett continued to make plans for the new university soon to open in Houston.

In nineteenth-century America most colleges had been planted in rural locations or in decidedly small academic towns, in the hope that the (mostly male) students would thereby be isolated from demoralizing urban influences. Johns Hopkins and Chicago were exceptions, but most state universities were not in the major cities of their state, which Lovett was coming to see as a mistake. On August 14, still in Edinburgh, he recorded this insight: "We are fortunate in being located in a city. From whatever place the student may come they will be citizens of the city, but more than this will they be citizens of the college commonwealth within the city. I am beginning to believe that we may be able to combine the finer features of the college in the city and the college in the country."

J. Theodore Merz, a historian of European thought, with whom Lovett dined at New Castle-on-Tyne, England, strongly urged that "we make a larger place for theoretic than for practical science. Although progress would be slower it would pay in the long run if we attended more to pure than to applied science." Lovett had begun his journey with the typical Progressive-era view that universities should serve utilitarian purposes, but the new emphasis he was hearing on pure research was convincing. Merz also emphasized that the new university should incorporate originality in its planning and not "copy even the best models." Moreover, he insisted, "women should be admitted to the institution," though that was not at question because the Rice charter required it. The following day Lovett and his party set off for St. Andrews, where there was another round of meetings, inspection of facilities, and searching for good ideas. From there they went to Aberdeen, thence to Melrose (where Professor J. A. Gibson of the University of Glasgow had recommended "a considerable plant to start with . . . so constructed as to admit of additions." He also stated his belief that the "Academic scope and content [was] conditioned by two things: what the students are prepared for on entrance; what they should be prepared for on leaving"). Near Melrose the three Americans paused for a bit of touristy sightseeing, visiting Abbotsford, the home of Sir Walter Scott. How often over the course of the next few months would they act as regular tourists? Very rarely is there any mention of such pleasant interludes, but the record shows that they frequently bought guidebooks and maps, and they returned home with thousands of postcards that they had purchased but not sent. It is easy to imagine that at times the journey took on aspects of the Grand Tour that had in the previous century been the apex of a person's education.

But whatever the case, quickly after paying homage to the author of the Waverly novels, it was back to business, and they were off to Leeds, and from there to Manchester, which Lovett termed "the first industrial city in Great Britain." Lovett visited the University of Manchester and the Municipal Institute of Technology. True to what Lovett had told the Houston newspaper reporter, the Rice delegation showed particular interest in the new urban and technical institutions, whose curricula accommodated more engineering and practical science than did those of more traditional universities. (In truth, throughout the trip he seemed not to miss a single technical institute, although the visits surely became somewhat redundant. He somehow seemed constantly open to the possibility that he might learn something new and valuable at the next institution.) The next day they were in Liverpool. Again there was the usual round of meetings, consultations, building tours, letters to be written. Three days later Lovett interviewed there in Liverpool Professor Simon Newcomb of Johns Hopkins University, whose advice seems remarkably ill informed. Newcomb thought the United States already had enough universities, though he conceded that perhaps the South needed more. He said that the professors should be only Americans, "preferably of southern stock." Thankfully, neither Lovett nor the Rice trustees proved to be so provincial. Newcomb—from Johns Hopkins, remember—"thought it would be impossible to interest other men in the undertaking [in Houston] because the institution bears a man's name and is local." Of course, under Lovett's direction, the university would be anything but local.

On the way to Dublin, Lovett had an appointment on August 31 with Woodrow Wilson, who was vacationing at Grasmere; Lovett stayed over Sunday with the Wilsons. Wilson had sent Lovett a handwritten note on August 11 asking Lovett and his party to visit them at their English Lake Country vacation retreat. Wilson wrote his wife of the Lovett visit that while the two of them walked, "we saw the valley at its loveliest,—at least I did. I am not sure he took anything in very consciously, so absorbed was he in the questions he had come to discuss." For Lovett this was truly a journey of investigation and reflection, and he was concentrating almost exclusively on the project at hand.

In Dublin on September 1, the Rice delegation continued as usual. The British Association for the Advancement of Science was meeting in Dublin, and to its members Lovett read a mathematics paper entitled "Conservative Systems with Prescribed Trajectories," which was, he pointed out to the Rice trustees, "the first scientific paper from the Rice Institute . . . presented to the public." On the evening of September 3

Lovett had dinner and extended conversation with a half dozen English academicians, including eminent physicist J. J. Thomson of the Cavendish Laboratory of Cambridge. (On this and similar occasions over the last few weeks Lovett had met with Dr. W. N. Shaw, head of the Meteorological Office of the British government; Dr. A. E. Shipley of Cambridge; Professor A. E. H. Love of Oxford; Professor W. E. Dalby, dean of the Guilds' Technical College in London; Sir Robert Ball of Cambridge; Professor E. T. Whittaker, Astronomer Royal for Ireland; and many other faculty from University College, Cardiff, Manchester University, and similar distinguished institutions and agencies.) The whole group unanimously and strongly recommended that we "should consider men before mortar and brains before bricks." "Pay good salaries and especially to the junior members of the staff was the advice of all." Various members of the dinner party suggested "courses theoretical with not much shopwork," argued that meteorology now deserved a space on the faculty, insisted that research was important, and even emphasized that "the best teachers are the researchers who have time and facilities for their own investigations." On this last point everyone agreed. Here and on similar occasions Lovett asked for suggestions for faculty members, and names were often presented. On the night following the dinner conversation with the six academicians, Lovett greatly enjoyed the garden party sponsored by the Association for the Advancement of Science, where a highlight was meeting the Astronomer Royal. In a letter to Raphael dated September 6, two days later, Lovett mentioned that "the men with whom I have sought interviews have been uniformly interested and suggestive, the magnitude of our foundation [endowment] arresting their attention and the scope of our problems firing their imagination." In truth, nothing more important was being accomplished by Lovett than this placing of the Rice Institute on the mental screens of distinguished European academicians.

On the evening of September 7 the party set out by train to London, where they would remain for over a month. By now Lovett had tired of the routine of filling out many of the blanks in the record book, often only inserting the date and location, with perhaps an itemized expense such as "Kodak supplies." In addition to buying postcards and maps, they (almost certainly Carrington Weems) took innumerable photographs. On September 29 Lovett listed receipt of a bank draft of £200 from Rice Institute's business manager, A. B. Cohn; over the next few months other such infusions of funds would arrive. Finally on October 15 there was a notation that the group was packing up to leave London for Scandinavia the next day. Before departing, Lovett mailed the first of several boxes of books back to Houston, intended for the new institute. He also sent a long letter to Raphael describing their last weeks' activity.

Lovett especially praised the new municipal universities that were bringing high-quality technical and humanistic learning to the future captains of industry. These innovative new universities, "resolutely refusing to imitate established types . . . have boldly developed a system of education, adapted to the demands of their environment . . . thus meeting local obligations." Yet Lovett made clear that "in so bringing to a wider public the opportunities for a higher education, these later universities have maintained the high standards of English scholarship." These institutions, he also emphasized, by no means neglected the teaching and doing of science, and in fact the universities were doing remarkably well in conducting creative research—exactly what he had recommended to the Rice trustees when they had interviewed him in April 1907. Realizing that the trustees back in Houston were at the moment considering the site for the institute, he also lauded the decision of the University of Birmingham to move from its crowded downtown location to a far more spacious acreage three miles away, which not only allowed "large athletic grounds for the outdoor sports of the students" but would also make possible additional buildings and growth in the future. Lovett used the example of Birmingham's relocation to strengthen the Rice board's resolve to find a new and more ample setting for the Rice campus.

Aware from his student days of how cold Scandinavian nations could be in the dead of winter, Lovett decided that the Rice delegation should make preparations to visit there next. Going by way of Hamburg, they arrived at Gothenburg on October 19, and from there traveled on to Christiania, Norway, where Lovett had studied with Sophus Lie back in 1896. Of course, Professor Lie was dead, but Mrs. Lovett at least visited with his widow, who warmly remembered the young student

Lovett. Dr. Lovett did meet several times with Carl Störmer, a young Norwegian mathematician and astrophysicist who had already done pioneering work on the aurora borealis and who later would be invited to attend the formal opening of the Rice Institute. Here, as in many other stops, Lovett noted that he spent some time working in the university library, but there is no indication that he walked in the nearby woods, as he had during his student days on restful Saturdays. Through the good offices of Lovett's friends at Christiania, the king of Norway granted Lovett an interview, and he found that the king had already been briefed on the purpose of Lovett's journey. After three weeks the Lovett party left for Stockholm, arriving on October 30. Here among other buildings Lovett visited the university's observatory. Perhaps because he was already thinking seriously about the process of growing an infant Rice Institute into a full-fledged university, Lovett considered especially interesting the evolution of the University of Stockholm, writing that "I found that the beginnings of the new humanistic faculty furnish a most instructive example. However strong the original bent of the University was in the direction of pure science, as rapidly as its resources will permit, the institution is making provision for jurisprudence, civil law, letters and art."

While in Stockholm, Lovett on November 4 received a troubling letter from Emanuel Raphael, secretary of the Rice trustees. Lovett was glad to see from the first portion of the letter that the trustees were about to conclude negotiations to purchase the sizable plot out Main Street for the location of the institute, but the second part of the letter suggested that he terminate his trip in January 1909 and return to Houston and the active development of the institute; he could plan a visit to Japan later, the trustees proposed. Replying on November 12, Lovett explained to Raphael that he had taken a week "to think the matter over . . . [and] canvassed the situation thoroughly." Lovett wrote that he could fully understand the impatience of the people of Houston; indeed, he said, "my own impatience at times is almost uncontrollable." But Lovett cautioned that "to make haste where haste should not be made" would not convince the local citizens that the trustees were in earnest about erecting a great institution. He pointed out that the trip had been very carefully planned, and that the portion of it already completed "demonstrates the wisdom of the Board in this feature of their programme, and shows the advantages to be expected from the later events of the journey." He simply was learning so much he did not want to foreclose acquiring information from the more distant, less familiar portions of his planned itinerary. "There has been already too much time, money, and energy invested," he argued, "to fail of getting a proper return. The experience gained convinces me that we can hardly overestimate the value to our future plans of an exhaustive study of this kind."

He then stated that the continuation of the trip as planned was the shortest way practical to realize the goal for which the board had sent him abroad in the first place. He went on to state that his opinion regarding the wisdom and utility of the trip was seconded, "without exception, by the educators I have met in Europe." He concluded by saying that he appreciated that the board left the final decision up to him, but that he hoped that now that he had decided to continue as planned, "I still have their full approval." Like the indefatigable researcher who does not want to miss one archive, Lovett had set himself an exploratory timetable and wanted to extract every bit of information from the sources, always believing that new pearls of insight were possible. His letter apparently convinced the board, who in their meeting of November 25 discussed his letter and directed the secretary to communicate that approval to Dr. Lovett. Meanwhile, of course, the Rice party kept traveling, and after a quick stop at Lund, Sweden, where they saw the newer university buildings, they traveled to Berlin, arriving on November 10. Several days later their trunks arrived from London, and the party checked into a comfortable pensione for their Berlin stay. But no doubt Lovett remained worried at least to a degree about his relationship with the board of trustees and their true feelings concerning his insistence on completing the trip as originally planned. He knew how essential their mutual trust would be for the successful development of the new university.

There was much to see in Berlin but little was recorded in the daybook, except notice on the 16th that they visited the various buildings of the Technical Hochschule. Later there are references to visiting the University of Berlin, but astonishingly little—often nothing at all—was recorded in the daybook except date and location. However, by now Lovett was sending his impressions and conclusions to Raphael in the form of letters, neglecting to say much on the printed pages of the daybook. He was very taken with the technical institute in Berlin, located in Charlottenburg (then a western suburb of the city proper), which he pointed out "in a single generation has come to occupy the first place among institutions of this kind in the world." Although they were sometimes called technical high schools, he made clear that they were truly universities. He of course expressed great admiration for the University of Berlin, with its astounding enrollment of 14,000.

On November 20 Woodrow Wilson wrote Lovett that he had written to the U.S. Secretary of State Elihu Root, and Root had prepared a letter of introduction for Lovett to use when meeting with "officers of our Diplomatic and Consular Service" around the world. In fact, Root had had the letter prepared on November 17, which stated that "at the instance of Doctor Woodrow Wilson, President of Princeton University," he took "pleasure in introducing to you Doctor E. O. Lovett." "I cordially bespeak for Doctor Lovett such courtesies and assistance as you may be able to render, consistently with your official duties," Secretary Root had continued. Lovett did meet the American ambassador to Germany, Dr. D. J. Hill. Lovett occasionally mentioned correspondence sent and received, but nothing was recorded of the intellectual riches of the city. They left Berlin on December 6 and arrived in the famous old university city of Göttingen on December 7, where they stayed for two days. Göttingen had been the home of the brothers Grimm, writer Heinrich Heine, and explorer Alexander von Humboldt. The high point of the trip to Göttingen was an appointment with mathematician Felix Klein, once the collaborator with Lovett's former teacher Sophus Lie. Lovett was much impressed by the way Klein had arranged his research center in the "mathematical and physical sciences in such a way that they are coordinated and at the same time opportunities are offered to students specializing in these subjects to take liberalizing courses in letters, art and philosophy." Again Lovett was impressed with the combination of technical and liberal learning—a balance he would seek to establish in Houston.

On December 10 the Rice travelers were back in Berlin. There were constant meetings with scholars, and one notes that quite often, here and elsewhere, Lovett managed to meet with astronomers and the directors of observatories, no doubt names and places he was acquainted with. At last on December 16 the group set out for Leipzig. Was Lovett eager to see his old university city? Did he have special sites in mind to show his wife? The record is silent. He did write to Raphael that the "city is one of the centres of the book trade of the world, and I took occasion to make the Institute known to several of the leading firms." They stayed only a little more than a day in Leipzig, and then, by way of Dresden (and the Technical High School there) they journeyed to Munich. Here too they visited the university and the Technical High School.

What impressed Lovett about the Technical High School of Munich—which had just surpassed that at Charlottenburg in enrollment—was its decision to give "priority" to "theoretical over practical training." Lovett noted that this was a controversial point, but he seemed to agree with the Munich educators that the men best prepared for modern "large engineering enterprises are those who have been trained to think with their heads fully as much as with their hands." He would remember this when planning the engineering curriculum at the Rice Institute. Of course earlier in his trip Lovett had heard from other scholars that theoretical science—what today would be labeled pure research—should be emphasized, so the Munich example only drove home the point. This was, no doubt, one of the most important lessons he learned from his extensive travels.

Lovett wrote to Raphael on December 21, 1908, from Munich that of all the universities they had visited so far, one of the three most impressive was Göttingen (founded in 1737) precisely because "it combines in itself the advantages of an university with those of a technical institute, and that in spite of the rigid system under which German education is organized." Wanting to make this point very emphatically to the Rice trustees, Lovett continued to write of the glories of Göttingen. "Göttigen possessed exceptional facilities for teaching and advancing the mathematical and physical sciences, and yet the liberalizing influences are not wanting. I felt the spirit of the place at a dinner of mathematicians where metaphysics, world politics, and mathematics were discussed with equal relish." Unmistakably Lovett was developing a broad conception of a university in his mind. While the title *institute* suggested narrowness in focus, Lovett's vision of the mature university was anything but narrow.

Then it was on to Zurich, where they stayed through Christmas. Zurich too had a university and a Technical High School, representing the cutting edge of European education. On December 26 the three departed for Milan (and its "celebrated Technical Institute"), then on to Padua, Bologna ("the seat of perhaps the most ancient university in Europe," founded in 1139), Pisa, and Turin (again with a technical institute) in quick succession—but with meetings with scholars in every locale—and arrived in Paris on January 1. (Probably because she needed the rest, and perhaps too because her love of art made her want to spend time in Rome, Mary Hale Lovett had left her husband and Carrington Weems at Milan and journeyed to the Eternal City to stay for several weeks while Dr. Lovett and Weems continued on to Paris and beyond. Several days later a solicitous Lovett wrote his wife: "I hope you have recovered from the fatigue of your journey from Milan to Rome.") There followed visits to the Sorbonne, the Academy of Sciences, the University of Paris, and the Polytechnic Institute.

On January 3 Lovett wrote to Mary in Rome that while he was growing impatient to get back to Houston, "I am more than ever persuaded that it would have been a mistake for us not to complete the Tour du Monde while we are about it." For Lovett and Weems, this was university travel, not a vacation, so on January 7 the two men left dear Paris en route to Brussels and the École Normale. That same day Lovett received a letter from his wife's father in which he said that he was "Glad to hear of her improvement in health and spirit." Clearly this trip was for her, and no doubt for her husband as well, a continuation of her recuperation from those many months of deep depression following the death of their daughter. (Mary clearly appreciated the restorative value of the trip. An old friend of hers, referring to an earlier letter from Mary, commented that she was "delighted with your last letter, telling the great benefit the trip had been to you, giving you a new lease of life, as it were.") The next day found Lovett and Weems at The Hague—where they admired the "new building being built for the

Peace Conference, which Mr. Carnegie's liberality made possible"—the following day they were in Leiden, and then, on the night of January 9, they pushed on to London, arriving on the 11th. The schedule is tiring simply to read about, but in London they stayed in the comfortable Morley's Hotel, overlooking busy Trafalgar Square. They had already spent much time in London, but there was still so much to see and so many people to meet. They inspected the facilities of the Imperial College of Science, met with Professor J. J. Thomson, director of the Cavendish Laboratory, with Professor Glaicher of Cambridge University (during a quick day trip to Cambridge), then took a day trip to Oxford, and continued meetings in London with scholars representing a wide range of fields. Although Lovett never mentioned it, perhaps the most valuable part of this trip were the interviews time and time again with the leading scholars and academic administrators of Europe and beyond. Lovett was seeing and learning how the best minds thought, getting their ideas about leadership and administration, and simply coming to recognize uncommon individual merit. This growth in his understanding was a largely unanticipated result of his travels, and the experience would bring enormous returns several years later when Lovett actively recruited the initial faculty for the institute. And of course, everyone with whom Lovett spoke also learned something of the great new institute being planned.

On January 15 Lovett visited Eton College and Windsor, but the next day he was in Paris en route to Spain. January 18 found Lovett and Weems in Burgos, in northern Spain, and by the 19th they had arrived in Madrid, where Lovett quickly visited the university. On the next day they journeyed to Toledo, and at 9:05 p.m. on January 21 took the night train to Lisbon. The next day Lovett visited Coimbra and the university there, Portugal's oldest (founded in 1307) and most prestigious, and on January 23 he inspected the Technical High School and the Academy of Sciences in Lisbon. From there they went to Seville and its university. On the 26th they left for Cordova, having to spend the night there because there was no immediately available train. That evening an exhausted Lovett wrote to his wife, still in Rome, that he was really looking forward to continuing the work on planning the new university. Wearied by travel and lonely, and no doubt to a degree worried about his status in the eyes of the board in Houston, Lovett admitted to Mary that he was "finding it hard to be patient. There seems to be so little coming, for all the effort. It may, however, yield results later on, I am hoping so. It's right hard to keep from getting blue at times." Then, remembering the difficult time she had had in 1906 and 1907, he counseled: "I hope you are taking the best care of yourself. I'll need you and all your strength when we get back to our work. I'm more than glad," he added, "that you are going along to Japan. It will round out the whole journey just right, and we'll have the memory of it all our days together." The next morning, invigorated by a good night's rest and the blues vanquished, Lovett and Weems traveled to Granada, where they visited the beautiful "Mosque for Granada." The following day they visited the spectacular Alhambra, the last Moorish stronghold in Europe. On January 29 they left Granada, stopped for several hours at Ronda near the southern tip of Spain, and then pushed on to the Rock of Gibraltar.

As they waited for a steamer to Italy, they visited the massive limestone outcropping, and Lovett wrote a letter to Mrs. Sophus Lie. Also while waiting Lovett sent a long letter to Raphael summarizing the results of their journey of investigation over the last month. While he noted that the quality of educational institutions in Spain was behind that of most of the rest of Europe, he wrote that their travels in the Iberian peninsula "yielded most in the way of architectural suggestion. The winter climate strongly resembles that of Texas: bright sunshine and a clear sky and not too cold. We also found in the flora of the country a striking similarity to the Gulf Coast. . . . The widely prevalent live oak and the magnolia trees met with in the better watered areas were reminders of the more splendid specimens of the Magnolia City. The peninsula is rich in architectural remains. Spanish Gothic, or Renaissance, and Moorish—the acme of this latter at the Alhambra—are all represented with innumerable variations and combinations." These observations would later bear fruit when the architectural design of the Rice Institute was being considered. Lovett proudly pointed out in his letter to Raphael of January 31, summarizing the last month of travel, that while in Paris he had heard Professor Henry van Dyke of Princeton present a lecture on "the growth and spirit of American education, and among his illustrations was a very gratifying reference to the Rice Institute of Houston."

On February 1 Lovett and Weems boarded the SS *Corvania* for Genoa, arriving on the 3rd, but then they instantly journeyed on to Rome, checking in that evening at the Hotel Bethell in the Eternal City—Lovett and his wife were reunited after a separation of just over a month. Over the next several days Lovett visited the National Library and the University of Rome, conferred with Professor Vito Volterra of the university, met the architect of the university, the minister of public education, the president of the Italian Academy of the Lyncei, and two faculty from the engineering school. Lovett, who had made clear in his pre-trip interview with a newspaper reporter in Houston how important he felt consistency of architectural style was when planning a university, took pains to reemphasize this point in a letter to Raphael describing his meeting with the architect of the University of Rome. The university was embarking on a campaign to construct a series of buildings, and "when completed they will furnish a striking example of architectural unity without an objectionable uniformity in the treatment of the prevailing type. The type is a combination of classic and renaissance." On the evening of February 8 the three of them boarded the night train to Naples, first having purchased the Baedeker guide for Greece.

February 9 found them in Naples, where they, becoming tourists for the moment, visited Mount Vesuvius, climbing "to the highest edge of the crater." The next day, after a stop at the University of Naples and the School of Technology, they went to the port at Brindisi and boarded the SS *Bruenn* for Athens. The ship touched briefly at the Peloponnese port city of Patras, where they boarded a train to Athens, arriving on the 12th. Over the next three days Lovett inspected the University of Athens, the École Polytechnique, and the American Classical School, interviewing faculty along the way. Lovett especially admired the architecture of the Greek universities and scientific academies. The expense account shows them buying guide books and photographic supplies, so one can imagine that more sightseeing was occurring than the official record book indicates. Then on February 16 the group embarked from Pirasus aboard the SS *Reine Olga* for Constantinople because it was more convenient to get a train from there to Budapest and Vienna rather than going directly from Athens. Again on the way they touched shore very briefly at Liguria. They reached Constantinople (actually the city had been renamed Istanbul in 1453, though Lovett, like many others, continued to use its ancient name) on February 18 but were prevented from landing that day by unusually rough weather. Two days were scheduled for sights in this ancient city at the boundary between two continents (Lovett noted that "the museums were instructive and the mosques curious," but he was unimpressed with the educational institutions), and then their departure for Vienna was delayed "on account of snow bound Orient Express." But by the 22nd they were on their way via that storied railway, which had been completed from Paris to Constantinople in 1889, with three departures weekly from Constantinople. They disembarked the next day at Budapest to see the university there and the Technisch Hochschule, where they inspected the new buildings and equipment.

That evening they boarded the train again, after having purchased the Baedeker guides for Austria-Hungary, and arrived in Vienna on February 25, rooms already reserved at the Hotel Sacher. Did Dr. and Mrs. Lovett enjoy a tasty sacher torte that evening in the hotel's fashionable dining room? The record is silent. Several letters were waiting for them there, and of course as usual Lovett mailed out other letters. During the day they visited the Institute of Technology, which he noted was "superbly equipped." On the 26th they visited the University of Vienna, met the American ambassador, and Lovett noted in the record book that he had mailed a "scientific paper" to the American Philosophical Society's annual meeting. The next day the party went to the Natural History Museum. A notation at the bottom of the page suggests Lovett made a reservation for a rail car compartment for the long passage from Moscow to Vladivostok. There was obviously much to see in Vienna, for on March 1 they visited the Technological Museum and the Imperial Art Museum. Mrs. Lovett, with her love of art, surely enjoyed this respite from interviews and laboratory inspections. That evening they caught the train for Moscow, planning a stop along the way in Warsaw, where they already had a hotel reservation. The next day, in Warsaw, they made quick visits to the university and the Technical High School, but arrived in Moscow at 2:00 p.m., where they connected almost immediately with a train to St. Petersburg, arriving there on March 4.

In this beautiful city they visited the university, conferring with professors from it and the physical laboratory; the next day they went to the old Technological Institute and interviewed several faculty. They followed the same schedule for several days, looking with especial interest at facilities of the new École Polytechnique (with 3,500 students) as well. It had "splendidly appointed laboratories . . . and [was] administered by a man who recognizes the need for engineers of a training broader than the technicalities of their profession . . . [and] this institution," Lovett wrote to Raphael, "was to me a powerful object lesson." At 9:00 p.m. on March 8 the group boarded the train to Moscow, after having purchased additional Kodak supplies. In Moscow on the 9th, Lovett promptly began interviewing faculty at the university. The next day he met with the directors of the Moscow Institute of Technology and the Manual Training High School, and he spoke with the librarian for the university; he also sent a long letter to Emanuel Raphael in Houston.

And that evening, March 10, began the longest leg of their trip—at 11:55 p.m. they boarded the Trans-Siberian Express (having to pay an extra fee for excess baggage), which had only opened all the way to Vladivostok in 1905 as the longest railroad in the world. For the next twelve relatively eventless days they rode the train across the vast extent of Russia—"across snowcovered Siberia"—stopping each night for rustic hotel accommodations and dining, finally arriving in Vladivostok on Sunday, March 22. The very next day they boarded the SS *Mongolia* for Tsuruoka, Japan. They tarried there only one day, leaving the next for "Tokio," where they had reservations at the Imperial Hotel. This magnificent hotel, opened in 1890, was a huge, wooden, Victorian-style structure, directly across the street from the emperor's palace. After days on the train crossing the bleak landscape of Russia, Lovett and his party must have welcomed the American beds, English cooking (featuring beef and mutton), with English sterling silver cutlery, and fine French wines that were the hallmark of the hotel. They would stay in Tokyo from March 25 through April 1, when they journeyed by night train to Kyoto. In Tokyo there were discussions with Baron Bamao at the university and Professor Sakurai at the College of Science; the minister of public education; President Naruse of Japan Women's University; and President Kamato of Keigo University. Moreover, they made a quick trip to see Waseda University, and they met and conferred with the American ambassador to Japan.

In Kyoto on April 2, Lovett met with Baron Kikuchi, who would later be invited to the Rice opening ceremonies. They also visited the University of Kyoto. But they were in a hurry now to complete their trip, a voyage of learning as well as a public relations triumph for the Rice Institute, so on the night of April 6 the party took another night train, this time to Yokohama. The next day they set sail aboard the familiar SS *Mongolia* for Honolulu. While Lovett had been impressed by the changes underway in Japan and the adoption there of Western educational practices, he seems not to have learned anything particularly applicable to the future Rice Institute. En route to Hawaii, Lovett noted that April 13 was "Antipodes Day," when they crossed the International Date Line, whose exact location had been set in 1884 by the International Meridian Conference meeting in Washington, D.C. Finally, after ten days at sea, they landed on April 16 in Honolulu and spent the night ashore. But the very next day they were under way again on the *Mongolia,* sailing for San Francisco, landing there about 4:00 p.m. on April 23. Mary promptly took a train to Mayfield, Kentucky, eager to reunite with the children and her parents, but the two men had not yet completed the journey as they envisioned it. Over the next few days Lovett visited Stanford University and talked with President David Starr Jordan; at the nearby University of California, Berkeley, he conferred with President Benjamin Ide Wheeler, a fellow graduate of the University of Leipzig. Leaving San Francisco on the 29th, Lovett and Weems stopped briefly at Sentinel, then Wawona and El Portal, finally arriving at Los Angeles (after a several-hour layover at Merced) on the morning of May 4. On May 1 Lovett, who understandably had been wearied by their months of travel and had often found himself utterly exhausted, confessed in a letter to Mary in Mayfield "I have been discouraged frequently, as you know, in the course of the year, but Mary I am going to build the Institute yet!" Then he added, "Write me and tell me how the children are. You alone know how crazy I am to see them." Several days later, more rested and putting the months of travel in context, including unease about the squabble with the board over cutting the trip short, he wrote: "My head is getting clear about my plans—and my old-time hopefulness has come back." He was ready to begin building the new university. At noon he and Weems caught the Sunset Express for Houston, which they reached on May 7, having completed their circumnavigation of the globe for education's sake.

After several days of catching up on his correspondence, having meals at the homes of trustees Emanuel Raphael and James A. Baker and the parents of his traveling secretary, F. Carrington Weems, Lovett prepared to attend the trustee meeting on May 12. He already had a sense that whatever differences between him and the board that might have existed back in November had been erased. As he wrote Mary on May 9, after having seen several of the trustees, "As far as I can see things are working out right." At the trustee meeting he gave an extended oral report on what he had learned and how he had literally put Rice on the academic map of the world, and the board members listened with great interest. According to the board minutes, soon thereafter Lovett was going to give them a formal, written report, but if so, it has been lost. How might he have summarized what he had learned? One can imagine him saying, "Choose an ample campus, construct substantial, architecturally consistent buildings, hire the most outstanding faculty you can identify, have a curriculum that emphasizes—at least in the beginning—basic sciences and engineering but with enough courses in humanities and arts to guarantee that the students receive a well-rounded, liberal education. Make certain that the practical and technical emphasis is balanced with solid grounding in theoretical study, and, above all, insist that the faculty do research and add to the reservoir of learning as well as teach." It was inconceivable, after this trip, that Lovett could have accepted a model of a university that had only local or regional ambitions. The Rice Institute would always have a cosmopolitan character that set it apart from other southern colleges and universities.

Later in the meeting Lovett read a number of letters to the board that had been sent by architects who had been approached by Lovett via earlier correspondence concerning "tentative plans and designs to be made for the Institute buildings." After much discussion, the board asked Lovett—just back from a nine-month trip around the world on behalf of the university—to travel to the Northeast to "personally interview several eminent architects," and then report back to the board in about six weeks. After the meeting (Lovett had worn his frock coat and top hat for his report), he summarized the result of his presentation to Mary with a great feeling of relief and justification: "Laid before them a tentative programme of what I thought was the next thing to do, and they gave me a free hand." This incredible vote of confidence by the trustees says as much about their ambition and courage as it does their respect for Lovett.

Members of the Houston public might have complained in previous years about the slow pace of development, but plans were rapidly under way now. Edgar Odell Lovett would be furiously busy for the next three years, preparing to open a new university that incorporated the most innovative academic practices found around the world. No one in Texas or the South had ever seen such intellectual ambition set under way.

Edgar Odell Lovett at age fifteen, a freshman at Bethany College.
*Courtesy of Bethany College.*

Members of the Beta Theta Pi fraternity on the steps of their chapter house,
Bethany College, June 1890. Edgar Odell Lovett is the second from the right.
*Courtesy, Woodson Research Center, Fondren Library, Rice University.*

Mary Ellen Hale, "in dress worn for commencement exercises" at
West Kentucky College, June 1892. This is the coed Edgar Odell Lovett
fell in love with during his first teaching appointment.
*Courtesy, Woodson Research Center, Fondren Library, Rice University.*

Mary Ellen Hale in 1897 just before her marriage in December to Edgar Odell Lovett.
*Courtesy, Woodson Research Center, Fondren Library, Rice University.*

Edgar Odell Lovett, 1898, as an instructor of mathematics at Princeton University.
*Courtesy, Woodson Research Center, Fondren Library, Rice University.*

Ellen Kennedy Lovett on her first birthday, March 25, 1906.
Photo taken in Mayfield, Kentucky, at her grandparents' home.
*Courtesy, Woodson Research Center, Fondren Library, Rice University.*

Mary Ellen Hale Lovett with her three children; from left to right,
H. Malcolm, Lawrence Alexander, and Adelaide. Photo taken in
their home at 1218 Polk Street, Houston, in February 1912.
*Courtesy, Woodson Research Center, Fondren Library, Rice University.*

Rice Institute trustees, 1911, in the institute office in the Scanlan Building.
Front row, from left to right: James Everett McAshan, vice chairman;
Cesar Maurice Lombardi; and Captain James Addison Baker, chairman.
Standing, back row: Benjamin Botts Rice, treasurer; President Lovett;
Emanuel Raphael, secretary; and William March Rice, Jr.
*Courtesy, Woodson Research Center, Fondren Library, Rice University.*

Several original faculty and trustees of the Rice Institute, September 23, 1912.
From left to right: W. F. Edwards, Francis Ellis Johnson, Thomas Lindsey Blayney,
Phil H. Arbuckle, President Lovett, Benjamin Botts Rice, William Ward Watkin,
Emanuel Raphael, Griffith C. Evans, J. E. McAshan, John T. McCants,
Captain Baker, H. A. Wilson.
*Courtesy, Woodson Research Center, Fondren Library, Rice University.*

Original class members, Rice Institute, on registration day, September 23, 1912.
*Courtesy, Woodson Research Center, Fondren Library, Rice University.*

The delegates to the formal opening of the Rice Institute, having begun their march from their gathering place at South Hall (now Will Rice College), are crossing the still unfinished campus grounds and approaching the south end of the administration building (now Lovett Hall); they will enter through the Sallyport into the academic quadrangle for the festivities.

*Courtesy, Woodson Research Center, Fondren Library, Rice University.*

Edgar Odell Lovett delivering his keynote address, "The Meaning of the
New Institution," at the opening ceremonies, Saturday, October 12, 1912.
*Courtesy, Woodson Research Center, Fondren Library, Rice University.*

Group picture of the delegates and distinguished visitors to the
formal opening ceremonies, October 10–12, 1912. Photo taken from
the south side of South Hall at 1:00 p.m., October 12, 1912.
*Courtesy, Woodson Research Center, Fondren Library, Rice University.*

Maria Elizabeth Spreng Lovett, President Lovett's mother, in 1916.
*Courtesy, Woodson Research Center, Fondren Library, Rice University.*

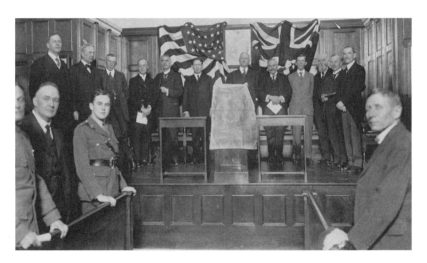

The British Educational Mission to Rice, meeting in the Faculty Chamber (now
Founders' Room), Administration Building, November 25, 1918. On platform, from
left to right: President Lovett, E. F. Simms of Houston, William Marsh Rice, Jr.,
Edward Walker of Oxford, Dr. John Joly of Dublin, Governor William P. Hobby of
Texas, Captain James A. Baker, Sir Arthur E. Shipley of Cambridge, B. B. Rice,
Sir Henry Jones of Glasgow, Sir Henry Miers of Manchester, Dr. Joseph Muller of
Houston. Left, below: half visible, Brigadier General Guy V. Henry, in command of
Camp Logan, Professor H. A. Wilson, Lieutenant Beverley St. Clair.
*Courtesy, Woodson Research Center, Fondren Library, Rice University.*

Members of official mission of French scholars to Rice, December 1918.
Left to right: Mr. Charles Koechlin, composer and music critic; Mme. Cazamian;
Mrs. Edgar Odell Lovett; Dr. Louis Cazamian, literary scholar; and President Lovett.
*Courtesy, Woodson Research Center, Fondren Library, Rice University.*

General John J. Pershing visiting the Rice Institute, February 5, 1920.
Walking in front of the physics laboratory, from left to right: General Pershing,
President Lovett, and Professor Thomas Lindsey Blayney.
*Courtesy, Woodson Research Center, Fondren Library, Rice University.*

Henry Malcolm Lovett received his B.A. degree from Rice Institute
at the 1921 commencement; here he stands, diploma in hand, by his
father under the cloisters of the administration building.
*Courtesy, Woodson Research Center, Fondren Library, Rice University.*

A matronly Mary Ellen Hale Lovett; photograph taken in Paris, 1922.
*Courtesy, Woodson Research Center, Fondren Library, Rice University.*

*Inset:* Group passport photo of Mary Ellen Hale Lovett, Adelaide, and Alex, as they prepare to visit France in 1921–1922.
*Courtesy, Woodson Research Center, Fondren Library, Rice University.*

Dedication of the statue (by John Angell) of William Marsh Rice, on
June 8, 1930. From left to right: Francis Vesey (president of the Rice Students'
Association), Lillian Elizabeth Horlock (president of the women's council),
President Lovett, Benjamin Botts Rice (reading; secretary of the board of
trustees), William Marion Standish (president of the Rice alumni association),
Ralph Adams Cram (hands before him; the commencement speaker), and the
Reverend Dr. James Gordon Gilkey (the baccalaureate speaker).
*Courtesy, Woodson Research Center, Fondren Library, Rice University.*

President Lovett, undated, but probably late 1930s.
*Courtesy, Woodson Research Center, Fondren Library, Rice University.*

President Emeritus Lovett, left, and President William Vermillion Houston, March 1946.
*Courtesy, Woodson Research Center, Fondren Library, Rice University.*

Dedication ceremony renaming the administration building,
Lovett Hall, December 4, 1947. From left to right: Harry C. Wiess,
Lamar Fleming Jr., Harry C. Hanszen, President Emeritus Lovett,
William Alexander Kirkland, George R. Brown, President Houston,
Gus Sessions Wortham, and Dr. Frederick Rice Lummis.
*Courtesy, Woodson Research Center, Fondren Library, Rice University.*

President Emeritus Lovett in 1954.
*Courtesy, Woodson Research Center, Fondren Library, Rice University.*

President Lovett and Adlai E. Stevenson at
Princeton upon receiving honorary degrees, 1954.
*Courtesy, Woodson Research Center, Fondren Library, Rice University.*

# CHAPTER FOUR

# THE LAUNCHING OF THE NEW UNIVERSITY

WHEN THE RICE TRUSTEES ENGAGED Edgar Odell Lovett as president of the Rice Institute for the Advancement of Literature, Science, and Art, they fully expected him personally to plan and lead the development of *all* phases of the new university, and that is precisely how Lovett understood his role. So when, at his initial board meeting following the round-the-world trip, he in his own words "laid before them a tentative programme of what I thought was the next thing to do," and they gave him "a free hand," Lovett began to take action on an interrelated series of initiatives. He understood that an architect had to be chosen and a general design plan for the university agreed upon. He knew that he had to seek and gain commitments from a range of faculty members that covered the fields initially to be taught. And he knew that qualified students had to be recruited to be in place when the buildings were ready and the faculty on hand. At the culmination of these three efforts would be the beginning of classes, but Lovett was soon planning a grandiose opening ceremony quickly to follow that would announce to the world the birth of an infant university that he was confident would one day be an academic giant. These were large tasks, and with public pressure in Houston mounting to see the fruition of William Marsh Rice's dream, Lovett well knew in the spring and summer of 1909 that it would take equal measures of hard work, creativity, and good luck to bring to life the vision of a university he had begun to fashion during those months of tiring travel.

The idea most firmly in Lovett's mind from the beginning about planning the new university was its architecture—but the consistency of architectural vocabulary, not any particular design. Lovett's insistence on unity of architectural style was probably a result of his having studied at the Thomas Jefferson–designed University of Virginia, with its exquisite lawn and two ranges of secondary buildings, all of the

same color brick, connected (on the lawn) by white-columned porticos
and (on the range) by brick cloisters. In 1892 the whole effect must
have been stunning to young Lovett, whose prior collegiate experience
had been at two small colleges without such an architectural heritage.
Afterward he had spent a summer at the University of Chicago with
its impressive and handsomely designed plant underway, and in 1907,
before Lovett left Princeton, it had signed an agreement with a prominent American architect, Ralph Adams Cram, to develop a long-range
master plan for campus construction. And of course during his world
trip Lovett had been much taken with the architectural unity being
proposed for a new series of building at the University of Rome. So
this much was set in Lovett's mind from the moment he began thinking
about the construction of facilities for the new Rice Institute. By now
the Rice Institute had offices on the eleventh floor of Houston's new
tallest skyscraper, the Scanlan Building, at 405 Main Street between
Preston and Prairie.

Shortly before embarking on the world tour, Lovett had written a
letter to several architectural firms (only the draft of his letter is extant), dangling before them the prospect of a spectacular commission
that they would no doubt be glad to know about; he obviously expected
that the firms would reply, as they did. This letter, in draft form at
least, pointed out that "this institution starts with an endowment of
seven million dollars, and should rank eventually with the representative universities of the country. We hope to have an equipment as conspicuous for its beauty as for its utility, in an architecture adapted to
the climatic conditions of its environment as well as to the educational
ends of its foundation." It was the responses to this letter announcing
what in essence became an informal architectural competition that the
board laid before Lovett on his first meeting with them after the world
trip, and on the basis of these replies the board asked him to travel to
the Northeast to meet with several of the firms.

The location of the new university was finally established at the same
time. For several years the board had been discussing the optimal size
of a campus, having quickly determined that the existing downtown
location was too small. Lovett had even been shown several possible locations during his first interview with the trustees in April 1907, and by

early 1908 it was clear that the leading contender for the campus was a large, level, very sparsely treed site along Main Street about three miles southwest of downtown Houston. In June before Lovett embarked on his round-the-world trip he had discussed the desired size of the campus with the board, and the consensus was that from two hundred to three hundred acres would be appropriate. It was following this meeting that William M. Rice, Jr. (Will Rice), was authorized to begin negotiations to buy the requisite acreage along both sides of Main Street at not over $1,000 per acre. It turned out that George Hermann, who owned much of the land, would not sell any part of his holdings east of Main Street, so owners of adjacent land were contacted; at the September 30, 1908, board meeting Will Rice was authorized to buy about 175 acres from Hermann and two additional owners. Over the next several months more land was acquired, so that eventually, on April 7, 1909, the board could vote to finalize (with a small exception) the entire campus, a five-sided plot consisting of 287.233 acres at a total cost of $177,408, which turned out to be $618 per acre. The land was perfectly flat, had a few trees in the northeast corner along Main Street, and at its western end was bisected by a stream known as Harris Gully. When Lovett returned to Houston in early May, the land deal was all settled. Trustee chair James A. Baker had purchased a car while Lovett was abroad, and on May 7 he drove Lovett out Main Street to inspect the site. The next day Lovett officially announced the location of the Rice Institute to the press, a story that garnered large headlines in the next day's *Houston Post* and *Houston Chronicle*. Clearly the people of Houston were eager for the new university to open. The papers announced also that the city would widen and extend Main Street into a gravel (but not paved) boulevard to the campus site, and the streetcar company stated that the car line would also be extended along parallel Fannin Street to the site as soon as campus construction began.

Lovett did journey to the Northeast that summer and meet with several architectural firms. When he reported back to the board at their July meeting he said that he had narrowed the possible firms down to three or four "eminent architects." He said that he planned to go back to the Northeast and, after another round of interviewing, select one of the architects who would then be asked to come to Houston, inspect the campus site, familiarize himself with Houston, and then submit some preliminary plans. If these proved acceptable to the board, it could then decide whether or not to extend the architect and his firm a contract to design at least the first phase of campus construction. He also announced that he had assembled an advisory team of prominent scientists to help the university and the architectural firm selected to design laboratory space, which he wanted to be as good as any in the world. The eminence of these consultants suggests the ambition Lovett was already developing for the Rice Institute. The advisory committee consisted of physicist Joseph Sweetman Ames of Johns Hopkins University; biologist Edwin Grant Conklin of Princeton; chemist Theodore Williams Richards of Harvard; and engineer Samuel Wesley Stratton of the National Bureau of Standards in Washington, D.C. Ames, Conklin, and Richards were members of the National Academy of Sciences. The board accepted with appreciation the work and suggestions of Lovett, giving him full support to carry on as he planned.

By the end of July Lovett had decided to choose the firm of Cram, Goodhue, and Ferguson, and he made his recommendation to the board at their August 5 meeting. He had at first been hesitant to select Cram because of Cram's association with Princeton, and Lovett was aware that he should not appear too beholden to Princeton practices. But Cram's intellectualism and enthusiasm for the project—not to mention the overall quality of his work—overcame Lovett's reluctance. Moreover, after much thought, Lovett suggested that the first four buildings to be constructed should be the administration building, a laboratory (for all the sciences at present), a power plant (Rice would for the time being have to generate its own electricity), and a residence hall for male students. The board accepted Lovett's recommendations and instructed him to travel to Boston, ask the architects to sketch out "the entire group of buildings en bloc, showing the four buildings which are considered necessary to be erected at first," and then bring back preliminary drawings to the board for it to consider at its regular October 1909 meeting. Lovett must also have been thankful that the board then gave him a paid leave for vacation until October 1.

Ralph Adams Cram was a decided medievalist, a prominent public intellectual, and author as well as architect. He was known primarily at the time as the designer of a number of prestigious churches, including St. John the Divine Cathedral in New York City. His fame had grown immensely in the last decade after he had been asked to develop the master plans for both the U.S. Military Academy at West Point and Princeton University. Cram had traveled widely in Europe, especially along the Mediterranean Sea, and he was particularly enamored of the English and French Gothic style, though he was fascinated with imagining the relationship of that style to the one found in the southernmost nations of Europe whose shores were lapped by the warm waters of the Mediterranean. Cram's partner, Bertram Grosvenor Goodhue, an especially skilled draftsman, headed the firm's New York City office, while Cram ruled the Boston office. On major commissions both offices proposed drawings, competing with themselves and gaining creative spark from the competition. The scope and importance of the Rice commission excited the architects; the firm wrote Lovett on August 30, 1909, that "We have seldom been more enthusiastic over any project than over this of the Rice Institute. West Point alone rivals it in interest." So when the firm was shown the shape and size of the intended campus (as of yet an eight-and-a-half acre section along Main Street had not yet been purchased, its owner holding out for a much higher price, so there was an ungainly bite taken out of the southern boundary of the campus near what was to become the main entrance), both Cram and Goodhue began a series of drawings that featured the complete layout of the campus, oriented in slightly different ways on the site. Lovett examined these various proposals with extraordinary attention, sending questions and suggestions by telegram to the architects, who were clearly nonplussed by the intensity of his engagement in the design process.

At the time the architects had not visited Houston, so there was an abstract quality to their various conceptions of the layout of the campus buildings. Although the Cram office offered three different plans (prepared by a highly skilled young Pennsylvania-trained draftsman, William Ward Watkin) and the Goodhue office but one, the original Goodhue version was far closer to the layout ultimately chosen. It consisted of a longer east-west orientation of buildings, set forth in graceful quadrangles, with a shorter north-south axis bisecting the longer axis.

The buildings were as of yet indicated only as shaded-in rectangles, but there were tentatively suggested locations for science and liberal arts buildings, residential buildings, law and medical schools, an amphitheater, faculty housing—a grandiose scheme. Lovett responded to every version, pushing to move the main administrative building farther to the east and nearer the ultimate Main Street entrance. He was very concerned to position the buildings so as to maximize the free circulation of breezes, a necessity in the Houston climate before air conditioning. Over the next few months Lovett made several trips to Boston, where he pored over the drawings. He made a number of detailed recommendations, not all of which the architects appreciated, but Lovett was determined and persistent, and he generally got his way. For example, he did not want wings of buildings to connect flush with the original building but rather to be separated to improve air circulation. This tedious back-and-forth went on for months, long after Cram had begun to draw detailed plans for the first actual buildings, with the final overall campus plan approved at the end of May 1910.

In late November 1909 the architects made their initial trip to Houston and visited the property recently purchased for the campus. It was not, at first glance, a propitious site—primarily a flat prairie, with no defining features save some trees at the northeastern end. Cram later recalled it as "a level and stupid site." Cram also noted that there were no other buildings around, no architectural context for the campus construction to respond to. He did not think the Spanish-Indian style was appropriate, and of course the Georgian or faux-Gothic that constituted the canon for East Coast collegiate architecture also seemed out of place. The climate in late November struck Cram as Mediterranean, so he decided "to invent something approaching a new style," a synthesis of the styles he had admired in his travels in Mediterranean lands. Hence he proposed to reassemble "all the elements I could from southern France and Italy, Dalmatia, the Peloponnesus, Byzantium, Anatolia, Syria, Sicily, [and] Spain." The style chosen predated the Gothic with which Cram was especially associated; rather, using rounded arches, the buildings drew their primary inspiration from tenth- and eleventh-century Byzantine and Lombard sources and an eclectic synthesis of other Mediterranean forms. Lovett mentioned in a letter to Harvard

President Charles W. Eliot in September 1910 that the architects were even considering the use of reflecting pools in the main quadrangle "and thereby heightening the Venetian effect, for which they strive." Surely Lovett played a role in this choice of styles, for he had noted the similarity of the Spanish climate and flora to that of Houston and had much admired the architecture he saw there, thinking in 1908 that here was inspiration for the design of the new university. Cram does not mention any suggestions from Lovett, but knowing Lovett's views, and his willingness to express them forcefully, certainly it is probable that on this point of architectural style Cram and Lovett saw alike, with their common views mutually reinforcing one another. And while Goodhue's campus plan had shaped the general layout of the campus, Cram's aesthetic primarily shaped the actual design of the buildings themselves, though Lovett's hand would be involved to an extent that Cram ultimately found annoying.

Lovett kept the Rice trustees informed of the progress being made, and at a specially called board meeting on November 30 the general conception of the plan was approved; the architects also presented a preliminary sketch of some of the buildings, which the board members found to their liking. On December 1 the architects also offered preliminary cost estimates for the first four buildings, totaling $880,000, and the board authorized them to "proceed with plans and specifications without delay." There was already talk of hiring contractors, and a Houston engineer, Wilmer Waldo, was engaged to study the campus site and make recommendations about soil stability, road surfaces, sewage, and drainage (a local civil engineer, a Mr. Dorman, was also consulted on the last two matters). Several deep wells were drilled to provide water. As with the generation of its own electricity in a coal-burning power plant (a special rail spur brought in train-car loads of coal from the Midwest), Rice was outside the city limits so had to provide for its own potable water. Early January found Lovett in Boston going over the architectural plans—"I have had a perfectly glorious day in with Cram," he wrote Mary. The work was now going so well that Lovett waxed exuberant about the prospects that lay ahead. "This is wonderful country up here, but we have gone where opportunity is great, and a magnificent life of service is ahead of us." In a few days, back in Houston, Lovett met again with the board (on January 14), and went over with them the architectural and planning details. Subsequently, a formal contract was drawn up with the Cram and Goodhue firm on February 2, 1910, for preparing the working plans. But extremely detailed correspondence continued between Lovett and the architects for months, with much attention being given to the color of the bricks and mortar, the marble, the Texas granite, every single aspect of the design, large and small, and no consideration of the final look of the campus can be made without factoring in Lovett's ideas. But his meticulous concern drove the architects to distraction, leading the firm to write him on March 17, 1910, a special plea:

> Now can you not place some reliance in us as your chosen architects when it comes to a matter that, like this one, is one almost wholly of design? It seems to us that it is really our function to determine more or less questions of this nature. Where cost, practical considerations, or the sacrifice of valuable space is concerned, it is, of course, your duty to pass upon everything we suggest, but while we welcome every particle of assistance you can give us from an artistic standpoint, we must admit that this case of the Rice Institute is the only one we have ever had in our experience where the highest authorities were so exceedingly conscientious as to strictly architectural considerations.
>
> We repeat, this is not a criticism, for no one welcomes more than we do the really penetrating criticisms you have made, or who recognizes more fully the motive that underlies these criticisms. All we are trying to do is to take upon our own shoulders some of the responsibility that belongs there, and so we seriously ask you to leave us, as far as you conscientiously can, the determination of questions which in themselves are strictly architectural.

The letter worked in getting Lovett to back off just a bit from his involvement, and he soon approved the plans for the administration building, but the tone of the letter also suggests the influence Lovett's constant communication and comment had had. And within a few months a bid of $319,478 was accepted from the Wm. Miller & Sons Company to construct the administration building. Finally William Marsh Rice's long-awaited institute was to take form in the southwestern suburbs of Houston. Lovett would stay closely involved with the construction phase too, and nothing escaped his notice. He had completely internalized the role of head of the institute, and his involvement reached from the ultimate academic concept of the university to the most minute detail of construction—and to such matters as the design of the official university stationery; the selection of the university colors, blue and gray (the "Confederate gray enlivened by a tinge of lavender, with a blue still deeper than Oxford blue," so subtly distanced from a southern identification and with a hint of internationalism), intended to mediate any lingering sectional feelings; the choice of the university mascot (the owl of Athena as depicted on a particular fifth-century BCE Greek coin); and even the exact alignment of the live oaks that today so characterize the campus. (One of the few times he was ever seen to get angry was when groundkeepers misplanted some trees. Normally he kept his emotions totally under control.) This was the role of Lovett expected by the board of trustees and accepted by him. Clearly Lovett had gained the complete confidence of the trustees. In mid-1910 they formally named him to membership on the board, filling the place of the deceased Frederick Rice—the founder's brother. (In 1908, in response to a request for information from Captain Baker, Lovett had reported that at most major American universities, the president was a member of the governing board.)

Cram, Goodhue, and Ferguson recommended, as with all major projects, that an architect from their firm move to the construction site to supervise construction, making sure that the designs were faithfully executed. The Rice trustees of course accepted this recommendation, so in April 1910 William Ward Watkin, who had been preparing most of the drawings, was sent, and the remarkably tall and thin Watkin, almost a stick figure of a man, opened offices in the Scanlan Building adjacent to the institute offices themselves. Not only would he supervise all the building, but also he would end up becoming the first professor of architecture and would spend the remainder of his career at Rice, making a substantial impact not only on architectural education but also through his later private practice on the architectural heritage of Houston itself. Shortly before Watkin moved south, the firm sent A. C. Perry to serve as clerk-of-the-works, essentially overseeing construction details on the ground each working day. With these men on hand, and the plans coming to fruition, and a contractor signed up, the Rice campus became a flurry of activity over the next two years. The formal dedication of the laying of the cornerstone occurred on March 2, 1911, Texas Independence Day, and Lovett had chosen to have carved on the 6,500 pound marble cornerstone, below the Rice and Texas shields, a quotation from Democritus rendered in Greek: "Rather would I discover the cause of one fact than become king of the Persians." (The quotation was adapted from an epigram, authored by Eusebius Pamphili, found in an ancient Byzantine monastery in central Greece.) Lovett intended for research—discovery—to be a central part of the educational endeavor of the Rice Institute, not merely practical training or the transmission of information, and the cornerstone inscription emphasized that point.

In early 1911 the Rice trustees signed a contract to sell the more than a billion feet of lumber on its 47,000-acre tract of virgin longleaf pine in Calcasieu Parish, Louisiana, for a sum of almost $4 million, far more than enough to pay construction costs without touching the original endowment. Lovett of course stayed involved in every aspect of construction as always—for example, choosing the scholars of various fields whose faces (including that of Sophus Lie, his old mathematics teacher at Leipzig) would be carved on the capitals of columns of the administration building—but in the capable hands of Watkin and Perry, work progressed satisfactorily. There were delays, frustrations over getting satisfactory materials, periodic flooding, disputes over building details, and many other problems, but within months the pace of construction was changing forever the prairie landscape. (The administration building—years later renamed Lovett Hall—would prove to be the masterpiece of Cram's entire body of secular works.) Lovett found delays difficult to accept, but there was no way around them, and soon he realized that his initial expectation of opening the university in 1911 was impossible, so the fall of 1912 became the target date. As the opening date loomed and construction lagged, there was a furious whirlwind of activity to get everything ready. But of course it takes more than buildings to make a university.

Even if Edgar Odell Lovett had not already believed it, the advice he received over and over again in the course of his world travels would have convinced him that nothing was more important to the life of a university than the quality of its faculty. This idea was central to his conception of the Rice Institute. Although he did receive some advice that the faculty members would have to be southern in order to be accepted in Texas, Lovett repudiated that idea from the beginning. He understood that having some tie to the region could be mildly advantageous, but by no means was it determinative. After all, the trustees had chosen him, a non-southerner teaching at a northern institution, to be the first president. Once Lovett had been chosen, the trustees allowed him carte blanche in the matter of selecting the teaching staff. He was predictably systematic and unrelenting in his search for faculty, not simply in identifying the men he wanted (and in this age, all the faculty were men) but more important, convincing them to come to a university that had not yet opened in distant Texas, then as often even now a place assumed to be hostile to—or at least a relative stranger to—academic endeavor. Nothing Lovett did is more impressive than his persuading an international group of accomplished scholars to join the Rice faculty in its first couple of years. Lovett foresaw Rice as a national and international university *sited* in Texas (and thus the South), but he never imagined it as southern in any defensive or provincial sense.

As he interviewed academicians throughout England and Europe on his round-the-world trip, Lovett not only piqued their curiosity about the future opening of the Rice Institute but also asked in general terms for the names of possible prospective faculty. After returning, he—a consummate networker—sent letters to prominent faculty at leading American institutions asking their advice. Although he had assembled a consulting group of scientists and engineers to advise him and the architects on constructing laboratories at the new university, he did not put together a committee of distinguished scholars to assist his search for new faculty. He did, however, confer individually with many such men. For example, the letter he sent to Edward Capps, a noted professor of classics at Princeton, on December 18, 1909, is typical, and it deserves to be quoted in full:

At this stage in our work of organization we are seeking those men for which every institution is looking, young men of some performance and great promise who are first-class men already, or, in the opinion of first-class men, are destined to reach the front rank. My search would be greatly facilitated, if you would allow me to make a draft on your extensive personal knowledge of men, both in your field and in the wider University world. We expect to be able to offer appointments of unusual opportunity in mathematics, physics, chemistry, biology, engineering, history, philosophy, political science, and literature, ancient and modern. In the final choice of men for these positions we are restrained by no ties of affiliation with State, Church, or University, and, accordingly, we are free to go for the most promising man wherever he is to be found, although it would be in his favor should he prove to be of the South or the West, either through birth, education, or teaching experience.

Lovett generally played his cards close to the vest when trying to locate and interest prospective faculty, though sometimes he would indicate in letters to his wife particular individuals on whom he was seeking information or planned to interview. For example, as early as December 1908 he heard favorably of "Huxley's grandson" from a friend in the Princeton biology department, and in October 1910 he mentioned to Mary that his friend William H. Echols at the University of Virginia advised him that he did not want historian Thomas Jefferson Wertenbaker. In September 1911 he wrote that he had "Blayney on one of my slates," but he knew it would be several months before he could visit with this scholar in comparative literature whom he had met years before in Frankfurt when both were graduate students in Germany. But the faculty search became practically a full-time occupation in January 1912, when he sailed to Europe aboard the *Kronprinzessin Cecile* of the Norddeutscher Lloyd line of Bremen, beginning three months of touring the Continent, England, and Scotland to interview personally prospective faculty. Over the next several months Lovett went to London, Glasgow, Paris, Berlin, Leipzig, Göttingen, Amsterdam, Rome, and Madrid, putting together his faculty list and seeking high-profile speakers for the academic celebration that would mark the formal opening ceremony. The students admitted the first year would only be freshmen, and over the next three years the faculty and course offerings would grow as the student need required. So when selecting faculty to fill out the academic program, Lovett understood that he had several years to attract the scholars who would teach the courses necessary for graduation. That meant he was interviewing scholars who he knew would not be able to come for a year or more. The result, then, of this recruitment trip should be measured not solely by the faculty on hand when classes opened but rather by the full roster of those available to the initial students at the end of their undergraduate career.

This was the second major European trip for Lovett, in addition to his 1900 sabbatical year in Paris, and it clearly brought back memories of the previous trip on behalf of Rice when Mary had accompanied him. Shortly after arriving in London he wrote back to her, reminiscing warmly about their having walked "arm in arm" along "Regal Street and Piccadilly and Oxford and Hyde Park and Pall Mall and St. James" a little over three years before. But Lovett was even more busy this time; his letters reveal conversations with and recommendations about such men as Griffith C. Evans, Julian Huxley, Harold A. Wilson, Max Freund, Albert L. Guerard—all of whom became early members of the faculty. Evans was touted by his professors as one of the best math prospects ever to come out of Harvard; Wilson was praised by the leading physicists of England; Huxley engaged in a prolonged correspondence with Lovett in addition to their several meetings—"a splendid fellow he is," Lovett exulted about young Huxley. Huxley was curious about the state of civilization in Texas and the climate; was Lovett "going to aim at a Cosmopolitan staff, not one fundamentally American?" Somehow Lovett convinced them all to come.

He also was consulting with very eminent scholars trying to persuade them to make the long trip to Houston to participate in an elaborate opening ceremony. Sometimes he was unsuccessful, as, for example, with historian Karl Lamprecht, with whom he spent a day in Leipzig. (Did Lamprecht remember signing off on Lovett's final dissertation paperwork in 1899?) And he was distressed to learn in Göttingen that mathematician Felix Klein was "almost broken down & I don't believe he will come." (By now Lovett's mentor Sophus Lie was dead.) But whenever he got an acceptance, he would gleefully write Mary about his newest triumph: "I saw Sir William Ramsay this morning and I think he will be coming to the opening." "Mary just a line to say that

Sir Henry Jones of Glasgow is coming to the opening. That makes six acceptances to date." "Mackail (the hardest one to land) has finally consented." "You must begin to exercise your wits to devise a means whereby we can all brush up on French during the summer. Perhaps a governess. Borel is coming and will bring his wife. They speak nothing but French. Volterra may bring his wife, and that means French. If Poincare comes, and I am still hoping that he will, that will mean more French." Perhaps more remarkable than the so-called landing of these scholars is that the Rice trustees accepted Lovett's vision of an international convocation replete with visitors who only spoke French. This was Texas in 1912, and even today there would likely be some Texans who would object.

Lovett was unrelenting in his efforts to build the faculty. On one rainy day in Madrid, he wrote Mary, he penned fifty-three letters. Several weeks later he wrote her from London that "I have broken the Sabbath today by working until my tongue is hanging out and my tail sore." On still another occasion he complained "Mary, you never saw your old man as tired as he gets these nights." Many of these letters that he was writing were sent to potential faculty in a number of fields at universities all over Europe and America. And these efforts paid off. When classes opened in 1912, Lovett had assembled a beginning faculty of twelve representing the following fields: English literature, German, applied mathematics, pure mathematics, French, physics, biology, electrical engineering, physical education and athletics, chemistry, and architecture. These men had earned their doctorates at such universities as Heidelberg, Paris, Harvard, Cambridge, London, and Leipzig. Huxley would not have to worry about the provincialism of the faculty. Because Lovett was planning a faculty for a four-year curriculum, building one class per year, he was interviewing faculty from the beginning that he knew would not actually be in place for another year or two; after all, freshmen and sophomores did not need senior classes and the professors to teach them yet. But Lovett had within his mental framework the entire four-year faculty, and by 1916 the fruits of his initial faculty searches were in evidence. In their senior year the initial students would find a faculty of thirty-one members, covering such additional fields as mechanical and civil engineering, philosophy, history, architectural drawing, and added depth in such fields as modern languages, physics, and chemistry. There would also by that year be eight graduate fellows. All in all, not exactly the size Lovett had imagined in 1908, but the distribution of fields reflected that plan, and the graduate institutions represented proved that he had learned the lesson to hire only first-rate scholars: in addition to the universities where the initial twelve faculty had trained, now the list of Ph.D.-granting institutions included Princeton (two faculty), Johns Hopkins, Cornell (three faculty), Chicago, Columbia, Liverpool, Berlin, and Bonn. This was the most international faculty, and the best trained, in the entire South at the time.

How did Lovett persuade these men to leave institutions like Princeton and Stanford and Oxford to come to Texas? Certainly he possessed energy and charisma, and he convinced them that something truly exciting and novel was happening in Houston at the infant Rice Institute. They were attracted both by his personality and confidence and by the exhilarating boldness of his vision. In a 1907 commencement address at Drake University, Lovett had commented, "I am idealist enough to believe in the power of an idea." Now he was seeing that truth made manifest in his building of the Rice Institute. Remember that when Woodrow Wilson had proposed transforming both teaching and scholarship at Princeton with his preceptorship program, dozens of highly talented young professors applied for positions, with each of them testifying to the attractive power of Wilson's vision. A more contemporary example of the attraction of a good idea is equally illustrative. Eighty years after the Rice trustees had sent Lovett around the world, they in 1998 signed an agreement to help create a new private university in Bremen, Germany, in effect helping to shape Germany's first private university on the explicit model of Rice. When the officers of International University Bremen initially advertised for twenty-seven faculty positions at this infant university, an astonishing total of 1,600 faculty applied—captivated by the vision of a new university that might by example reform the moribund higher education system of Germany.

What Lovett was projecting, with uncommon eloquence and the endowment to back up his ideas, was a far-reaching vision of a university that represented the most advanced thinking available about higher education. As he had written to trustee Emanuel Raphael while in England in September 1908, the scholars with whom he had spoken were "uniformly interested . . . the magnitude of our foundation [endowment] arresting their attention and the scope of our problems firing their imagination." Lovett's genius was to have distilled the best available thought—from the United States and abroad—about universities, teaching, research, and community service and synthesized the whole in a way that immediately excited idealistic faculty. One of Lovett's earliest faculty recruits, philosopher Radoslav Tsanoff, sent a letter back to his mentor at Cornell, Frank Thilly, in the fall of 1914 describing President Lovett, and his mentor (who had been a colleague and Prospect Street neighbor of Lovett's at Princeton) forwarded that letter to Lovett. Tsanoff captured the essence of Lovett's appeal: "The Institute is strangely like Dr. Lovett—enthusiastic but steady, solid and ambitious for genuineness and 'nothing but the best.' One feels that here an honest endeavor is being made to build up, not the gaudy shell of a university, but a real seat of scientific learning and culture." That vision that later inspired Tsanoff Lovett would spell out in detail in his major address at the formal opening in October 1912, and it would be a vision that largely directed the development of the university over the course of its first century.

Lovett knew full well that a university required able students as well as faculty and facilities, and he expected to work hard making the soon-to-be university widely known. Immediately after returning from his faculty recruitment trip to Europe, he would go to work recruiting students. (At the time, fewer than 3 percent of the U.S. population ages eighteen to twenty-four attended college.) It took longer to finish up in Europe than he originally expected ("I am just so heartsick to see you," he wrote Mary on February 29, "that I can hardly keep going"), and his letters to Mary reveal that he kept watching and then missing the departure schedules of ship after ship: first the *Olympus,* then the *Mauritania,* before finally booking passage on the *Lusitania* for March 9. Credible family tradition holds that a ticket agent in England tried to persuade Lovett to wait a few weeks until April 10 to catch the maiden voyage to America of a giant new luxury ship, but Lovett was too eager to get back to Mary and the children and begin the next phase of preparations for the Rice Institute to wait for the *Titantic*. The *Lusitania* would make this particular voyage successfully.

Lovett engaged in a multi-prong effort to spread the news of the university that he hoped to open in Houston, originally in 1911 but soon pushed back to the fall of 1912. First, he conducted a huge, actually heroic, campaign of letter-writing to educators and publicists across the nation but especially the South and East—he even sent a letter enclosing sketches of the administration building to Booker T. Washington—and his description of the plans for the Rice Institute characteristically stirred admiration for both the new university itself and what it could do for the region. For example, in May 1910 Randolph Hall, the president of the College of Charleston (and a fellow mathematician), responded to a recent letter from Lovett with a sense of vicarious excitement: "Your letter had in it the glow of the Golden West. . . . my, what an outlook you have! It was good to hear of the widening horizon and the substantial state of your resources. You have an opportunity well worth the best effort you can bring to it; and with a virgin field & untrammeled hands your chance is limitless. I look forward, old man, with keen interest & fullest confidence to the story of your progress." Other such letters had a hint of pride that such was occurring in the South and a hint of envy that it was not occurring with their institution. A year later David Spence Hill, the president of Tulane University, replied to another letter from Lovett, "You . . . are laying foundations broad, deep and fit for a superb and unique superstructure. . . . I believe that in the educational field you are perhaps in the best strategic position in the world, considering the work to be done and the means and personal vigor at your command." It would not be inaccurate to state that many in the South viewed Lovett's opportunity with a sense of awe. Not atypical was the view of Salem College president Howard E. Rondthaler, as reported in the *Winston-Salem Journal* on February 12, 1913. Having just visited the Rice campus, Rondthaler reported himself "amazed and delighted at what I saw. . . . It is a wonderful sight to see an institution spring fullfledged into active existence." "Dr. Lovett has at once an opportunity unprecedented in history." Such was the impact of Rice's opening.

Lovett obviously knew something about public relations, and he made every effort possible to place stories about Rice in newspapers and periodicals local and national. He clearly was behind an article entitled "The Progress of Science" that appeared in the December 1910 issue of *Popular Science Monthly;* the article was replete with fulsome praise of the new university being planned for Houston. Practically the entire issue of the November 1910 *Southern Architectural Review* was filled with a long essay by William Ward Watkins on the designs for the Rice Institute, with pages depicting the major buildings, detailed architectural plans, and a learned discussion of the origins and nature of the architectural vocabulary being employed. Lovett managed to get a long, fulsomely illustrated story on Rice published in the *New York Times* in February 1912, which pointed out to its readers that Lovett and the trustees had "a rare and interesting opportunity." Lovett also had printed a small, pocket-sized pamphlet entitled *The Rice Institute: Preliminary Announcements,* which he distributed widely. He even reported back to Rice officials while on his faculty recruitment trip to Europe in early 1912 that "the booklet makes a fine impression everywhere." And when the Southern Educational Association met in Houston in December 1911, Lovett had printed up a handsomely illustrated booklet describing the history, purpose, design, and facilities of the soon-to-open university to be distributed to participants at the conference. Given the small size, poverty, and limited potential of most southern colleges and universities, the Rice Institute as presented in this booklet must have seemed impressive almost beyond imagining.

At the time Lovett was considered a remarkable orator, and he never missed an opportunity to speak on educational themes; he also never failed to work in references to the expansive mission and ambition of the Rice Institute. His schedule in the three years before the opening show him addressing the Hellenic Banquet in Houston in 1909, giving the Phi Beta Kappa lecture at the University of Virginia in 1910, discoursing on "The Education of the Southern Girl" at the Southern Educational Association meeting in Houston in late November 1911. On other occasions he lectured on "The Appeal of Music" and "The Spirit of Science." He gave commencement addresses at the University of Texas, Texas A&M, and Texas Christian University. But he did not confine himself to academic audiences. In Houston, for example, he spoke to the "First Annual Banquet of the Houston Real Estate Exchange," the "Quarter Century Convention of the Lumbermen's Association of Texas," and the "Town and Gown Club" of Austin. His talks were always meaty, serious, intellectually challenging, with never a pandering to local prejudices—and he always opened with humor.

This energetic public relations campaign succeeded, and as the contractors rushed to finish the last-minute preparations for the campus (and the final acreage was acquired), both students and faculty journeyed to Houston. The dormitory ("of absolutely fire-proof construction, heated by steam. Lighted by electricity, cleaned by vacuum apparatus, and equipped with the most approved form of sanitary plumbing, providing adequate bathing facilities on every floor") was for men only. Women students would have to live at home (or, soon afterward, in approved boarding houses), though this was thought at the time to be merely a temporary inconvenience. Faculty found housing in nearby neighborhoods, although several of the young male faculty would live in the faculty tower of the residence hall—Julian Huxley, for example, lived there in 1913 and complained bitterly of the food. On Monday morning, September 23, 1912—twelve years to the day since the death of William Marsh Rice—the university opened. Students arrived on campus and began a series of admission tests, although some had already gained full admission because of their record at better known high schools. For the next several days, as the contractors rushed to finish the dorm rooms and other details (the screens were not yet installed on the windows, and a member of the first class recalled eighty-nine years later that mosquitoes invaded the rooms in full force; the *Houston Chronicle* admitted that the students would "find themselves facing a 'camping out' experience for some days"), students and faculty made last-minute preparations for classes. The students scurried to pick up their class assignment cards—that is, they registered—on the afternoon of Thursday, September 26, with actual class lectures beginning the next day. But earlier that morning on Thursday, the initial fifty-nine admitted students (eighteen more arrived in the next few days) had climbed the marble steps of the administration building and entered—to warm and sustained applause—the faculty chamber, the room now called the Founders' Room. Present already were the faculty, the members of the board of trustees, various city dignitaries representing government, business, and religious leaders, and of course President Edgar Odell Lovett, who shook every student's hand. Everyone immediately sensed the auspiciousness of the occasion.

A cold front had come through the previous night, and by 9:00 a.m. the weather was delightfully cool and the sky brilliantly blue—a newspaper reporter called the day "Venetian." When all were present, Lovett stepped upon the podium, raised his hand to command silence, and looked upon the audience, his countenance showing how moved he was. As he began to speak, he even faltered a moment, but he quickly regained his composure. After a scripture reading and a brief prayer, he spoke feelingly on the history of the institution—on William Marsh Rice's gift, on the careful planning, on the architecture of the campus—he introduced the faculty, and he predicted the impact on the community, state, and region of the new university whose promise seemed almost without limit. Lovett announced to the cosmopolitan faculty that they would find Houston—a small city of about 85,000 people—a surprisingly cosmopolitan place, "where the old South grows into the new West. You will learn to talk about lumber and cotton and railroads and oil; but you will also find every ear turned ready to listen to you if you really have anything to say about letters or science or art." Then directing his gaze to the students, Lovett said, his voice dropping to a conversational tone and speaking slowly and deliberately:

> I trust that we begin here today co-operation in high and noble tasks, with the common sympathy, affection, and energy which would characterize the members of a growing and immense family. I require that those who listen to my words should hold one faith with me. They must believe in the value of human reason; they must love beautiful things and consider them important; they must be enthusiastic for their fellow men. They must believe that it is possible to learn and that it is also possible to teach.

Sharing those beliefs, Lovett said they could together build a great university. At last the Rice Institute had been launched.

Yet Lovett had long been organizing a more formal opening ceremony, a bold public relations gamble intended to set forth enormously ambitious plans for the new university and to gain it almost instantaneous worldwide renown. And it would be on this occasion and before this audience that he would lay out his mature vision for the Rice Institute and effectively establish the trajectory of its future development. Clearly Lovett had been making preparations for this event—at least in his mind—for several years, and during his faculty recruitment trip to Europe in early 1912 had been asking scholars to participate, but it was not until a special meeting of the board on May 2, 1912, that his plans were officially approved. In a nutshell, the board resolution outlined the program. There would be "appropriate ceremonies" on October 10, 11, and 12, of that year, to which they would "invite delegates from celebrated universities, colleges, scientific foundations and learned societies of the world to be present . . . to invite several scholars of international reputation to participate in these proceedings by contributing papers . . . to offer each inaugural lecturer an honorarium of one thousand dollars . . . and to request the privilege of publishing the lectures in a volume commemorative of the formal opening of the new university." Lovett envisioned an event of unprecedented grandeur in the South and perhaps the nation, and literally no expense was spared. Would it work? Would scholars of such magnitude come to the infant university? (Lovett's letter of invitation to Leipzig chemist Wilhelm Ostwald had laid out the intended purpose of the visits: "Your presence would be of everlasting value to us in establishing high traditions. Your coming would serve as a constant inspiration to all future associates and students of the Institute.") Would the facilities be completed? Would the weather cooperate? How would the event be perceived—as Texas-sized presumptuousness or a signal moment in the history of American higher education?

Lovett had designed and printed a grand invitation, printed on calfskin, measuring 18 by 23.75 inches, with an embossed seal of the university. This stunning document was then mailed, rolled up (along with a paper version of the program) inside an exquisitely milled hollow wooden tube (20 inches long, 3 inches in diameter), shellacked to a fare-the-well, and more than a thousand of these were sent (a corps of secretaries and clerks worked for weeks in three rooms next to the institute offices in the Scanlan Building addressing and mailing them out) to individual scholars and such institutions as The Royal Danish Academy of Science, the Reale Academia Delle Scienze di Torino, the Imperial Medical Academy at St. Petersburg, the Polish Academy of Science, and every well-known university in Europe and a scattering of other places on the globe. To write that the recipients were impressed would be an understatement. John William Mackail of Oxford called it "a most magnificent document," while James Hampton Kirkland, chancellor of Vanderbilt University (and, like Lovett, the holder of a Leipzig doctorate), commented, "I do not know that I have ever seen so elaborate an invitation." And when scholars read the program, the real lavishness became even more apparent. Lovett had not been able to get every speaker he requested—Rudyard Kipling, for example, turned down the invitation to write and deliver an ode for the occasion—and several very eminent scholars declined on the grounds that they did not have the available time required for such a trip. Several statesmen such as Woodrow Wilson and Theodore Roosevelt also declined for scheduling reasons (it was a presidential election year). But even so, it was the greatest—and most international—academic assemblage ever held in the state or region.

On October 10, with the weather again perfect, and the campus almost completely finished and tidied up, with potted plants and shrubbery hurried into place, the more than 150 delegates from universities and learned societies from around the world had gathered in Houston. In addition to the eminent foreign guests, the chief academicians from a number of leading American universities attended, including such luminaries as David Starr Jordan of Stanford, William James Battle of the University of North Carolina, Robert Sharp of Tulane, Richard C. MacLaurin of the Massachusetts Institute of Technology (MIT), James Hampton Kirkland of Vanderbilt, Ira Remsen of Johns Hopkins, Sidney E. Mezes of the University of Texas, Harry Pratt Judson of Chicago, and at least a dean or faculty member from every other important American university. When the delegates perused their program, a large (12.75 by 18 inches) folio beautifully bound in calfskin, with the seal of the university embossed on the cover, and illustrated by tipped-in pen-and-ink or watercolor drawings of the buildings, they must have sensed the rigorous round of activities before them. The day began with a breakfast at the Bender Hotel downtown hosted by the trustees, following which the delegates were ferried to campus, where beginning at 10:30 in the faculty chamber—made unusually festive by the hanging of flags of the various nations represented by the visiting speakers—lectures were delivered "or presented by title" (meaning the writer was not actually present and only the title was given). At this morning session Professor Rafael Altamira y Crevea of Madrid and Professor Hugo de Vries of Amsterdam read their papers, while those of Professor John William Mackail of London and Professor Frederik Carl Störmer of Christiania, Norway, were presented by title only. After a noon luncheon at the banquet hall of the city auditorium, where welcoming remarks were made by Mayor Horace Baldwin Rice of Houston, Texas Governor Oscar B. Colquitt, and many others, the delegates returned to campus for papers delivered by Professor Emile Borel of Paris and Professor Sir Henry Jones of Glasgow; the papers of Senator Benedetto Croce of Naples and Privy Councilor Baron Dairoku Kikuchi of Tokyo were presented by title. The long and surely tiring day continued with a garden party at 5:00 p.m. in the academic court of the administration building, then a slide lecture at 8:30 p.m. at the Majestic Theater downtown by Professor de Vries, and finally ended with a reception at 9:30 p.m. in the home of Mr. and Mrs. James A. Baker.

Friday, October 11, was equally demanding, again beginning with a breakfast at the Bender Hotel hosted by the Houston Chamber of Commerce. Then to campus for lectures given by Professor Sir William Ramsay of London (a Nobel laureate) and Professor Senator Vito Volterra of Rome. The paper by Privy Councilor Professor Wilhelm Ostwald of Leipzig (another Nobel laureate) was presented by title, and Professor Volterra also gave an appreciative commentary on the life and work of the late Professor Henri Poincaré of Paris, who had just recently died. Lunch was at the Thalian Club, hosted by Mr. and Mrs. Jonas Shearn Rice, then at 3:00 p.m. a concert at the Majestic Theater by the Kneisel Quartet of New York City (Lovett had attended one of their concerts at Princeton a decade before), followed at 5:00 p.m. with a garden party at the stately home, "The Oaks," of Mr. and Mrs. Edwin Brewington Parker. (Several years later the Parkers sold their home to Captain Baker.) Somehow the delegates found the stamina to return to campus for another concert by the Kneisel Quartet and afterward, "supper" at the residential hall commons. Mercifully the events on Saturday, October 12, started a little later, beginning with an academic procession from the residential hall assembly site across the still almost completely bare campus to the academic court on the west side of the administration building. After an inaugural poem by Dr. Henry van Dyke of Princeton, short addresses by the honorable Thomas Jefferson Brown, the chief justice of the supreme court of Texas, and Dr. Thomas Frank Gailor, the Episcopal bishop of Tennessee, Dr. Lovett himself gave the speech of his life, entitled "The Meaning of the New Institution." After a quick photo session by the south wing of the residential college, there was at 1:00 p.m. a luncheon in the commons at which congratulatory messages from universities around the world were presented. Hugo de Vries later wrote that Lovett was "visibly touched" by the greetings and good wishes that were read. Finally the event was drawing to a close, and following a farewell reception at the Houston Country Club hosted by Dr. and Mrs. Lovett, all the delegates boarded a specially chartered train to Galveston, where they enjoyed a "shore-supper and smoker" at the sparkling new Hotel Galvez. Breakfast was served promptly at 8:00 a.m. the next morning, after which the delegates returned to Houston by chartered train again and at 11:00 a.m. listened to a sermon at the city auditorium by Reverend Dr. Charles Frederic Aked of San Francisco. That concluded the opening ceremonies, and the delegates must have returned to the Bender Hotel (or local attendees to their homes) both exhilarated and exhausted.

Lovett's inaugural address on October 12 is the ultimate summation of his vision of the purpose and possibilities of the new university that was in every way but monetarily his creation. "For this fair day we have worked and prayed and waited," he said. "In the faith of high adventure, in the joy of high endeavor, in the hope of high achievement, we have asked for strength, and with the strength a vision, and with the vision courage." And finally, today, "the Rice Institute, which was to be, in this its modest beginning, now has come to be." He predicted great things for the university and the city, for "great trading centers have often been conspicuous centers of vigorous intellectual life"—"Athens,

Venice, Florence, and Amsterdam" come to mind, and it was easy to imagine a "similar vision" for Houston. Then, after a brief sketch of the history of the university's founding, he outlined its characteristics. It would live on its endowment income; it would initially give prominence to applied science and engineering (carved on the cornerstone of the first science lab was the phrase "science in the service of society") but would emphasize research at least as much as instruction and utility. It is difficult today to realize how ambitious such an emphasis on research was in 1912. Just two years before the president of the "Association of Colleges . . . of the Southern States" had admitted that "Looking at the situation in the South . . . no university [is] well enough equipped to do genuine research work. . . . it is simply disheartening to contemplate our situation." Given Rice's location in a new country with practical needs, it would understandably begin its program "at the science end," but it would develop the arts and letters component of its purpose as soon as possible. Attention would be paid to architecture, developing a physical setting of "great beauty."

"The new institution . . . aspires to university standing of the highest grade"—it would not be merely a technical or training institute. "For the present it is proposed to assign no upper limit to its educational endeavor"—the ultimate goal was to be a world-class university. It would be coeducational, "for the present" no tuition would be charged, and for its able students "the best available instructors and investigators are being sought wherever they may be found." The expressed hope was that "the Institute should speedily take a place of considerable importance among established institutions." The title *institute* suggested the important role of research; the university would teach and contribute to knowledge, combine theoretical and practical scholarship, and support technical as well as liberal (humanistic) learning. Humanities meant far more than the old classical curriculum and now were attentive to "modern civilization and modern culture." Drawing ideas from the best practice around the world, the new university would promote research and teach in order to create "knowledge-makers." Teaching alone was not sufficient: "no university can live without the vitalizing reaction of original investigation." But more was expected of the faculty: "To the privileges of research and the duties of administration must be added the pleasures of teaching and public lecturing." Lovett made clear that teaching and research were not antagonistic but complementary: "the best man to lead the learner from the unknown to the known is the man who is continually leading himself from the unknown to the known . . . in point of new knowledge contributed by himself to the store of learning." The university must be a true learning community, with the first-year students being mentored by senior faculty and all, undergraduates, graduate students, and faculty, interacting and learning together. Lovett called for an honor system of self-governance for students; he called for a residential college system; he called for students living and dining together in democratic fashion. At present housing would be provided only for men, but it was expected that soon housing would also be available for women students.

Lovett wanted students to be well-rounded, combining scholarship with exercise and an appreciation of music and art. Warning of the overspecialization of team sports, he urged students to engage in intramural competition. He intended to generate funds for scholarships and develop opportunities for student jobs in the city so that the advantages of a collegiate education could be "brought within the reach of the promising student of slender means." He particularly insisted that undergraduates interact with and learn from and with graduate students, just as he held it essential that "the most distinguished teachers must take their part in undergraduate teaching." Courses for the first two years would be rather general, with specialization occurring in the final two years. The engineering courses would have a decidedly theoretical orientation. And while at present there would be no medical, law, or business schools, in the goodness of time the university would offer instruction in all the "brain-working professions" of modern life. Under neither state nor church control, the university would be extraordinarily free, each professor "a freeman to teach the truth as he finds it, each man a freeman to seek the truth wherever truth may lead." Moreover, Lovett realized that education did not end when one had attained a degree; rather, "it is a matter of life, the whole span of life." Lifetime learning would play an important function in the university, and the university would offer an elaborate set of extension lectures in the city, free to the public. Lovett foresaw the day when graduates and citizens would return to the cloisters and groves of the campus to contemplate, to think more deeply, to rediscover the great traditions of scholarship and spirit.

Lovett understood what was at stake in establishing a new university. Speaking on October 12, he reflected that "on the anniversary of Columbus's arrival, we too are setting out on a voyage of discovery." He was hesitant to prophesy, but he could not resist: "This academic festival provides the first alignment of the Rice Institute with other institutions. It is the placing of a new university on the map of the earlier universities. The new institution comes as a rival to none, but as a child hoping to grow in favor, to gain the confidence and to win the respect of older foundations. It is the advent of a man-child that we have witnessed, and some of us believe we have discovered in its form the features and bones of a giant." But only time would tell.

The formal opening was covered extensively by the local press, and even the national press found it notable, the *New York Times* calling it "an array of learning such as has seldom been assembled in the United States," featuring what Julian Huxley later recalled as "a galaxy of outstanding savants." Those who actually attended were extraordinarily impressed. Hugo de Vries, the Dutch botanist, wrote to Lovett in December from aboard the SS *Nieuw Amsterdam,* returning to Europe, that he admired the buildings, Lovett's "masterly address," and the "complete and careful preparation" that was so evident. He praised Lovett for "not only founding a great university on a large campus, but in founding it in the hearts of the citizens of Houston, and in giving it a wide reputation all over the world of learning." (The following year Vries published a book in Dutch on his recent trip to the United States, *Van Texas naar Florida: Reisherinner,* which contained a long and favorable descriptive chapter on his visit to the Rice campus and opening ceremonies.) Earlier Lovett had received an equally effusive letter from Sir William Ramsay, and he would be pleased several years later to read in Ramsay's official biography a section on the opening (prepared by Lady Ramsay) that stated that Sir Ramsay "had been present at several of the gatherings in this country [England] to commemorate centuries of university history, but none were more impressive than this, looking forward to a great future." It was, Lady Ramsay had told the compiler of the biography, "different from anything ever experienced before. It was indeed a great experience." Robert S. Lovett, chief counsel to the Southern Pacific Railroad (and no relation to President Lovett), wrote to Dr. Lovett that he had received a long telegram from Dr. Aked of San Francisco saying how satisfied he had been by his visit, how impressive and dignified he had found the ceremonies, and Robert S. Lovett confided to President Lovett that "I think Houston and the character of the Institute were a revelation to him." Many who had been present had similar feelings.

No visitor more vividly described the entire experience than Julian Huxley, who attended in part to check out the situation before actually joining the faculty one year later. Seeking to tell a British audience what the event had been like, he published a colorful essay entitled "Texas and Academe" in the July 1918 issue of *Cornhill Magazine*. Huxley set the scene for his readers, telling of the flatness of the prairie and then giving some idea of Houston society. He no doubt pleased architect Cram when he stated that there "in Houston was being celebrated the birth of a new University, and celebrated in the same spirit as might have been the dedication of a new Cathedral in the Middle Ages." Huxley explained that while an "uninstructed Englishman, or even an arrogant New Yorker," might have expected the Texas school to be little more than a very local, "ultrapractical," and provincial institution, in fact the Rice Institute was "a real University," "the reverse of parochial in all its ideas." He pointed out that the university would emphasize research, that it would be coeducational, that fraternities were forbidden, that academic standards would be high, and that the faculty would be highly qualified. But perhaps his most powerful writing came when Huxley tried to convey to his British readers the unexpected beauty of the architecture. Driving out the primitive dirt road, all of a sudden before them stood "an extraordinary spectacle, as of palaces in fairy-story. The Administration Building was before us, looking exactly as if it had risen miraculously out of the earth." After a detailed depiction of the building, "almost Moorish in feeling," Huxley concluded: "Here it stood, brilliant, astounding, enduring." No reader could have failed being impressed, as surely was Huxley himself.

Soon after the opening ceremonies Sir William Ramsay had written to Lovett from Boston on October 31, 1912, en route to London, that "everyone is speaking of the Rice Institute." After praising the ceremonies and arrangements for all the guests, Ramsay concluded that "you carried out everything in a most impressive manner; & and now it remains, I suppose, to settle down into routine." That would indeed be the major task for the next decade, but Lovett as yet had some unfinished business with the opening to settle. Remembering the large book he had seen at Princeton in 1897 memorializing the previous year's celebration of Princeton's sesquicentennial, Lovett was determined to do the same for Rice, only threefold. He collected all the papers, the toasts, the programs of the three-day event; he compiled lists of all the delegates; he acquired photographs of many of the congratulatory scrolls that had been sent—and all this he compiled into three massive volumes collectively entitled *The Book of the Opening of the Rice Institute,* elegantly printed by the De Vinne Press that had produced the Princeton volume. The commemorative volumes were "inscribed by special permission to the Honorable Woodrow Wilson, Ph.D., Litt.D., LL.D., Man of Letters, Leader of Men, Thirteenth President of Princeton University, and the Twenty-Eighth President of the United States of America." Lovett thus acknowledged his fealty and intellectual debt to his former colleague.

Lovett had over 1,200 copies of this set of volumes sent to scholars, universities, learned societies, and research libraries around the world, with review copies mailed to major publications. Back came dozens of letters expressing thanks, amazement at the grandeur of the opening, and praise for the promise of the new institution. A. E. Shipley of Christ's College, Cambridge, described the books as "beautifully got up," and President Andrew D. White of Cornell said of them "it seems to me to be the most perfect tribute of the kind that I have ever seen." The *Sewanee Review,* after lavishing praise on the "magnificent" work of the De Vinne Press, stated that "it is doubtful whether any other institution of learning, either in this country or abroad, opened its doors under more auspicious circumstances." Edgar Odell Lovett had to have been pleased over how the ceremonies themselves had gone and over the favorable attention they created internationally for the new university.

This was exactly the outcome for which he had worked so tirelessly and so intensely. He had put Rice on the academic map of the world. Several commentators at the time remarked that Lovett was obviously moved, almost overwhelmed, by the course of events on those three days in October 1912. Perhaps the letter of R. W. D. Bryant, the president of the University of New Mexico, to Mrs. Lovett on October 23 best captured both the sentiment of the days just past and the work yet to come:

> As I saw on several occasions during those wonderfully interesting inaugural exercises, the emotions of your husband and how hard at times it was for him to control himself, I realized how much the consummation of long years of thought and endeavor meant to him, especially when he felt that the thing he has dreamed of and planned for was even greater than his anticipations. I am sure that you have reason to be very proud of your husband and I trust that you will long be spared to be an incentive and a help to him during the coming years when there will be painstaking drudgery to build up and perfect the institution.

Edgar Odell Lovett had opened the Rice Institute, but as Bryant understood, there was still much to be done, and not all of it would be as exciting and emotionally fulfilling as the last few years had been. There *would* be drudgery ahead. But Lovett was duty-bound to the task; he had found his life's work.

# CHAPTER FIVE

# ACADEMIC ADMINISTRATION
# IN PEACETIME AND WAR

THE FORMAL OPENING CEREMONIES had been filled with academic glamour, intellectual excitement, and the buzz of great expectations, but after those heady days invigorated by the presence of important visitors and expansive visions came the steady, hard work of actually getting a university underway. Moreover, Edgar Odell Lovett had a family, with a devoted wife who had a history of illness, and part of his attention and psychological energy had to be directed toward establishing a home in Houston. Sensing that this was his final move and that the development of the new university would occupy his thought and energy—and his patience—for the remainder of his life, Lovett took care to fit himself and the university into the ethos and ambition of the rapidly growing city on the plains of Texas. The region had no experience with a university of the quality that Lovett envisioned, nor did it produce students all of whom were prepared for the academic challenges the Rice Institute offered. And in the midst of these founding years, the European world collapsed into a maelstrom of war, destruction, and death—an event terribly upsetting to the quintessentially cosmopolitan Lovett, who had strong ties to scholars in all of the contending nations and, moreover, had a close personal relationship with Woodrow Wilson. Within less than a decade Lovett was having to deal not only with the quotidian problems of creating and sustaining a new institution but also with the vexing problem of how the university should respond to the exigencies of wartime.

One issue of unexpected difficulty was finding a home for the Lovett family. From the beginning Lovett desired to have a house built on campus, but before that could be done, of course, he needed a place in 1909, after returning from the round-the-world trip. In the first months after the return, as he hurried back to Houston to work with architects and the board, Mary returned to Mayfield, Kentucky, to rejoin the children, and then in the later summer and early autumn she went with the children to Atlantic City. It was feared that Houston was too hot for her to arrive in July and August, she still was extremely careful about her health, and she understandably felt the need to bond anew with her children after being absent from them during her long illness and then the voyage. They were, after all, at impressionable ages—Adelaide turned eleven that fall and Malcolm was seven. During the summer and early fall Edgar Lovett wrote to her often, with frequent references about looking for a house in the city for the university to either rent or buy. He also sought—unsuccessfully at first—to enroll the children in a good private school, and he remarked to Mary how much the various wives of trustee members and other prominent citizens were looking forward to meeting her. "Everyone is asking when you and the children are coming. . . . And Mary, it's going to be another honeymoon for us when we do get under our own roof again." Sometime in the fall he rented a house at 1218 Polk Avenue (at the intersection with Caroline), and by November Mary and the children were there. Almost a half century later another Houstonian, William Kirkland, recalled "Mrs. Lovett welcoming boys and girls to her home with patience, understanding, and enthusiasm," and he remembered as well how "easily" the Lovett children "fitted . . . into the neighborhood." Before the house was found, Lovett stayed in a hotel, and even after the house was acquired but before Mary arrived (and he had not yet found a servant), he took his meals at the hotel.

For the next few summers and early autumns, Mary and the children escaped the Houston heat and humidity by returning to Mayfield for a while and then longer visits to either Atlantic City or Asheville, North Carolina, in the mountains. Lovett meanwhile stayed mainly in Houston, working on institute matters, though he often traveled to New York City, Boston, or Princeton to confer with the architects and interview prospective faculty. He traveled exclusively by train—Lovett never drove an automobile—the trip to New York City from Houston, for example, typically taking two days and three nights. While he was enormously busy, he often wrote to Mary about the issues he was facing and the progress being made on various projects. He asked her advice about inscriptions he was preparing to have carved onto the buildings and sought her approval of his design for the official university stationery; he commented on things about the house on Polk Street—"The chickens are doing well and the old hen setting"; he mentioned how much he missed her—"Thumbed the piano awhile before leaving the house. Imagined I was getting out of it some of the things you have put in it, even to your voice. And left utterly miserable"—and often his letters were filled with longing for her.

He missed the physical intimacy, referring to it often (but resorting to a code language in French when doing so), and his craving at times almost seem to have driven him to distraction. He would write her expressing his desire to hold and touch her on a Sunday afternoon, which seems to be the day they normally reserved for themselves. (And she responded in kind, once writing: "Sweetheart, . . . I'm going to tell you how wicked I think it is of you to remain away over *Sundays*—What's a lady to do at home all day Sunday alone?") He would write such things as "I don't believe that you can even faintly imagine how much I want you—and in the flesh! Just to fondle and cuddle and kiss and caress partout!" (And the French continued in a much more intimate manner.) Another time: "Mary, it's a cool and rainy Sunday. Just the sort of day to snuggle up close in married blessedness." He even suggested she keep careful notice of her periods so that together they could calculate the best time for him to make occasional trips by train to Mayfield or wherever she happened to be. He respected and drew upon her aesthetic tastes, he admired her musical skills, he enjoyed her companionship, and he deeply treasured their sensual relationship.

Sometime in October 1910 Mary conceived again, an event that filled both parents with excitement and concern in the light of the death four years before of Ellen. Mary very much wanted Miriam Bowles, her old nurse from 1906, to join her, and though Ms. Bowles confessed that she was not "a maternity nurse, know precious little about it," nevertheless she agreed to "stay by and fight battles if need be for you, like I did at the University Hospital." After some wrangling with Ms. Bowles's present employer, the Lovetts gained her services. Both Lovetts were cautiously optimistic, conferred with doctors, and waited nervously for the time of delivery. On July 22, 1911, a healthy boy was born, whom they named Lawrence Alexander. Obviously with the sad memory of little Ellen starving to death, they kept close watch on Alex's growth and reported with pride his steady weight gains. When he was a little over a month old, Mary wrote that he was "gaining weight and doing so well," and Lovett wrote soon after to a friend that Alex had been "gaining uniformly since his birth: a quarter of a pound the first week, a half the second, three quarters the third, a half the fourth, and nearly a whole pound the fifth." Within a few months Lovett would triumphantly write his former secretary who had circumnavigated the world with Mary and him: "Dear Weems: Alexander weighs fifteen pounds!" What a joy it was to have a healthy baby once again in the family.

In the midst of the excitement and sense of expectancy over the birth of a child, Lovett came to realize that despite repeated attempts to juggle size requirements with budget considerations, a stately president's house would not be built on the campus in the foreseeable future. The immense volume of correspondence between Lovett and the architects on the matter, the repeated consultations with both Mary and the board members, and the strong desire for a university home fitting the architectural ambition of the rest of the campus buildings, made this deeply disappointing to Lovett. (A tiny group of critics claimed that Lovett simply wanted a palatial home for himself, but Lovett saw the house as an instrument to help advance the reputation and ambition of the new university by means of receptions and other public events.) He and his family would never live on the campus. They continued to live at the Polk Street home through the academic year of 1914–1915, and then—though Lovett had earlier expressed reservations about living in a hotel (it was expensive, there was a lack of privacy)—in the fall of 1915 they took a suite of rooms in the Bender Hotel, the city's leading hostelry, where they lived for several years. In 1918 they moved again to a rented private home at 3904 Brandt Street, but after two years they returned to the Bender. Never again would the Lovetts live in a house; in 1928 they rented a suite of rooms on the eighth floor of the new Plaza Apartment Hotel on Montrose Boulevard, much nearer the campus (the university provided him at the time a $300 monthly allowance), and there they would live the remainder of their lives. Their suite was on the eastern wing of the Plaza, near the street, with views also to the north and south, and there was enough room for a grand piano. Looking southwestward, with the new (1926) Warwick Hotel looming nearby, one could see over the canopy of trees the administration building of the Rice Institute. To the northeast, three miles distant, was the central business district, whose skyline was dominated after 1929 by the thirty-seven-story Gulf Building that would remain the city's tallest until 1962. Both Lovetts were inveterate readers, and eventually all the shelves were bulging, with the books double shelved, and there were shelves in every room.* On several of the bottom shelves there eventually was a collection of children's books, handy for the grandchildren. It was a comfortable apartment, providing an elevated view of both the Rice Institute and the growing city. Later, students would remember often seeing President Lovett walking the short distance of just under a mile to the university, a book strap over his shoulder.

Lovett's efforts to recruit faculty did not cease with the opening of classes, as was discussed earlier. He was pressured by both students and the existing faculty to accelerate the enlargement of the faculty, but doing so was no easy task. Lovett still assumed that this was a matter solely up to him, and at least for the first few years the existing faculty played no role in the selection of additional faculty. There were no search committees, although Lovett wrote to his wife in May 1914 that he had "a splendid committee [on courses of study and schedules] at work on the curriculum," and of course curricular decisions helped determine the disciplines of the new faculty sought and their number. Soon there were also committees on examinations and standings, on the library, on outdoor sports, on non-athletic organizations, on entrance examinations, on recommendations, and on student advisors. All these committees sent recommendations and resolutions to the general faculty meetings, which then acted upon committee reports. But Lovett assumed that it was solely his responsibility to hire faculty. The Rice

---

* Eventually Dr. Lovett's private library, consisting of the books in the Plaza apartment and from his university office—over seven thousand books in all—would be integrated into the collections of the university's Fondren Library, each book identified with a special bookplate.

Institute was in every way his creation, and he had shaped every aspect of its development so far, down to the last detail, even including the university seal and shield. Moreover, he had been named a member of the board of trustees in 1910, and although he still had to make presentations and attempt to persuade the board to accept his recommendations, he did not see his relationship to the board as antagonistic, even when—as on the matter of building a presidential house on campus— they rejected his wishes. On most matters the board, and especially its chair, James A. Baker, was completely supportive. So Lovett continued to see the institute as his project, his conception, and he oversaw its operation in a manner that could be considered that of a benevolent dictator or a wise patriarch, according to one's viewpoint, but he was so benevolent, so fair-minded, so obviously devoted to creating a university of the highest standards, and commanded such loyalty from the faculty and students that most—with few exceptions—accepted his leadership. Over time there would be gentle suggestions that committee structures be enlarged and there be more faculty input, but Lovett understood his role to be the leader, and the faculty (and students) were expected to follow. Usually they did, but not always. And of course because Lovett was known to be essentially in charge of everything on campus, he was the target of complaint and anger whenever anything did not live up to expectations. One prominent faculty member even wrote to him about holes in a tennis net on campus.

Perhaps the first friction developed because the pace of hiring did not appear to keep up with enrollment growth and the expectation of continuing students that class offerings would increase as they proceeded through the four-year curriculum. For example, on April 16, 1914, President Lovett was handed a petition signed by 101 students "respectfully" requesting that they be provided "an outline of the courses which will be offered at the Rice Institute next year" and "The formation of a definite policy as regards engineering courses." The petitioners feared that they were "not getting the courses in the branches of engineering which will lead to a degree in four years," so they asked "what branches of Engineering will be offered and the outline for each course that is offered." The petition had been originally sent to the trustees, and they simply forwarded it to President Lovett. Chairman

Baker replied to the students that the board was referring the issue to the president, "who no doubt will take up the matter with the petitioners either in a body or severally, or both." Lovett followed that implied suggestion, and his written response was made with the polite formality that characterized all his exchanges with students. Lovett wrote that "in reply to this courteous communication [the petition], I have pleasure in saying," and then he promised that as soon as he had the information together that the students requested, he would communicate it to them in "printed form." He then promised to meet each signatory of the petition personally and go over the curricular plans and their personal course list. Then followed advice that today sounds almost avuncular: "I confidently hope that the same spirit of earnestness and loyalty which prompted this petition will constrain all students to meet squarely the opportunities of the present session in the faith that the new Institute will meet as squarely all obligations it promised, with all earnestness, to its students." That settled the matter. The students obviously took Lovett at his word, and perhaps some of the faculty counseled them that Lovett was working as hard as possible to bring in the requisite faculty. The curriculum would grow with the student body, and during the first two years even prospective engineers would take mostly basic science and mathematics courses. By their last two years the entering class would have engineering courses. The Rice catalogue for 1915 listed three instructors in the field of engineering; that of 1916 listed a total of seven; and by 1920 there were nine faculty teaching various branches of engineering.

At least some of the faculty too grew impatient at what to them seemed the dilatory nature of faculty recruitment in their fields. Potential faculty did not come to Houston to be interviewed; rather, Lovett spent a great deal of time traveling to the major cities and academic centers of the Northeast to interview both prospective faculty and senior faculty at established institutions to get their recommendations for persons he might want to approach. This extensive travel, and the fact that only Lovett was involved in the process, meant that faculty recruitment was an ongoing process literally for years. In the spring semester of the first academic year physicist Harold A. Wilson complained to a fellow physicist in London that "Prof. Lovett seems very slow about getting more members of the faculty. I can't make out whether this is due to mere slackness or to some reason he wishes to keep to himself." Wilson may have underestimated both how hard Lovett was working at the task of recruitment and how hard it was to find people of the ability he wanted who were willing to leave their current institution—Lovett was unwilling to compromise on quality. But Wilson's complaining letter the following fall probably did reflect some of the frustration that later would motivate students to send a petition to Lovett. Wilson commented that "the chief difficulty here seems to be to get instructors. President Lovett says he will get them all the time but just puts it off in an aggravating way. Then we never have any faculty meetings & every thing is done without any attempt at proper organization. There is no curriculum or anything & no regulations about courses." Again, this may represent nothing more than growing pains at an instant university, and within three years Wilson was bragging that "the Institute is doing rather well." He also was by then lauding several of the "quite good students" who were taking "honours in physics." Apparently Lovett had corrected the perceived problems by the fall of 1916. Certainly by 1915 there were regularly scheduled faculty meetings twice a month and a number of faculty standing committees that reported to the general faculty meetings.

By no means was Wilson the most troublesome member of the faculty; that position was held by a lecturer in chemistry, William Franklin Edwards, who possessed only a B.S. degree from the University of Michigan and was a native Houstonian. Edwards was disgruntled over what he saw as the leadership and visionary failings of Lovett and nearly every aspect of the Rice Institute that bore the impress of Lovett. Edwards began on June 1, 1914, sending anti-Lovett letters to trustee chair James A. Baker. Lovett mentioned in a letter to his wife in July 1914 that "Edwards had given me a great deal of trouble and is planning more." Lovett suspected that Edwards "inspired" the petition earlier that year from students. Writing from New York City, Lovett confided to Mary that "I'll certainly get rid of him a year hence and perhaps immediately upon my return." Later that summer, back in Houston, Lovett commented to Mary that he had not seen Edwards, but clearly Edwards was still working to undermine the trustees' confidence in Lovett. On April 5, 1915, Edwards sent Baker an eleven-page typed letter summarizing his charges against the president, with another seven-page letter continuing the vendetta on May 20. These two letters, containing approximately 6,500 words, attacked every aspect of Lovett's leadership. Lovett reportedly so cowed the faculty that they were "comatose," the university barely functioned, the faculty were overpaid and did no legitimate research ("degrees do not always insure scholarship"), they were an undistinguished lot, far too many of them were "foreigners," there were not enough engineering and practical courses and too many pure science and mathematics courses, too much attention was paid to fancy architecture, all the emphasis on academic quality instead was intended to "build up an institution of learning for developing a snobbish intellectual aristocracy," advanced degrees were overrated, the public lectures presented were second-rate ("cribbed from encyclopedias"), Dr. Lovett was not in sympathy with the stated purposes of the university, and everything seemed intended to "emphasize medieval architecture and the president."

Dr. Lovett was charged with intentionally holding engineering back, with being primarily concerned with building for himself a palatial president's house, and in every way was destroying the prospects of the university's future. In summary, according to Edwards, "from every point of view except, perhaps, as an architectural museum, the Institute is a failure," and Lovett was the reason for that failure. On May 29 Mr. Baker simply sent the letters on to Lovett, sardonically adding that "the enclosed letters will explain themselves," adding that "we should have an early conference in respect to them." Later in the summer Edwards took his complaints to the *Houston Chronicle*, who published some of them in a front-page article on July 16, 1915. The newspaper quoted Edwards as saying in summary that the Rice Institute was "unique as a masterpiece of mismanagement and indefiniteness." (The editor subsequently told Lovett that a subordinate had published the material without the editor's approval.) But soon the furor subsided, for the trustees as expected saw through Edwards's intemperate complaints and found them unpersuasive. For the next few days or so Lovett found widespread support from the public; he even reported that "Janitors, engineers, stenographers, and gardeners" were "all indignant" at Edward's charges, "and in every move show a desire to help." Lovett finally could write with relief to his wife on August 5 that he had received "a rather successful issue out of my recent troubles [with Edwards]." The last Lovett heard of him, Edwards was said to be moving to Philadelphia.

Edwards had despaired of what he called the slow pace of development of the university, but if Lovett's letters are any indication of his activity, he was constantly involved in faculty recruitment and the faculty steadily grew in numbers. His letters to his wife are filled with comments about his hopes, which were sometimes dashed, that this or that promising candidate would be coming to Rice. Repeatedly he referred to his attempts to attract engineering faculty, or a "corking good" chemist or physicist, and he carefully cultivated Stockton Axson, a professor of literature at Princeton who had been repeatedly chosen the most popular teacher there, to come to Rice permanently, where he would become beloved to many citizens as well who took in his free public lectures. Perhaps no potential faculty member occupied more of Lovett's time than the young Julian Huxley. Lovett had begun communication with Huxley in 1909, answering question after question from the hypochondriacal young British prima donna who was filled with concern about coming all the way to Texas. "Is there any malaria or yellow fever or other unpleasant tropical or semi-tropical disease against which one has to be continually guarding?" queried Huxley in February 1912. Lovett even agreed to bring him over for the opening ceremonies so that he could get some sense of the opportunities here. Finally Huxley agreed to come to teach, but he did so tardily in the fall 1913 semester. He seemed always to be complaining ("The food [he lived in the faculty tower of the residence hall, now Baker College] is very monotonous, & often ill-cooked; & there is far too great a use of canned vegetables & fruit. The meat in particular is most unappetizing, & the bread often of poor quality, & a little more imagination in the kitchen, would help a great deal"), wanted to arrive late and leave early in the academic year, and generally was what today would be termed *high maintenance*. Huxley was a brilliant scientist though, and did shape the biology department in such a way as to make the department more than one of, in his own words, "glorified technique & diligent plodding." Huxley missed the excitement of London but came to appreciate the "open warm-heartedness & and freedom and the earnestness of the Texans," but with the onset of World War I Huxley felt his mother country calling him. In the summer of 1916 he asked Lovett for a leave of absence the coming academic year, and then in April 1917 he submitted his formal resignation. He admitted that he had learned a lot in Houston, had "'come of age intellectually,'" and would be homesick for Rice, but he also did not like the climate or the flatness of the land. He told Lovett that he felt he had established the department "on right lines," and he assured Lovett that the faculty member remaining, Hermann J. Muller, was first-rate (actually, some years later, having left Rice also, Muller would win the Nobel Prize). Huxley's original teaching assistant, Joseph Ilott Davies, stayed on at Rice for decades, eventually earned his doctorate, and became a legendary teacher of freshman biology.

By all means impatient students and disgruntled faculty were not the only ones who criticized President Lovett. Then as now a university president's life was complicated by the importuning of parents. Lovett handled such issues with formal courtesy, but he never gave in and was confident that the board of trustees would support his (or the faculty's) decisions. In an era when there were no standardized testing procedures for student applicants and the quality of high schools varied immensely, choosing qualified students was even more difficult in 1912 than today. Few parents had received the benefit of university training and hence knew what to expect in college classrooms, and the high academic standards insisted on by Lovett and his small cadre of hand-picked faculty were based on the practice current at the best institutions in the world. Perhaps then it is no surprise that the academic work load and faculty expectations stunned many of the students, dozens of whom failed out after the first of the year's three semesters. One disgruntled parent, J. M. Wilkinson, sent a long and impassioned letter to the trustees (one of whom, of course, was President Lovett) on January 4, 1913, protesting on behalf of three students who had been informed that because of "deficiencies in scholarship" they would not be permitted to enroll in the next semester's courses. Mr. Wilkinson thought the exams too rigid and too difficult, and he argued that the faculty should simply work with "the material at hand" and slowly build up the academic skills of the students.

Lovett replied, first expressing his "appreciation both of the spirit in

which you have written and of the feelings which prompted your protest." But Lovett did not back down; he knew the standards had been
set high and intentionally so. He continued to Mr. Wilkinson: "The action called into question by your inquiry was taken upon mature deliberation. Moreover, the Institute's aspirations in service and scholarship
demand the maintenance of just such standards as have been set. Accordingly I am compelled to adhere to a policy to which you have been
constrained to take exception." Wilkinson hoped the trustees would
overrule Lovett, but that possibility was scotched by trustee chair
James A. Baker's letter to him on January 13. Baker simply acknowledged receipt of the communication and then, closing the matter, said,
"if there is anything further to be said or done, I will write you again."
Of course he never did.

Far more insistent was J. Thos. Hall of Nacogdoches, who had received a letter from President Lovett on November 16, 1914, informing
him that his son, G. Martel Hall, had been "suspended from residence
in the Hall for the remainder of the present academic year." Lovett
stated that this action had been initiated as a result of the recommendation of the board of representatives of the residence hall, although
Lovett said that he concurred with the decision and "greatly deplore[d]
the necessity of this action." Mr. Hall wrote Lovett that his son had explained to his parents that it was all meant as a joke, intending no harm,
and the father appealed to Dr. Lovett's memories of his own childhood,
when surely he too must have done something foolish. So, in the spirit
of forgiveness, Hall asked that the ban from residence on campus be
lifted. Mrs. Hall also sent Lovett a plaintive letter, though it has been
lost. Thanking them both for their correspondence, Lovett replied on
November 20 that he regretted "to say that any further discussion of
the decision made would be fruitless in the way of any revision. The action, which was not taken hastily, was promptly and unanimously confirmed by the Faculty of the Institute." But Mr. Hall was not to be put
off, so he wrote Lovett again asking for a "full statement of the charges
or complaint against the Accused."

Now the whole story was to come out. Lovett replied to Hall on
November 28 that at 2:30 a.m. on November 13, his son had been ap-
prehended with several other boys on the roof of the residence hall pre-

paring to set fire to two gallons of gasoline, having first entered the office of the residence hall manager and also the administration building to disable the telephones. Hall wrote back, saying essentially that since they had been caught and the "prank" therefore not accomplished, no punishment should be administered—a "no harm, no foul" position. Lovett responded again, simply referring Hall to his previous comment that "further discussion . . . would be fruitless." After another letter to Lovett protesting the severity of the punishment for such a minor prank, Mr. Hall gave up on the president and wrote a long letter to James A. Baker. In this letter Hall said the boys had also carried to the roof several pails of water, and that they intended to pour some gasoline on top of the water so the flames would not come into contact with the actual structure of the residence hall, and besides, he said, they had picked a rainy night for their prank. And they did not actually cut the telephone wires but merely disconnected them. As to the issue of entering offices that they were not supposed to, Hall said the boys had "never been told" that these offices constituted a "'Sacred Arc' or a 'Sanctum Sanctorum'" that were off-limits to students. Hall concluded that the "expulsion was excessively severe, humiliating to students and parents." That last phrase perhaps explains the insistent protest of Hall. Then he asked to visit Baker in Houston. But when Hall came by Baker's office, the trustee chair was out of town. Meanwhile Baker had replied blandly that he would look into the matter. Hall then proposed to raise the stakes of the battle, mentioning that his son had had a "conference" with a "leading Editor [a writer for the *Houston Chronicle*]," and in fact the story did get into that paper. Mrs. Hall then wrote Chairman Baker, arguing that some of the students who had been on the residence hall governance committee now thought the punishment too severe and were circulating a petition among students asking President Lovett to relent. Mrs. Hall asked Baker to interview several of these students who were defending her son. Baker wrote back promptly that "it would not be in order for me to put on foot any such inquiry as suggested in your letter. Such an inquiry comes entirely within the jurisdiction of Dr. Lovett and the faculty, and not with that of the Trustees." Both Mr. and Mrs. Hall wrote several more times, with Mrs. Hall remarking that she was sending clippings from the *Houston Chronicle* to the president of Texas A&M. But neither Lovett nor Baker backed down under pressure, and Baker apparently closed the matter in his final letter on February 13, 1915, pointing out to Mrs. Hall that the disciplinary action taken against her son "grew out of nothing that reflected upon his integrity, good name or character," so he should be able to gain admission to "any other educational institution." In the face of what the Halls deemed a matter of family honor, the trustees stood squarely behind President Lovett and the faculty.

Of course, by all means student life was not dominated by pranksters and complainers. As with any new college, the first several classes of students were busy forming organizations, establishing traditions, fielding athletic teams, and shaping the character of the student experience. The student-run newspaper, the *Rice Thresher,* was begun in 1916 and quickly established its independence.* A yearbook staff had already begun work, and in 1916 the first edition of the *Campanile* appeared. In its pages the rich panoply of student activities were displayed: YMCA and YWCA clubs, a Menorah Society, Les Hiboux, Goethe-Verein, the Riceonian Debating Society, the Owl Literary Society (men), the Elizabeth Baldwin Literary Society (women), and many other organizations, including a band. The Honor Council, adopted by student vote in 1916, was supervising an important part of university life, academic integrity. A Rice college culture had been fashioned within a few years.

The strong support Lovett received from the Rice board complicates understanding of a brief episode in 1915 when Lovett was unofficially approached about accepting the presidency of the University of Texas. The backdrop to this development consisted of a series of events playing themselves out in the state capital. President Sidney E. Mezes, a Harvard-trained philosopher, had resigned the presidency of the University of Texas on November 4, 1914, to accept the presidency of the College of the City of New York. A few days later, the regents named classics professor William J. Battle as acting president, effective December 15, and appointed a "Committee on Presidency" to begin a search for a permanent head of the university. Houston civic leader and philanthropist Will C. Hogg, a university regent, served as secretary to

---

*Because the paper has always been called simply the *Thresher* on campus, I use that title hereinafter.

the search committee. In the meantime the regents as a whole and the acting president became embroiled in a terrific fight with the legislature and Governor James E. Ferguson over budgets and, essentially, control of the university. Ferguson claimed that Battle had misled the legislature about the university's budget, and the governor tried to dismiss Battle from the faculty. (Battle would later announce, in October 1915, that he did not want to be considered for permanent appointment.)

Amid this turmoil various candidates were promoted for the university's presidency, including an especially vigorous effort on behalf of the university's founding dean of engineering, Thomas U. Taylor. Apparently Hogg—who had great respect for Lovett—in the early summer sent a feeler to the Rice president (probably very similar to a later effort Hogg made to another potential candidate "to ascertain if he would be in a susceptible mood if a definite position were made to him"). Hogg had a tendency to act on his own, without bothering to get authorization for his actions or go through the proper channels, and his dangling of the Texas presidency before Lovett may have been an example of Hogg's precipitateness. Lovett wrote to his wife on August 1, 1915, however, that he feared the recent controversy over the Edwards charges against him "may have affected the University question, for I have now been here two weeks and Mr. H. has not been to see me."

Then, two weeks later, on September 5, Lovett sent his wife an update. "Will Hogg had me to dinner with him & his brother Friday night. Battle has gotten in bad this summer, but to avoid the appearance of politics the Board of Regents will not act at once. Hogg declares . . . that I am still his first choice . . . . said that they could pay ten thousand, and he certainly hopes I'd accept if they made the offer. I could only say that until they made me an offer I was at a great disadvantage in talking about the matter. I really doubt very much if I ever hear any more about it." But apparently Hogg did broach the matter again, because on October 12 Lovett wrote Rice board chairman James A. Baker to say that "Until I had this double assurance [?], I had been hesitating to tell you that a proposition looking towards my leaving Houston has come to me in such a form that I am obliged to consider it." The correspondence is silent on what happened next, but clearly shortly thereafter Lovett was no longer even an unofficial candidate for the position. Did Baker persuade him to stay at Rice, or did Lovett find the fiercely politicized presidency of the state university not to his liking, or did he simply understand that his duty lay with the infant Rice Institute? Or was it the instant $3,000 raise the trustees provided, retroactive to October 1, that made all the difference? (His annual salary thereafter of $12,000 would be equivalent to $236,000 in 2006 dollars.*) Perhaps all four factors entered into his decision, although of course it is possible that Hogg met opposition from other members of the search committee when word leaked that he had approached Lovett without committee authorization. Or other objections may have arisen to Lovett. Whatever happened, by the end of October the search committee in Austin was sending letters to academic leaders across the nation to get suggestions, and by mid-November they seemed to be favoring a candidate from outside the state. On November 3 Lovett wrote Hogg approving a list of possible candidates that Hogg had sent him to vet, and Lovett offered to use his contacts to try to get "inside information of some value" on a shorter list of actual nominees. So he was clearly still on good terms with Hogg. But the committee determination to seek someone from outside the state faded, and on April 15, 1916, Robert Ernest Vinson, president of Austin Theological Seminary, was named president of the University of Texas. The still out-of-control Governor Ferguson was soon at war with the board of regents over Vinson and attempted to veto almost the entire university budget. The ensuing legislative fight with Ferguson energized the faculty, alumni, and other supporters of the university to such an extent that Ferguson was eventually impeached over the matter. Watching this unseemly fight from Houston, Lovett must have been thankful he had stayed at Rice. He became even more appreciative of his university's independence of state interference—never again would he entertain the possibility of leaving Rice.

Then, as now, a university president finds his time absorbed in an almost daily routine of settling disputes, solving problems, symbolically putting out fires, responding to student, faculty, and alumni concerns—at least there were not many alumni yet—and addressing issues

---

* Based on figures produced by the Inflation Calculator at htpp://data.bis.govt/cpicalc.pl.

that arose from the press and public. There was no end to unanticipated problems. For example, when a hurricane slammed into the Texas coast in August 1915, Lovett arranged for Rice to serve as a temporary shelter for those whose homes were damaged or destroyed. As he wrote to Mary on August 18, 1915, "we took care of about a hundred refugees from the prairie in the Residence Hall last night." Telephone and telegraph service was down for several days. "I have never experienced anything like it except at sea," he reported. When Lovett's old friend from Princeton and now Rice colleague Stockton Axson had written Lovett in May 1914 that "the position of a college president is a rather lonely one," Lovett surely nodded in agreement, especially when Axson referred to "all the practical and pressing problems before you." And yet, despite the everyday tedium of his position, Lovett throughout his presidency found time to write countless thank-you notes, letters of congratulation or condolence, and brief acknowledgments of meetings or conversations, all handwritten in his delicate script. His thoughtfulness in such matters became legendary.

Another perennial issue developed within the first few years, an issue that would continue to emerge over the decades, and this was the fear on the part of some in the larger community that the Rice Institute was anti-Christian or atheist or pro-Darwinian, which were essentially synonymous charges. For example, the Houston Ministers Alliance, meeting in a regular session at the downtown YMCA building on January 7, 1918, passed a set of resolutions addressed to Dr. Lovett in which they "respectfully" requested of him a statement "concerning the character and quality of instruction authorized and approved by the authorities" concerning the following issues:

First,—Do the President and Board of Trustees of Rice Institute endorse and approve the teaching of Atheism, agnosticism or infidelity by the Professors, teachers or instructors of this Institution, in the Class rooms to students looking to these accredited leaders for guidance in the realm of education?

Second,—As understood and interpreted by the President and Board of Trustees of Rice Institute, does "academic freedom" guarantee to your professors, teachers and instructors, the privilege of publishing and declaring as truth, certain individual views which ignore the being of God, discredit the belief in the inspiration of the BIBLE and repudiate the thought of faith in the Divinity of Jesus Christ?

The Ministers Alliance went on to say that they were cognizant of the "aims and purposes" of the institute as set forth by its charter, and that they had "no just cause in asking the professors, teachers and instructors . . . [to] declare or publish their personal allegiance to any doctrine or creed in Christendom or without." And they also recognized that Rice had the legal right to employ as faculty persons who might be "Mohammedan, Buddhist, pagan or Christian." Nevertheless, the ministers on behalf of the Christian community believed they were "well within the bounds of courtesy, fairness and right in asking that a statement be made" by the appropriate Rice authorities as to the "character of teaching and instruction to be given in the class rooms . . . under the authority, approval and endorsement of the President and Trustees of the Institution."

This was neither the first nor last of such inquiries, sometimes put in the form of a charge. For example, a clipping from an unidentified Houston paper for May 12, 1916, carried a letter from one S. F. Tenney attacking the Rice Institute for blasphemous teaching about religion and for teaching evolution. "Would it not be wise for the directors of the Rice Institute to bear in mind that many of the patrons of Rice Institute are Christians, and do not wish the minds of their sons and daughters to be misled and prejudiced against Christianity? Such teachings as I have referred to will not help to bring students to Rice Institute from Christian families, and that portion of the patronage the institution receives is not to be despised." These protesting Christians simply assumed that both the Rice Institute and its president were anti-Christian. No one could have made this suspicion more explicit than Methodist minister C. M. Myers in 1919. He wrote the Rice trustees that "The ministry has never thought much of Rice. When an Institution wants to be broad and liberal enough to take in German kultur with its philosophy of naturalism, materialism, and rationalism it is getting sure enough broad. We have always considered it un-american, un-scientific and un-christian. In the first place it needs a man at its head that possesses something else beside scholarship."

Despite these charges, President Lovett had from before his Bethany College student days been personally quite devout. Later, in an 1896 letter from Germany to his mentor at Virginia, astronomer Ormond Stone, Lovett had acknowledged the influence on him of Stone's Christian faith, and Lovett wrote that "It's the same faith that keeps me down on my knees with my sleeves rolled up. You can't keep a man down who works and prays. You'll be glad to know that my experience abroad has confirmed rather than unsettled my convictions relative to spiritual things and the part that character plays in education and the life of the educator." Now an educator himself, he and Mrs. Lovett soon after moving to Houston became members of Central Christian Church at the corner or Main and Bell streets, where they contributed regularly and Lovett wrote of attending worship; he carried on for most of his life correspondence with leaders of the Christian Church, the denomination he had joined during his student days at Bethany College; he occasionally gave addresses on special occasions in churches of that denomination; and he even momentarily considered preaching at Rice. Writing to his wife on July 29, 1917, he asked her: "What would you think of my trying to preach a half hour's sermon weekly in the Faculty Chamber on Sunday mornings this coming year? And have a communion service monthly in the afternoon for such as desired it, and conducted in turn by local ministers? It's rolling over in my head and I may have to decide it again."

But after further consideration he apparently thought better of the idea, whether because of limitations on his time or because he came to see such preaching to be inappropriate. To have done so, even with rotating ministers, would have clearly given the university a sectarian tone inappropriate in terms of the original charter (the university was to be "non-sectarian and non-partisan") and Lovett's often expressed views. He did frequently address the topic of religion in a university setting, and more generally, religion in the modern age. In one of his very first talks in Houston, an address to the Hellenic Banquet on December 29, 1909, he had noted that "The Hebrew was hounded by the mandates of the moral law, the Greek was haunted by the mystery of the material world. . . . And to my mind," he emphasized, "the supreme problem of our modern civilization is to realize, in the life of society, the reconciliation of the Spirit of Hellenism with the spirit of Hebraism."

Lovett made clear that the founders and leaders of the Rice Institute fully appreciated the role of religion in life. "While the new university is free of any ties of direct affiliation either with State or Church," he wrote in 1914, "all those who have been responsible for the development of its plans have felt that patriotism and politics, reverence and religion, are indispensable and invigorating elements of the atmosphere of any educational institution." But religion was a matter to be considered freely by every student—Lovett was unalterably opposed to "dogmatic theology" and praised the university's freedom from "sectarian authority." He prepared a careful response to the 1918 inquiry of the Houston Ministerial Alliance. Before he sent them his reply, however, he sent an even more detailed statement to the members of the Rice board, rehearsing what he planned to say to the ministerial alliance and putting that response in a broader philosophical context of the role of the university in such matters.

Here he was in effect putting into words the rationale for the university's position. "The President and Board of Trustees of the Rice Institute," he wrote, "in their corporate capacity neither approve nor disapprove the teaching of atheism or theism, agnosticism or gnosticism, infidelity or fidelity, by the professors, teachers or instructors of this institution." Perhaps anticipating other similar charges, he made clear that "We are building a university, not a school of Hebrew theology, nor of Christian theism, not a school of rationalistic philosophy, nor of mechanistic interpretation of the universe, nor of any one of a hundred other special systems of thought or speculation or knowledge or faith." Here as in many other places both before and later, Lovett spoke of how privileged Rice was to be free of support or pressure from either the state or the church. "We are all determined, I believe, to preserve to this university not only intellectual freedom but also the religious and political freedom guaranteed to all American institutions. In my judgment, we should be false to our trust if we sought to impose upon the university our individual views, whether scientific, political, philosophical, or religious. To that trust we should be even more ignobly false if we sought to impose our individual views upon our colleagues of the faculty." After all, he concluded, "It is only in an atmosphere of freedom that learning thrives."

Yet with this philosophical foundation made explicit, Lovett went on to remind the trustees of the many ways the university was supportive of religion: the long-range architectural plans had a proposed site for a university chapel; there were religious inscriptions on the buildings; religion had a place at each year's commencement convocations, as it had at the opening; almost from the beginning students established branches on campus of the YMCA, the YWCA, and the Menorah Society; and at the beginning of each academic year the leaders of all the city's religious groups were sent the names and addresses of students who had indicated their religious preference. The board evidently approved Lovett's proposed reply, which incorporated most of the discussion of the ways Rice had promoted religious values and concepts on campus and in its ceremonial life, although the undergirding philosophical rationale for its neutral stance to any one religious viewpoint was minimized. On that point Lovett simply told the ministerial alliance in March 1918 that "the Trustees in their corporate capacity cannot commit the University to the advocacy of either side of controversial theological questions." Whether or not this satisfied the unhappy ministers, there is no record of their reply to Lovett's formal response to their original set of resolutions. (Likewise, with Lovett's words surely ringing in his head, James Baker on June 12, 1919, responded to the Reverend Myers's charges against Lovett and the Rice Institute by writing that they were "not justified by any single fact in connection with the history of the Institute from its organization to this good day," and were simply "mistaken." Myers never replied.)

Six months after his reply to the ministerial alliance, Lovett on October 3, 1918, spoke to Rice's YWCA organization on the topic "Rice and Religion." Here again he summarized the various ways that the university was friendly to religion and respected its role in the lives of individuals and the nation. Although his own personal remarks about religion—for example, Lovett offered prayers at the commencements—were explicitly Christian (and Protestant), he made certain to indicate to his YWCA auditors that he had spoken in the city to a wide variety of religious audiences, including Catholic and Jewish, and appreciated their differing faith traditions. Somewhat later, when the issue arose in 1923 as to whether the university should contribute to the support of

Autry House, a community center for the university sponsored by the Episcopalians, Lovett wrote Chairman Baker that "Not even in the best of causes can this university afford to place in jeopardy its freedom from political and religious affiliation. To maintain this freedom a middle-of-the-road policy is the only course practicable. We dare not seem to discriminate in matters of religious faith. I have quite as much fear of this in education as I have of the fanaticism that religion becomes when it is mixed with politics. To no one religious communion can we as a university offer recognition that we are not prepared to offer to all."

In an age when the city of Houston was not nearly so religiously and culturally diverse as today,* Lovett made some effort to reflect the other religious traditions that were present. For example, in 1920 the baccalaureate sermon was preached by "the Very Rev. Father Kirwan of the Catholic Church" and in 1926 by Rabbi Henry Barnston of Congregation Beth Israel. Lovett, however, saw no contradiction between his own use of Christian language—even when speaking in an official capacity—and his determination that Rice as an institution be and remain absolutely nonpartisan in terms of religion. And as to the old bugaboo about religion being at war with science, Lovett told a 1916 meeting of the YWCA that people should realize that "the Bible is neither a treatise on astronomy nor a text-book of geology." Two years later he made the point in another way: "In our day there are multitudes of men and women who combine in the same personality a sympathetic comprehension of modern science with a profound and reverent faith; and who find that the acceptance of the teaching of science in no wise disturbs their personal religious life." (Lovett himself, for example, fully accepted Darwinian evolution.) In these direct and indirect ways Lovett answered the Ministers Alliance and others who questioned whether Christianity was attacked or evolution taught—an issue irrelevant to faith—in the classrooms of the Rice Institute. But by this time the so-called war between science and religion was not the conflict that loomed largest in Lovett's mind.

---

* The religious affiliation of Rice students in 1922—based on their religious preference cards—was as follows: Methodist, 257; Baptist, 168; Presbyterian, 128; Episcopalian, 110; Catholic, 78; Disciples of Christ, 68; Jewish, 42; Christian Scientist, 18; Lutheran, 16; Congregationalist, 2; Unitarian, 2; Evangelical, 1; no preference given, 44.

During the century before 1914 somewhere on the order of nine thousand American scholars had earned Ph.D.s from German universities, where they had come to admire much of German culture and especially its research and educational institutions. Lovett had not previously been an Anglophile, even writing to his wife from London in 1912 that though he loved the vitality of the city, in a way he found himself despising many of the Englishmen he saw on the streets. Lovett's feelings were not atypical, for during the prior century the United States had had a number of diplomatic squabbles with England, and many Americans felt condescended to by the British. Consequently, when Germany invaded neutral Belgium in August 1914, she fully expected the American professoriate to be her defender. But Germany grossly miscalculated: Americans were morally appalled by Germany's flagrant disregard of Belgium's neutrality. Instantly Germany was put on the defensive, and her military decision soon thereafter to conduct unrestricted submarine warfare that killed thousands of civilians solidified the image of Germany as an immoral, militaristic nation bent on world domination. Slowly the American nation moved from an official position of neutrality to increased moral support for the Allies to finally declaration of war against the Axis powers on April 6, 1917, with President Woodrow Wilson establishing the tone of America's position: Germany was engaged in a "warfare against all mankind" and the United States was to embark on a crusade to make the world "safe for democracy."

Lovett was deeply affected by the decline of Europe into the maelstrom of total war. The Germany he had admired now seemed ruled by power-mad militarists whose guiding principle appeared to be that might makes right. When a German U-boat torpedoed the *Lusitania* off the coast of Iceland on May 7, 1915, killing 1,198 people (including 128 Americans), the barbarism of the German war strategy came home to Lovett in a personal way, for he had returned from his European faculty-hunting trip in 1912 aboard that ill-fated British passenger liner. The Europe Lovett had so admired now seemed almost doomed, shattered beyond recognition; the words British foreign minister Sir Edward Grey reportedly said in August 1914, that the "the lamps are going out all over Europe; we shall not see them lit again in our lifetime," would have captured Lovett's perception of the world tragedy. Former Stanford president and now its chancellor emeritus, David Starr

Jordan, a prominent pacifist, gave the first Rice commencement address on June 12, 1916—he had been asked long in advance—and that address represented the last defense of neutrality in the midst of the world calamity that would be heard at Rice for several years, and it must have to an extent embarrassed President Lovett at the graduation ceremony. (Somehow in the midst of his other activities Lovett had finally perfected his design for the distinctive Rice diploma, first presented in 1916. He had dashed off a letter to Mary from New York City in May 1916—after having watched a military preparedness parade—that "today I have written the first diploma over about twenty times and have it about whipped into shape.") Jordan argued that "The greatest evil in the world is that of International War." Then he warned that "we are going to see the phenomena of nationalism very differently in a short while. We shall be ashamed of that fever of so-called patriotism, that excited stimulation which forces a man blindly to hate another nation and to brand its citizens as inferior and wicked. Europe has been perverted by this patriotism of lies. . . . This has made it possible for a very few men to drag Europe into a war that is, in a way, wrecking the whole civilization of Europe." But he held out the hope that eventually mankind would turn against war, though maybe only after "one grand horror." Yet these prescient cautionary words soon came to seem naively inappropriate to most Americans and to Lovett as the German war machine ground on and casualties mounted into the millions.

Lovett had already rejected Jordan's message. Speaking to a Rice YWCA meeting on February 25, 1916, he had told the students that "there are worse things than war, and I for one would like to think that out of this war there is coming to be another stage in human progress, a stage toward the elimination, perhaps the final elimination, of despotism from politics and dogmatism from religion." Already by the spring of 1916 a goodly number of male students had formed themselves into two military-like companies, received instruction in drill and tactical formation from Herbert N. Roe, a physical education instructor, and were taking organized hikes and looking forward to getting uniforms. The reality of a Europe at war alerted most Americans to the possibility that they too might be called upon one day to defend their nation. Clearly the unprecedented calamity of the war had shaken Lovett, and, he believed, all thinking persons. As he put it in his matriculation address to incoming students on September 25, 1916, "the War has set the world to taking stock. . . . individuals and institutions have been brought sharply face to face with elemental things. Civilization, commerce, culture and the conduct of life have suddenly been called to take and give account of themselves." Within two months about a hundred Rice male students were participating in the two quasi-military companies; by December 1916 they had devised a system of demerits to simulate military life, and they drilled twice daily. It was all a volunteer effort, but the students and the university were moving toward a more intentional military system of training and preparation.

Later in the course of that academic year, on April 6, 1917, the United States declared war. The *Thresher,* the student newspaper, announced the declaration of war and patriotically demanded that "the duties of all be stated and let all be required to perform those duties. Any man who can oppose himself to such a program as this is unworthy to be called an American." An editorial in that issue said that a few students had already left to go to war but that the faculty wanted them to stay enrolled, for they could best serve the nation that way—at least for the time being. Lovett, like most college presidents, instantly sought to have his university serve the nation's cause—after all, the ideal of service was central to the emerging state land-grant universities, it had been the hallmark of Wilson's call to Princeton for greatness in 1902 that had originally inspired Lovett, and Lovett's sense of the service Rice could render its developing region in 1912 had determined the curriculum's initial heavy emphasis on science and engineering. Recall the inscription in 1915 on the cornerstone of the first science laboratory building at Rice, "science in the service of society." So when the nation called, especially in the voice of Woodrow Wilson, Lovett—like most university presidents in the nation—was only too happy to devote his institution "to the nation's service."

Instantly after the declaration of war, Lovett traveled to Washington, D.C., on behalf of the Rice Institute to petition the War Department, pursuant to the National Defense Act of June 3, 1916, to establish an infantry unit of the Reserved Officers Training Corp (ROTC) at Rice. Although with the declaration of war the War Department had ceased authorizing any new ROTC units, the Rice application—on the recommendation of the chief of staff—was approved by "special dispensation of the Secretary of War." On May 12, 1917, Major Joseph Frazier was ordered to come to the campus to begin organizing and training students to become officers. But even before Major Frazier could arrive and arrange meetings with both men and women students, thirty-three male students were already in the process of withdrawing from the university and making plans to travel to Camp Leon Springs, in Bexar County north of San Antonio, to begin training in an hastily organized officers training facility. (Ironically, Leon Springs owed its origins to a one-time German nobleman who had immigrated to Texas in the early 1840s and founded a stagecoach inn at Leon Springs in 1846. The officers training camp was formed in May 1916, and subsequently trained some 1,500 men who became commissioned officers.) The May 4 issue of the *Thresher* had reported that "a great many [of the students] have become so steeped in enthusiasm that they have failed to fully appreciate the sacrifices to be borne by all." But the *Thresher* also reported that full credit for the courses enrolled in (with a passing grade) would be extended to all the early volunteers.

When Lovett spoke at the June 11, 1917, commencement, he emphasized that "our land has been compelled under moral compulsion, to enter" the conflict. "We enter it," he continued, "because some things are worth dying for." This was a time for individuals and institutions to step up to their duty and serve their nation and indeed all mankind. Following the graduation ceremony on campus, Lovett and his secretary John T. McCants traveled to Camp Leon Springs and there presented diplomas to eight Rice males currently undergoing military training. "It is with high hopes and great expectations," Lovett told the departing students, "that we now send you forth, our sons, on your great adventure." And the *Thresher* had written earlier, "the student body of Rice Institute is proud to be able to offer so many of its men in the present crisis. Whatever the sacrifice, our abnegation shall be complete."

In his matriculation address to new students on September 24, 1917, Lovett described the war as "a consuming fire. In its wake a new heaven and new earth will rise, from its wreckage a worthier world will roll." The students soon found, however, that the ROTC presence on campus meant a far different military atmosphere than they had experienced the previous semester when only a voluntary military program had been in effect. With no local precedents to work with, the university was being transformed into essentially a military institution. Four military companies were organized, three for the residence hall males and another for the town dwellers. A rigorous system of drills was established. Students were awakened by a bugle call at 5:45 a.m., followed by reveille, roll call, room inspection, and breakfast, then drill for half an hour before classes began at 8:30. This rigid schedule continued throughout the day, including afternoon drills. One had to be in his dormitory room twenty minutes after the evening meal. Major Frazier had succeeded in reshaping the university in a martial fashion, leaving little time for normal college life: as the *Thresher* sardonically described the routine for a Saturday night, the only free evening: "The cadets may go anywhere they please, dress anyway they please, provided they wear their uniforms, and get back any time they feel like it, provided they don't stay out after about ten and a half."

Understandably, the new regimen was engendering discontent and soon protest. The *Thresher* editorialized that some of this regulation was irksome, but it hoped that students would appreciate the opportunities offered for training and that essential academic features of university life could be retained, and it urged those with legitimate complaints to make use of the *Thresher* to air their views. But when the respected Major Frazier left to assume duties in Missouri, his replacement, Captain Taylor M. Reagan, proved not to have much rapport with student-soldiers. Discontent, even anger, about some of the excesses of regulation, needless red tape, drill, and the necessity to have a pass to leave one's room for any purpose, began to mount. An unsigned guest editorial appeared in the *Thresher* on November 10, 1917, blasting the extreme, even silly attention to military detail and rigor that was reportedly destroying the democratic nature of Rice, actually endangering its academic nature. Finally in January 1918 the university offered two new courses whose content seemed reasonable both academically and militarily, one in "wireless telegraphy" and another in "gas engines." But this was too little, too late. And there was still no

Red Cross instruction for women students. The students remained over-whelmed with needless and rigid rules that served no obvious purpose. Sarcastic comments began to appear in the *Thresher,* one of which even compared prison life favorably to that at Rice, and there were mocking remarks about military discipline to the nth degree. Was there any need for student sentinels standing in the hallways? In Houston, Texas?

Then on the morning of January 19, 1918, every resident student found outside his room the first (and only) issue of a protest newspaper, *Tape,* its bold masthead printed in red ink, that blasted the militariza-tion of the university, attacking bitterly the military supervision and the university administration. Captain Reagan was described as incompe-tent, the president's secretary, John T. McCants, who had been hired in late 1910 to replace F. Carrington Weems (who had resigned that September) as the president's personal assistant, was characterized as a stickler for meaningless military regulations, and Dr. Lovett—aloof and unreachable—scathingly portrayed as the unbending defender of a system even though, according to the authors of *Tape,* he had already privately admitted to the cadet commanders that the military organi-zation was a failure. Lovett had asked Washington in December 1917 for a replacement for Captain Reagan, but Lovett had been told that no replacement was available. He essentially asked the students to be patient and simply make do with the failed system—not what the dis-gruntled students wanted to hear. Clearly the matter was about to get out of control. The result was a mass meeting with the trustees of the university.

How had matters gotten so out of control on Lovett's watch that he lost the trust of the students? Even the students later admitted that he had often been out of town on university business, but Lovett was not one to be uninformed about affairs at the university. In the past he had warmly praised the democratic nature of the student life of the university, but now it was being administered in an authoritarian style. Previously he had insisted on the primacy of academics, but now mili-tary preparation was seemingly given precedence. He was normally a very hands-on president, although in truth during 1917 he had been ex-tremely involved with the publication of the three-volume *Book of the Opening* and the mailing of over a thousand copies to scholars, libraries, and learned societies around the world. Conceivably this task could have distracted him from paying his usual close attention to the daily operation of the ROTC program. Perhaps his devotion to the cause of the war temporarily blinded him to the military excess under his nose; possibly he thought such training was essential for military success even if it were almost antithetical to the rigorous academic purpose and the democratic nature of the learning process at Rice, both of which Lovett had often lauded. Perhaps correspondence from academic acquaintances in Great Britain so moved him by their depictions of tragedy and social disruption as a result of the war that the inconveniences at Rice seemed to him, by comparison, both minor and transitory.

If Lovett had any lingering doubts about the justice of the Allied effort, the letters he received in late 1917 from faculty in Great Britain (thanking him for sending them copies of the *Book of the Opening*) reinforced his belief that this was a war for a noble cause that had to be fought no matter what temporary changes in academic routine it required. From Professor A. E. Shipley of Christ's College, Cambridge, came a sad letter dated November 2, 1917, depicting life in the war-ravaged nation: "I confess I envy you the comparative peace of Texas. We are just entering on our fourth winter and the darkness at night is so appalling. It gets dark soon after 4 p.m. & no lights of any kind are allowed. Then the perpetual air raids mean that the electric light goes out during the hours of the evening & one has to sit in the darkness and do nothing. The streets are full of wounded, maimed and blinded men. For the last three years I have turned my Lodge into a convalescent home & have had an opportunity of seeing hundreds of wounded Officers." A month later Shipley again lamented, "It is perfectly terrible the way the wounded are pouring in." Sir William Osler, the Regius Professor of Medicine at Oxford, wrote in December that "these are troublous days . . . with the harassed old world." Letter after letter defended the Allied cause in moral terms. Professor Douglas Ainolie of Edinburgh spoke of hoping to see "the shadow of the Hun . . . vanished before the Sun of Anglo-Saxon liberty." George A. Gibson of Glasgow no doubt found Lovett approving: "The students are few and the staff is depleted. But there is no thought of peace on German terms. Unless right can be enthroned above might this earth would be a mere home of the devil. I regret the severance from some dear friends in Germany but I hope to see the Prussian militarism crushed once and for all." Letters such as these reinforced Lovett's determination that the Rice Institute should make every effort to contribute to the war, and these letters may have blinded him to the very real concerns of Rice students who were patriotic but simply considered much of the excess regulation imposed on them irrelevant to preparation for military service.

On Saturday, January 26, 1918, the cadet officers met with the Rice trustees, but as they began to lay out the issues, the board members deemed it advisable to come to campus themselves and have an open meeting with all the students. Accordingly, on Monday morning, beginning at 10:00 a.m. and lasting until 1:20 p.m., they met with the assembled students. Five male students and two women students were chosen to present the students' side of the matter, and they spoke with surprising frankness, specificity, and maturity. McCants came under special criticism. The board members listened carefully, were respectful of the views of the students, permitted them to send a formal petition to the board requesting certain changes in procedures, and said that students would be allowed to organize a Students' Association. As one student participant wrote in his diary account of the meeting, "We prepared a petition asking that almost all of the accessory stuff to the ROTC be abolished as unnecessary and incompatible to a regular University curriculum." The board then promised to take everything under consideration at its next meeting on February 6. At that meeting the board accepted every recommendation made by the students and authorized major changes in the military regulations. Drill for women was ended, a so-called proper Red Cross training class was put in place for them, and all the needless military regulation for men—call to quarters, guard duty, roll call at meals, taps—were scrapped. What was left in place was deemed reasonable and appropriate to a university. As trustee chair Baker said, "We all feel that the things asked for are reasonable and, under the existing conditions we granted them." It was total victory for the students. This was all announced to the students at a mass meeting on campus on Saturday, February 9, and Baker requested several times that the students give the Rice cheer: "Yea Rice, Yea Rice, Yea Rice, R-I-C-E, Rice!" It was a college again, not a military camp!

Dr. Lovett spoke briefly and movingly to the students, then, symbolically "extending his hand to the student body, said: 'May I not ask you to take the hand I extend and ask you to help me bridge the gulf.'" With that the students let out another Rice cheer, and after several students spoke accepting Dr. Lovett's offer and thanking the trustees, the meeting ended with renewed affection for the university.

As the *Thresher* editorialized, "the tide has ebbed, the storm has passed and the sun is out." The paper praised the trustees, Dr. Lovett, the military committee, and the faculty: "We take off our hats and call them gentlemen, for they have acted fairly. . . . We are ready to 'bury the hatchet.'" The future indeed looked brighter to the students: they had protested, made their case, convinced the trustees, and gotten the necessary adjustments in policy. Students supported the more restrained military training system under the auspices of the ROTC, and student awareness of the possibility, even the duty, of active military service, increased with American involvement in the war effort in Europe. A number of Rice men in the summer of 1918 attended ROTC camp in Fort Sheridan, Illinois, with the camp actually conducted by Major Frazier, who had introduced the ROTC program at Rice. The issue had never been a lack of student patriotism or disapproval of the war but rather a critique of the inappropriateness of the excessive military regulation under the direction of Captain Reagan. Rice students were fully prepared to serve their nation in its time of need. By the fall of 1918 the war-shrunken senior class had fallen to only thirty-three students, twenty-one of whom were women.*

On September 23, 1918, when Lovett welcomed another class of first-year students to Rice, he acknowledged to the students that "this year you have come to college at your country's call—the women to take the cross [Red Cross], the men to take the sword—challenged by your country's peril, charged with your country's defense. You have heeded the call, you accept the charge, you will meet the challenge. Not all of you will remain here long. Some of you may never return." Lovett so spoke because he knew that in a week the Rice Institute would, along

---

* Overall, there were slightly fewer than 200 women students out of a total enrollment of approximately 660 for the 1918-1919 academic year.

with practically every other college and university in the nation, be militarized and turned into an army training camp. In the spring of that year the War Department had begun to think about preparing enough technically trained officers to meet the expected need, and after some preliminary efforts, on May 8, 1918, the secretary of war announced a "comprehensive plan" (whose final details were revealed on June 29) to create a Students' Army Training Corps (SATC) at all colleges and universities enrolling a minimum of a hundred males of the age of eighteen or older. These male students would be enlisted in the army but put on furlough status without pay, and they would not be called into active service until they received their diplomas or turned twenty-one. But this policy was soon changed. By August it was determined that the male students would wear uniforms, their dormitories would be run as barracks, they would eat in a common mess hall, they would be subject to strict military discipline, and they would be paid thirty dollars per month. The normal academic year and curriculum was junked: the school year was divided into four quarters, the courses for men had to be explicitly relevant to military needs (for women and those males deemed physically unfit for combat, the courses remained mostly as before, although many fewer courses would be offered). Every student had to take a War Issues Course, which tended to become propagandistic. (But the anti-German hysteria that afflicted many colleges did not occur at Rice; instruction in the German language, for example, continued throughout the war.) Every able-bodied male had to drill for eleven hours a week, they marched to class, they had mandatory study halls at night—in short, colleges and universities were transformed into military camps. This national requirement affected every institution of the requisite size in the nation, and of course it applied to the Rice Institute.

Practically no college or university objected to these changes in the midst of a war widely seen as a defense of Western civilization. Lovett, with his devotion to the concept of service to the nation, his personal admiration of President Wilson, and his total dedication to the so-called noble aspirations of the war effort, completely supported this temporary transformation of the academic nature of Rice. By the order of the War Department, and approved by Congress, the moment of transition whereby 140,000 male students at 516 colleges and universities nationwide would become in effect soldiers-in-training was 11:00 a.m. (CST) on October 1, 1918. President Wilson issued a statement to the students, praising them for becoming "comrades in the common cause of making the world a better place to live in." At the appointed time the Rice students gathered in the main academic quadrangle, drew themselves into a hollow square formation, and were entered into the SATC by commanding officer Colonel Charles J. Crane. President Lovett then addressed the Rice students standing in military formation: "You have consecrated to the cause of freedom all that you are and all that you hope to be. By this solemn act, we become crusaders in a common cause, knights of a new chivalry, champions of a cherished civilization." Filled with patriotism and pride, Lovett hailed the students before him: "Gentlemen of Rice, I salute you, as you salute the flag. Four hundred strong, you are joining the ranks of the Rice men in service, ranks already nearly four hundred strong in volunteers from students and staff. I hail you as conquering crusaders, champions of the common weal of men and nations." There was not one iota of doubt in the cause before them. A new era had begun at Rice.

But changes almost as wrenching had already decimated the faculty even as the curriculum was about to be drastically changed to meet the needs of the SATC. Lovett himself had already sketched the effect of the war on the faculty when he spoke to the freshman class a week earlier. In his words,

> Our professor of English is National Secretary of the American Red Cross, loaned to that organization for the duration of the war; our professor of French is in the American Army on the Western Front; our professor of mathematics is on the Italian Front; our professor of physics is directing the work of several hundred men in an experimental laboratory of the United States Navy; our assistant professor of biology is on the Italian Front; our assistant professor of chemistry is in charge of a government laboratory with sixty researchers under him; our assistant professor of mathematics is with the ordinance department; our assistant professor of physical education is direct-

ing the athletic activities of Camp Logan; our assistant professor of physics is off the coast of England with a crew of thirty men; in addition, some ten or a dozen junior members are on leaves of absence in government service.

With such staff shortages, such curricular changes, and such a transformation of the student life as the SATC required, how would the Rice Institute operate during the duration of the war? To that task Lovett now turned his attention. But only five weeks later, on November 9, Kaiser William II abdicated, and two days later the Great War ended. Hence the necessity of the SATC program evaporated, and it was quickly dismantled. In its stead university ROTC programs were reinstituted, and although the ROTC program continued at Rice, it thereafter played a much smaller role. Rice was now ready to return to peacetime normality, no doubt to the relief of everyone. The transition back to the traditional academic programs was quick and painless, and soon the faculty (except for Julian Huxley) all returned to their teaching responsibilities at Rice.

With peace in the offing, British and French authorities wanted to ensure that in the future, American graduate students would consider pursuing their advanced training in the universities of their nations, not in Germany as had been the academic fashion for almost a century. U.S. government officials concurred in this desire. One immediate result was that in the fall of 1918—planning having been under way even before the worldwide conflict was over—two delegations of foreign scholars came to Rice. The first group, representatives of the British Educational Mission, visited on November 25–28, 1918. A contingent of seven eminent British scholars, including several known personally to President Lovett, were on a two-month tour of the leading American universities, with Rice the only institution visited west of the Mississippi River—convincing evidence that public relations–savvy Lovett and the faculty he attracted had already won for Rice a coveted position in American higher education. The stated purpose was to establish "closer relations in the future between the universities of Great Britain and those of the United States, through the interchange of instructors, students, academic credits, and educational experience." The program at Rice consisted of lectures by the visiting British dignitaries, lectures by faculty from Rice and several other U.S. universities (Princeton, Chicago, Virginia, for example), an address by the governor of Texas William P. Hobby, and a series of lunches and receptions. The whole was an academic festival celebrating the shared cultural traditions of the two nations. "We admire the enterprise of your mission," President Lovett told the British educators, "on a new form of international endeavor." And as trustee chair James A. Baker put it, "There was a time—not so many years ago—when the people of both Britain and America were disposed to look askance at each other . . . but, thank God, that day has passed forever, never to return."

A similar international bridge-building event, but more limited in scale, occurred on December 9 and 10 of that year when three members of an Official Mission of French Scholars visited the Rice campus. The explicit purpose of the visit was "to have representative French scholars interpret [to American audiences] the dominant elements of French culture, as a means of binding France and America more closely together in intellectual sympathy." Again there were lectures, receptions, and a formal dinner. Needless to say, President Lovett was in his glory amid such international academic convocations, and his gracious behavior always meant that visitors—for example, the Right Honorable Sir Auckland Geddes, the British ambassador to the United States, who spoke to the Rice students on May 12, 1921—left with an elevated opinion of the academic mission of the Rice Institute. The era of what became known as World War I can be said to have ended at Rice on February 5, 1920, when General John J. Pershing, who had commanded American troops in Europe, visited the campus. After speaking briefly to students (having been introduced by Rice German professor Lindsey Blayney, who had served on Pershing's staff in France), he was escorted to a site east of the administration building and ceremonially planted a tree as a token of hope for the future. That tree, "the Pershing pecan," flourishes yet on the campus of Rice University.

# CHAPTER SIX

# STEADYING THE COURSE
# IN THE ROARING TWENTIES

ALTHOUGH—or perhaps because—Edgar Odell Lovett had been born in a small town, had earned his first degrees at colleges and universities located in small academic villages, and had spent most of his career teaching at small-town Princeton University, he loved cities. His correspondence makes clear that he was invigorated by the pace, excitement, diversity, and cultural riches of cities like London, Paris, and Berlin, and he had often visited the bookshops and haberdashers of Philadelphia and New York City. He firmly believed that cities were the nurseries of intellectual life. In his 1912 address at the opening ceremonies of the Rice Institute he had noted that "great trading cities have often been conspicuous centers of vigorous intellectual life: Athens, Florence, Venice, and Amsterdam . . . stimulated and sustained the finest aspirations of poets, scholars, and artists within their walls," and considering the "commercial prosperity" of Houston, he optimistically concluded that "it requires no prophet's eye to reach a similar vision for our own city." The nurturing relationship between city and university was a theme to which he would often return in the following decades. This relationship was part and parcel of his ambition for the Rice Institute. As he wrote for the *Houston Chronicle* in October 1921, "The city is indispensable to the university, for the very simple reason that it is only in a great city that a great university can be built." But for Lovett the relationship was reciprocal: the university and its leaders should contribute to the city in every way possible. For that reason, from the very beginning, he was intimately involved in the cultural life of Houston, he promoted a series of public lectures offered free by the Rice Institute faculty to the citizenry of the city, and his wife was similarly active in the intellectual and artistic life of the city.

Lovett's activities ranged from participation in Houston's week-long carnival celebration entitled No-Tsu-Oh (Houston spelled backward), which had floats, balls, and other social festivities each November to honor King Nottoc (cotton spelled backward), to service on such committees as the Committee on Education of the Texas Welfare Committee to the Welfare Commission of the city's Commercial Secretaries and Business Men's Association. (Even Lovett's small son Malcolm served as a page to "Her Majesty the Queen" at the 1911 No-Tsu-Oh Coronation Ball.) Because of his renown as an orator, Lovett was asked to read the Declaration of Independence at the official Fourth of July celebration in 1913 at the City Auditorium. When the Houston Symphony Association was organized in 1913 to establish a permanent symphony orchestra for the community, Lovett was named to the board of directors. He accepted an invitation in January 1917 to serve on the board of the Houston Grand Opera Committee. He served on statewide commissions too, including one first organized in 1911 by Will Hogg to improve the public-supported universities of the state. Lovett's services were of course not confined to Texas. He was chosen to become a member of the American University Union in Europe in 1923; he was asked, along with Abbott Lawrence Lowell of Harvard, to speak at the inauguration of a new president at the Massachusetts Institute of Technology (MIT); and he spoke widely at university commencements and other special occasions (such as the installation of President Harry Woodburn Chase at the University of North Carolina in 1920) throughout Texas and the South. Recalling his 1908–1909 round-the-world trip to investigate the newest educational advances preparatory to establishing Rice, in October 1924 Lovett was invited to Brussels to represent Rice at the commemoration of the fiftieth anniversary of the founding of the École Polytechnique of Brussels, and he assisted in the laying of the cornerstone of the buildings given by the Commission for Relief in Belgium. He also spoke to every imaginable audience in Houston—business, cultural, educational, and otherwise. From newspaper coverage and introductions, it is clear that he became one of the best-known and most respected leaders in the city and state. And he fully supported those members of the Rice faculty who volunteered to serve the region by assisting various cultural and artistic organizations. Within a couple of years of Rice's founding its faculty were presenting dozens of lectures at several locations for the edification of the public, a prototype of what would later be termed *continuing studies.* Lovett promoted such city engagements and public lectures because—like many other progressive university presidents at the time—he believed that "service" was a cardinal responsibility of universities.

Mary Hale Lovett was, in her own rights, an educated and able woman, and she understood her role as wife of the president of the Rice Institute to include a public dimension. Of course as long as her health allowed, she was active in campus affairs, occasionally coming to have lunch with the women students, sponsoring afternoon teas for them, hosting a picnic luncheon following graduation exercises, giving garden parties for faculty, and attending all sorts of campus events. But she too became a civic leader, particularly in those areas that matched her interests and accorded with the socially appropriate roles for women at that time. Always a promoter of the arts, Mrs. Lovett quickly became a member of the board of directors of the Houston Art League (whose members were a Who's Who of Houston civic leaders), and was very active in the region-wide Southern States Arts League, presiding at a session during its 1926 annual meeting in Houston and serving as membership "chairman of the entire South." She played an important role in the organization and early governance of the Museum of Fine Arts in Houston, including membership on its board of trustees. (Art historian James Chillman, Jr., of Rice was for many years curator of the Museum of Fine Arts, another example of the service relationship of Rice faculty to the city and region that Lovett so strongly supported.) Mary also belonged to the Current Literature Club, where on February 27, 1917, she presented a program on "American Miniature Painters." She was quite progressive in her social and political attitudes, as indicated by her membership in the Houston Settlement Association.

In his official role as president of the Rice Institute, Dr. Lovett was so fully absorbed and so identified with the role that one easily forgets that throughout those feverishly busy early years he was also a husband and father, and the family were members of Central Christian Church at the corner of Main Street and Bell. Lovett's affection and respect for Mary has already been mentioned, but now that they were usually together, the epistolary record is not as extensive as it had been earlier. Most summer months Mary and the children retreated to the ocean breezes of Atlantic City, the cooler mountain air of Asheville, North Carolina, or her comfortable homeplace in Mayfield, Kentucky, where adoring grandparents assisted her with childcare. (Lovett himself grew to have a much closer relationship with his wife's parents and relatives than with his own.) Gone were those sad days in 1906 and 1907 when Mary had been unable to respond to her husband's frequent letters. Now when she did write him, she often referred to him as "sweetheart," and, quite typically, she closed a letter to him in the summer of 1910 "with great heaps of love, Your Mary." Lovett would get away from campus business for a few weeks, but in the meantime he wrote hurried notes to her describing activities and issues and seeking her advice, with frequent comments as to how much he missed her. The children—Adelaide, Malcolm, and little Alex—were growing, and later their days were filled with school, playmates, and summer camp. Adelaide and Malcolm formed easy friendships with the children of Captain James A. Baker and his wife, and over the years one notes that Adelaide is asking permission to visit Walter Browne Baker at Princeton (chaperoned, of course), and once Lovett noted that young Walter had come by the Lovett household to pay his respects but Lovett thinks he primarily came to see Adelaide. One reading the family correspondence is not surprised to learn that on December 23, 1923, Adelaide Lovett and Walter Browne Baker were married, further cementing the Lovett-Baker relationship that proved so instrumental in the development of the Rice Institute.

But that marriage is getting ahead of our story. In 1916 Adelaide had entered Rice as a freshman, majoring in academic subjects and earning what was called a general bachelor of arts degree. She was a member of the campus YWCA organization for four years and was active in the French Club, Les Hiboux, the Elizabeth Baldwin Literary Society (one of several social organizations that helped women students find a sense of community in the absence of residence on campus), and the Writing Club. She graduated in June 1920. Meanwhile her brother Malcolm, some three years her junior but, by virtue of when their birthdays occurred, only one year behind her at Rice, was even more involved in campus activities, including service on the Honor Council that administered the student-controlled honor system and captain of the basketball team. He graduated in 1921, but when he left for Cambridge and the Harvard Law School that fall, his mother, sister, and younger brother Alex had already gone to France for an extended, eighteen-month visit. Adelaide took courses at the Sorbonne and perfected her French, Mary improved her already excellent French and partook of the cultural and artistic splendors of the City of Lights, while Alex also took classes at the Lyceum Montaigne and became fluent in French. Mary was invited to attend meetings of the American Women's Club of Paris at which the American ambassador was to be the guest of honor. It was apparently in Paris that she had an almost full-sized portrait of herself painted by the artist August Lerout. It depicts her looking quite matronly in a handsome dress, with a square-cut, lace-trimmed neckline, and wearing two strings of pearls, the longer of which she fingers in her lap. Her slight hint of a smile and kind eyes suggest her sweetness of character. While abroad Adelaide treasured a visit to Venice, and the three of them enjoyed a guided tour of southern France, traveling in a great loop from Toulouse to Montpellier to Marseilles to Nice, and then sweeping back through such beautiful towns in Provence as Nimes, Avignon, and Orange with their spectacular Roman ruins, and thence via Lyon and Dijon back to Paris.

No doubt the trip brought back fond memories to Mary, of both the sabbatical year in Paris in 1900 and the round-the-world visit in 1908, yet this was to be her last trip abroad. Her interest in things French never lagged, and she was instrumental in establishing the Alliance Française de Houston in 1923, but her traveling days were over. (In 1928 the Central Federation of the Alliance Française in Paris gave her its premier award for leadership in promoting awareness of French culture.) By the early 1920s she had already suffered several bouts of sickness—probably kidney stones—with extended hospital stays, and these and other infirmities would reoccur until, by the end of the decade of the 1920s, she became bedridden with rheumatoid arthritis. On one of their several earlier trips to Atlantic City, the family had seen a style of large wicker chairs on wheels that were employed on the boardwalk. Dr. Lovett purchased one of these and had it sent to Houston. On occasion a strong porter at the Plaza Hotel named "Mr. Sam" would lift her from her bed and place her in the chair, and then her children could push her about. But soon the crippling arthritis made even that difficult because her legs were frozen into a locked position. Gone forever were those days when, as in 1922, she had been a member of a "Dancing Club" in Houston, or, even earlier, when she and her husband had jogged through the streets of London in 1908. Now a secession of registered live-in nurses were employed, but eventually the Lovetts found Molly Kleinfelder, R.N., and she came over the years to be considered practically a member of the family. Although "Mrs. K," as she was affectionately called by the grandchildren, often cooked, on occasion other cooks were employed. They would prepare old family recipes from Kentucky as well as the German food that Dr. Lovett had come to like when a student there: wiener schnitzel, sauerkraut, bratwurst, and apple strudel. (When in New York City he always tried to eat at least one meal at Luchow's, the legendary German restaurant founded there in 1882.) But they were homebound now. Dr. Lovett kindly turned down an offer in 1951 by their old round-the-world traveling companion, F. Carrington Weems, to visit him in New England: "we are utterly unable to encourage your extraordinary kindness because without an oriental monarch's entourage of servants and vehicles we could not travel by land, by sea, or by air. During more than twenty years Mrs. Lovett has not taken a single step. . . . In all that time she has not been out of Houston."

As his reply to Weems with its reference to "Mrs. Lovett" suggests, Dr. Lovett had about him the formality of an older generation. Decades later mathematician Hubert Bray would recall that when he was interviewed by President Lovett, "I remember how the stiff collar of his shirt creaked . . . [he was] an impressive figure in his Prince Albert coat." Even in the presence of their grandchildren, the Lovetts referred to one another as "Mr." and "Mrs." In yet other ways Lovett adhered to older values and practices even though he often was at the vanguard of educational ideas. Ironically, collegiate education of women was one of those issues toward which Lovett held old-fashioned if not conflicted views. Certainly he supported college education for women: he married a college graduate and was the father of one, and he obviously valued their education and opinions. He had earned his bachelor's degree at the coeducational Bethany College, and his first teaching position was at the coeducational West Kentucky College, where he first met the coed, four years his junior, whom he eventually married. But in both these small colleges women had taken a separate academic track that was deemed specifically appropriate for women and was less academically rigorous than that provided for men. Lovett's graduate work was at the all-male University of Virginia, and there were no women studying with Sophus Lie at Leipzig. (Women were not allowed to register for courses before 1896 at Leipzig, though a handful of them did informally attend some lectures.) Despite brief semesters at Johns Hopkins (all male) and Chicago, Lovett's formative teaching experience had been at the all-male Princeton. So he likely always associated coeducation with inferior "teaching colleges" and true higher education with single-sex institutions. In the fall of 1929 on two occasions he both wrote and spoke of his personal preference for separate women's undergraduate colleges (what were called *coordinate colleges*) that utilized the faculty and other facilities of the "neighboring institution with which they are affiliated." His idea was the kind of organization represented by Columbia and Barnard, Harvard and Radcliffe. And if he had had his druthers, he would have established such a separate women's college at the Rice Institute (he said that on several occasions he had attempted to raise sufficient funds for that purpose). For several decades on each side of 1900, Victorian conventions made such gender segregation common in many aspects of American life, and some women activists supported the separation because they argued that it enhanced women's autonomy.

Whatever Lovett's preferences, the Rice charter, vague as it was about the full nature of the proposed institute and with its references to a "thorough polytechnic school," did state quite definitively that it should be open to "males and females." All the early publicity about the institution made explicit that it was coeducational. However, Lovett in planning the university made no allowance for a separate women's academic track as he had experienced at Bethany College and that many women at the time seemed to desire. He insisted that all courses, majors, and laboratories be open to all students. His commitment to high academic standards could admit no watered-down or "domestic" courses for women. The result was that some people at the beginning interpreted the absence of special courses for women to be discrimination against them. Professor W. F. Edwards, the faculty member most critical of Lovett (and who was soon fired), wrote a long letter to the *Houston Chronicle* on July 26, 1915, attacking the president for not establishing a department of modern "domestic science" specifically for women, and Edwards criticized the institution for not developing on-campus housing for women. Similar charges were made in other newspaper articles, and the *Chronicle* editorial for July 27, 1915, questioned whether "sex prejudice or opposition to co-education" existed at the Rice Institute. Did Lovett feel that financial exigencies made provision of a women's dormitory at the moment unwise, or did he think that, since most women students were from Houston, there was insufficient demand, or did he already harbor hopes that soon an affiliated women's college would provide housing for women, or was he morally worried about the presence of women on the same campus with men, or did he hope to limit the number of women by making inadequate provisions for them? Anticipated financial pressure was probably the main factor in the decision not to immediately provide housing for women. Lovett did say in 1912 that "A little later in the history of the Institute similar colleges will be provided for the young women." That promise, however, was not fulfilled until 1957. In the intervening years there would be on rare occasions a renewal of the charge that Lovett simply opposed women students and hence on-campus housing for them, and there was a wildly inaccurate rumor as late as 1924 that he still harbored hopes of constructing a palace-like president's house and therefore wouldn't budget funds for a women's dormitory. Already Mrs. Lovett's arthritis made life in such a home impractical if not impossible.

Housing them on campus or not, Lovett was decidedly and uncharacteristically behind the times with regard to women's issues. While giving the baccalaureate address at North Texas State Normal College in May 1915 he said that although he believed "universal suffrage for women is coming in America," he also confessed that he was "a rather old-fashioned man" on this subject and so chose to "refrain from expressing on a public platform my inmost feelings on this subject." But we can certainly guess his feelings. Perhaps it was because he recognized that he was out of touch with the women students that he asked the board of trustees in September 1915 to appoint Sara Stratford (his stenographer) to be "advisor to women," but the women may not initially have had complete confidence in her because they likely continued to view her as the president's stenographer rather than their confidante. She actually seemed to serve more as an official chaperone than a student mentor. Nevertheless, Ms. Stratford continued as advisor to women until 1931.

Several times the student newspaper, the *Thresher*, reported that when explaining to Rice students the nature of the honor system and what it demanded of students, Lovett stated that such systems of honor had "been eminently successful in all universities where coeducation does not exist, and that where it has failed its non-success has been caused by coeducation. He stated that the unqualified success of the Honor System here at Rice has been made possible by the fact that, though Rice is coeducational, the men students are decidedly in the majority." Had he at the University of Virginia (or through his relationship with his father-in-law, a prominent former Confederate officer) so imbibed southern notions of honor as a male attribute only that he could not imagine women living up to its demands? Perhaps Lovett's experience at Rice subtly changed his mind. By 1920 when he spoke of the honor system he made no derogatory remarks about women, and in 1922 he said that such systems only failed at schools with a "lack of homogeneity in the students themselves," with no mention of gender.

Had the superlative performance of women students at Rice forced him to reconsider some of his earlier perceptions? In addition to his own daughter's academic promise, Rice women showed that they could excel in what were popularly considered male disciplines. For example, of the four students graduating with honors at Rice's first commencement in 1916, three of them were women—two of whom had majored in math. The only honor graduate the following year was a woman, again a math major. Women students also played an increasingly large role in supporting the honor system. For example, women made up two of the twelve members of the Honor Council in 1916, three out of nine (and the position of secretary) in 1917, and four out of eight in 1918. Events beyond the campus also indicated the evolving role of women in American life. Lovett—a lifelong Democrat—kept abreast of politics and could easily see that times were changing: in 1917 Jeannette Rankin had been elected from Montana as the first-ever female member of the U.S. House of Representatives, in 1918 the Nineteenth Amendment gave women the right to vote, and in the fall of 1924 both Wyoming and Texas elected women as governors. Lovett acknowledged these political changes and the advantage of Rice's coeducation in his 1924 matriculation address. First noting that in a recent presidential election, all three major candidates had been Ivy League graduates (Taft had entered Yale in 1874; Wilson, Princeton in 1875; Roosevelt, Harvard in 1876), Lovett commented to the incoming students that "Not all of you will become President of the United States, but the nineteenth amendment to the Constitution, coupled with co-education, gives Rice a double chance over Harvard, Yale, or Princeton!"

Over the years he continued to speak ever more positively of the men and women students at Rice, praising both together for their hard work, accomplishments, and "vitality to flesh and spirit alike." No doubt some women students originally resented the absence of special courses for them and especially the lack of campus housing, but most came to appreciate that all programs of study were open to them on equal terms with men, and in the same classrooms, and that there was, as Elizabeth Kalb, class of 1916, wrote to the *Houston Post*, "absolutely no discrimination . . . in the matter of library and laboratory facilities." Kalb spoke of the deep "love and loyalty" most women had for Rice, and another coed, Alma Nemir, writing in the *Thresher* in April 1921, after describing the equal access to all faculty, majors, and academic facilities, concluded that "A degree from such an institution is of highest value to the young woman, no matter what her aim in life." Ironically, Lovett's refusal to make special arrangements for women students resulted in a progressive educational setting for them. And he did slowly come to appreciate their presence.*

In other ways Dr. Lovett adjusted his attitudes and practices. At the very beginning he was, in effect, the only administrative officer of the

---

* There were no women faculty during Lovett's long administration, as was the case at most elite private universities then. Alice Crowell Dean, however, did teach Math 100 throughout the 1920s and 1930s while holding the title of Fellow in Mathematics. She had come to Rice in 1913 as a thirty-six-year-old sophomore, graduating in 1916 with a B.A. in mathematics. In 1919 she earned her M.A. in the same field. In 1914 she began working as a student assistant (the only employee) in the library under the direction of a faculty library committee chaired by math professor Griffith C. Evans. From 1914 until 1947, Alice Dean in effect was the university librarian. All the while she taught the introductory math course.

university, and this sufficed for several years. But almost immediately faculty began to urge a larger role for themselves through committees and regular faculty meetings. As we have seen from the grumbling of physics professor Harold A. Wilson, in the first couple of years some faculty were impatient over the pace of faculty hiring and construction of buildings. After all, for those trained in centuries-old English universities with mature administrative structures, it was unsettling to be, as it were, plopped down in the middle of a university being born. Like Wilson, young Oxford-trained Julian Huxley found the experience initially exasperating. Huxley wrote to his father that "Things move frightfully slowly here—Lovett is an awful man to get to act . . . However, if we could get a few more buildings, a vice-president, regular faculty meetings (to which L. appears to have an unconquerable aversion . . . and thus acts like a grand mogul with incredible [to English ideas] autocratic power) . . . we should get along." But Lovett was working as hard and fast as he could, and soon began to respond to such faculty criticism by delegating authority. Actually, within six months Huxley was writing his father that the "new Physics Building is very beautiful" and was soon praising the lab space provided biology—it just hadn't appeared instantly. And that November, after attending the first of what became regular fortnightly faculty meetings, Huxley complained that they were "devoted to pretty trivial business." Would that have surprised a more experienced professor?

English professor Stockton Axson captured the sense of Lovett's role in a letter written to the president on May 14, 1914. "I think the position of a college president is a rather lonely one," wrote Axson; "his membership in the board of trustees to some extent isolates him from his colleagues on the faculty, and his membership in the faculty must, I suppose to some extent, isolate him from his comrades on the board. He must be the advocate for each body with the other, must be always explaining to men who necessarily think in terms of money the apparent extravagances of men who primarily think in terms of ideas, and he must as far as possible justify to ardent theorists the apparent niggardliness of cautious financiers." Lovett must often have seen himself caught in precisely this bind.

In 1914 Lovett appointed a faculty curriculum committee to assist in the arrangement of programs of study, and within three or four years he regularly drew on the assistance and advice of the current professors to hire additional faculty. No longer was Lovett a committee of one making all faculty hires alone; he still was involved in and approved every choice, but the department heads were doing most of the searching and vetting of candidates. In the aftermath of the student protests in 1917–1918, he followed the advice of several faculty and helped develop a student council (with faculty participation) to better meet student concerns. One of Lovett's closest friends in the faculty, Stockton Axson, after mentioning his idea to Lovett earlier, sent a letter (with a copy to Lovett) to trustee chair James A. Baker proposing that Lovett appoint a dean of the college. Axson's rationale was persuasive. "A Dean would be an excellent 'shock-absorber,'" he wrote. "Young Americans want, not so much the particular thing they are asking for, as a realization that their views are receiving a respectful attention." He continued: "What seems large to them must often of necessity seem small in comparison with the constructive policy of the whole Institute, and it has always seemed to me that a college was best served by two officers, one devoting his energy and talent to the larger thing, and the other to the lesser." Axson knew how to make his case in such a way as to gain the assent of both Baker and Lovett. As Axson put it, "such an officer, fairly young, easily accessible to all students at all times, would be very helpful to Dr. Lovett in relieving him from petty annoyances and releasing all his energies for the larger constructive policies of the Institute."

Still, recognition of the need for such additional administrative assistance was surely hard for Lovett to accept, even though he knew, intellectually, that it made sense. The student unrest of the previous few months proved that he had been too busy to comprehend student attitudes fully, but he also knew himself well enough to realize that it would be difficult to give up control over any aspect of the university. Lovett was aware of his tendency toward micromanagement: mentioning to his wife in September 1918 that he had just read Julian Huxley's favorable article in *Cornhill Magazine* on the opening of Rice, Lovett found himself "with mixed feelings. Perhaps it's just my old desire to keep a hand on things," he confessed, "but I wish I had had an opportunity to suggest a few revisions." Despite his natural reluctance to surrender any responsibility, Lovett accepted the advice given and even exceeded what had been advised. At the final trustee meeting of the year, on

December 31, 1918, Lovett recommended that the university authorize the appointment of a dean (who would have "oversight of the attendance, conduct, and discipline of students"), a registrar (for the keeping of all student records), and a bursar (for the "oversight of the business and material equipment, as well as the discharging of the duties of a purchasing agent for all departments").

The trustees quickly accepted these recommendations, and at the February 26, 1919, meeting, Lovett asked confirmations of his candidates for each position: history assistant professor Robert Granville Caldwell as dean, Samuel G. McCann as registrar, and instructor of business administration John T. McCants (originally Lovett's personal assistant/secretary) as bursar. Each would serve for years and become beloved by students and alumni. One early member of the faculty, Raymond P. Hawes, with whom Lovett had corresponded about the efficacy of appointing a dean, replied to Lovett on January 3, 1919, in a letter that accurately suggested the positive impact on student morale of having a dean. "The dean," Hawes wrote, "forms a personal link between the administrative forces (which are largely impersonal: rules, laws, majority decisions of committees, faculties, etc.) and the student body. It seems to me that the average undergraduate student body lives largely on a personal level of experience and requires for its maximum efforts, inspiration, and loyalty to the institution just such a personal tie." Lovett clearly learned from the advice of faculty like Axson and Hawes, and their wisdom was soon validated. The 1919 *Campanile* was dedicated to Dean Caldwell, and the inscription read in part: "There is a man at Rice who knows our needs, close to his heart our aims and interests lie; he calls us Friend—for us no higher compliment can be. His sagacious counsel, his thoughtful generosity, his never failing geniality are always ours." Caldwell often proved his worth to Lovett. When in the spring of 1926 the trustees became upset over the publication in the *Thresher* of a three-part story the trustees considered obscene, they— after some discussion—wisely decided to let Dean Caldwell handle the entire matter. Lovett did not have to get involved.

This trio of advisors—the dean, the registrar, and the bursar—in trusted concert with Lovett essentially governed Rice for the next two decades. (In 1935 Caldwell left the faculty when he was appointed ambassador to Portugal, and chemist Harry Boyer Weiser replaced him as dean.) By modern terms Rice was still administratively lean if not starved, but it was a much smaller, less complex university than today (half the faculty, for example, of the current School of Humanities). Nevertheless, some professors still occasionally complained that there should be more frequent, and more substantive, faculty meetings, and that Lovett ruled in the fashion of a benevolent autocrat. Even some of his closest advisors such as Dean Caldwell gently suggested that Lovett ought to consult more frequently with the faculty gathered as a body and allow them to share more fully in the governance of the university. Caldwell reported (in 1922) that the faculty "are absolutely loyal to you personally and proud and happy to follow your leadership." Still, Caldwell suggested, "proper consideration of the faculty" would make them as a group more useful to the institute. Sometimes, he concluded, "the matter or the method is more important than the actual concrete policy." But try as he might, Lovett found it difficult to share authority. He continued to symbolize the Rice Institute for many faculty, for most students, and for much of the public. His personal style of polite formality—an aspect of his innate shyness reinforced by his learned skill of keeping his emotions at strict check at all times—no doubt was perceived by some students and faculty as coldness. Moreover, all university presidents have to decide upon a model of interpersonal behavior between themselves and faculty and students. For some today there is an easy collegiality as between equals; for Lovett, there was a reserve, a formality, that prevented a bonhomous, democratic relationship. While the faculty referred to themselves as "Mr. Wilson" or "Mr. Evans," it was always "Dr. Lovett." This form of "great man" leadership remained relatively common in universities before World War II. In general the Rice faculty accepted or at least understood that Lovett largely shaped and spoke for the university.

Both Julian Huxley and Harold A. Wilson discovered in 1913 that actually starting a university from scratch was harder, messier, and more frustrating than one might imagine simply from hearing or reading inspired words and perusing handsome prospecti. But more than anyone else, Edgar Odell Lovett experienced, over almost four decades, how difficult it was to achieve noble aspirations when one had to deal with real people and real needs in an era bookended by two World Wars with the Great Depression in between. Lovett found that he had to tack this way and that, had to make compromises, had to accept disappointment, but his ultimate aim never wavered. Lovett also understood from the beginning just how enormously expensive developing a complete university really was. Surprisingly, given the size of the initial endowment, the eventual lack of funding came to first impinge on faculty salaries and then the pace of construction and programmatic expansion, though it was perhaps difficult to assess accurately the long-range impact of the resulting financial stringencies until 1930 and afterward. The 1920s may have seemed like a temporary delay rather than the beginning of a two-decade-long halt in the upward trajectory of the Rice Institute, but Lovett kept the embers of institutional ambition alive in the hope that better times would eventually allow a return to something like the optimism of 1912.

Although the popular press at the time wrote as though the funds available to the Rice Institute at the moment of its beginning were practically infinite and would allow almost untrammeled development, Lovett and the trustees knew better. (One of the few faculty to grasp the budgetary problems fully was again Lovett's old colleague from Princeton, Stockton Axson, who in May 1914 had written Lovett that one of the things that made his task more difficult was "the fact that people suppose that the Rice funds are 'unlimited'—whereas you, with all the practical and pressing problems before you, feel daily how sharply and sternly they are limited.") It was their recognition of relative financial limitations that led them to begin the university "at the science end," with only the skeleton of a program in arts and letters, although it was assumed that over time, and with the acquisition of additional funding, a full university would emerge. Enrollment grew to the point that in the mid-1920s it was capped at approximately 1,200 students, though this was less the culmination of exact planning than a limitation based on the number of available faculty and existing facilities.* This size

---

* In 1909–1910, when Lovett was intensively planning the new university, Princeton enrolled 1,266 undergraduate and 134 postgraduate students, for a total of 1,400. So initially Rice Institute was roughly the size of other prominent private universities, unremarkable for its small enrollment.

was not intended to be necessarily permanent, and both the president and the faculty understood that as the city of Houston increased in population and the university grew in stature, future growth could be expected. As the Committee on Examinations reported to the faculty meeting on November 22, 1923, "With the rapid growth of Houston which we can confidently expect, the Rice Institute may very well increase from a college of one thousand to one of two thousand students. But such an increase will mean a corresponding expansion in building, equipment, and faculty." The institute as it existed in 1923 should not be considered the ultimate expression of the founder's vision but rather a stage in a continuous line of development. Hence there was a healthy open-endedness to Rice's future that challenged its leaders.

As Lovett put it in 1926 in an address to the local Kiwanis Club, referring to Texans' supposed proclivity for thinking big, "in Houston and Texas they could not do otherwise than plan for a great university" even though the trustees "recognized fully" that the "resources [then available were] far from adequate to the building of anything like a complete modern university." The entire point of the spectacular opening ceremonies was to lay a foundation upon which future greatness could be erected, to hold up a standard of excellence as a goal, and with selected emphases to launch a trajectory to achieve the highest ambitions over the course of decades. To conserve its resources, the leaders of the Rice Institute resolved early on to undertake no programs that other institutions in the city or region could, should, or were already fulfilling—there would be no duplication of effort. But perhaps sooner than Lovett had expected, monetary problems began to thwart his internalized schedule for development. As he wrote to trustee chairman Baker on April 2, 1923, "the university's immediate and prospective revenues are inadequate to the realization of the programme of instruction and research on which it has entered."

The budgetary limitations quickly affected faculty salaries, and once professors began to return to teaching after their wartime service, or, if they had not been called to service, with the nation's return to "normalcy," they all expected that their salaries would increase in proportion to the rise in prices. But already financial stringency, compounded by the trustees' desire to hold back from spending a sizable percentage of the annual revenue, meant that salaries were not significantly adjusted to reflect the new economic realities after the war, and the small (or nonexistent) annual raises meant, in effect, a loss of buying power. And disgruntled faculty complained to Lovett. For example, Arthur Llewelyn Hughes, an assistant professor of physics with a doctorate from Liverpool and prior experience at Cambridge's famous Cavendish Laboratory, wrote Lovett on June 25, 1919, pointing out that, in contrast to his expectations, he had received only one raise since 1913, and that 10 percent addition had not even allowed him to keep abreast of the increase in the cost of living. Lovett took Hughes's request to the board; soon the chair of physics reported to Lovett that Hughes was applying for a much higher-paying professorship at Queens University in Ontario and urged Lovett to do what he could to keep the promising young physicist, but Hughes apparently was already disenchanted with the prospects at Rice. On August 7 he sent Lovett his formal resignation. Physicist Harold A. Wilson—now with a major textbook, *Experimental Physics* (Cambridge, 1915), attesting to his growing eminence—was another who complained vigorously about his lagging salary. This turn of events became ever more frequent as the decade proceeded.

The Rice faculty was structured so that there was one full professor for most departments with most of the faculty consisting of much younger assistant professors and instructors. (The departments were so small at the time that most had only two or three faculty members.) Lovett seems to have regarded the younger faculty, on the whole, much as Woodrow Wilson had the preceptors at Princeton: they might stay only several years, their salaries were lower, and they could be easily replaced. But increasingly young scholars of great prominence began to leave—like the brilliant mathematicians Percy John Daniell, William Caspar Graustein, and Francis D. Murnaghan; student favorite John Clark Tilden of architectural drawing; and Hermann Joseph Muller in biology. (Daniell later became chair of the department at Sheffield, Graustein at Harvard, and Murnaghan at Johns Hopkins, and Muller would win the Nobel Prize in medicine in 1946.) Losses of this caliber hurt, even though no one could know at the moment they left exactly how distinguished their careers would turn out to be. But when the full professor of French, Albert Léon Guerard, who originally had been attracted from Stanford, resigned in 1924 to accept a professorship at UCLA, it was a real blow both to Lovett and the university.

Guerard had been one of the most respected founding faculty, a statesman and spokesman for the faculty known to and respected by the board of trustees—even if they did not follow his advice. In January 1918, while still in military service, he had written Captain Baker an eloquent letter supporting Rice's pursuit of excellence and advocating the critical importance of building up substantial library resources at the new institute. In words that would have warmed the heart of every other humanistic scholar on campus, he wrote that "We are far away from any good library, and books are our essential instruments." Lovett too was a lover of books, and though he similarly advocated the importance of building library collections, not until after World War II would a freestanding library building be constructed on campus. In the meantime, a central collection was housed on the north end of the second floor of the administration building, supplemented with various departmental libraries scattered across campus. In a stronger letter, addressed to the trustees in general and written after he had already offered his resignation and thus could not be seen as trying to feather his own nest, Guerard wrote a spirited letter urging the importance—the necessity—of substantially improving the faculty pay scale at the institute. Guerard pointed out that while Houston offered splendid opportunities for business, it was lacking in what he termed "the intellectual realm." Moreover, it was "fifteen hundred miles away from the chief centers or learning; and the climate is not conducive to scientific strenuousness." "So," he continued, at the beginning, "in order to get as good a Faculty as any, Rice had to make up its mind to pay as well as the best, *plus*." Guerard thought this need would exist for a generation, after which Rice would have acquired such academic cachet that the "new university could compete on terms of equality with the proudest in the East." But that time had not yet come, he stated, giving his own example where, after having taught at Rice for thirteen years, his purchasing power in 1924 was actually less than it had been in 1913. He explained that the original faculty had not come just for money, but "because the salaries seemed to show that the importance of the human factor was properly recognized." Sadly, he advised the trustees,

"This feeling of confidence has gradually disappeared. Until reports of my departure had started discussions among the Faculty, I myself had not quite realized how completely it had disappeared." In private correspondence with Lovett, Guerard reiterated his respect and affection for the president and emphasized his love for the institute and its founding mission, but clearly Guerard blamed the trustees for their shortsighted financial parsimony.

Guerard's departure was not the only significant loss in 1924. That same year the founding professor of German, Thomas Lindsey Blayney, resigned to become president of Texas State Women's College (two years later he moved on to become the longtime dean of Carleton College in Minnesota), and the influential professor of physics, Harold A. Wilson, left to assume the prestigious professorship of physics at the University of Glasgow. Of course every university president must to some extent deal with the problem of retention of his best faculty, and no one would want to have a faculty so undistinguished that other universities did not try to hire some of them away. That said, the loss in quick succession of three of the most eminent Rice faculty no doubt shocked Lovett (and perhaps the board), as it certainly did the remaining faculty; even the *Thresher* expressed worry about the necessary classes being offered.

To complicate matters even more, Lovett was engaged in a five-month trip to Europe from late October 1924 to late March 1925, but during that time he stayed as informed of university affairs as communications of the day allowed, and he conducted a whirlwind correspondence with scholars at leading academic centers searching for replacements for Guerard and Blayney. Wilson, it turned out, found Glasgow not to his liking and by spring of that year was already negotiating with Lovett and the trustees to return to Rice. (A few years later, in 1928, a second major college textbook, *Modern Physics,* sealed his reputation.) In January 1925 Professor V. Breul of Cambridge University warmly recommended an older scholar, Max Freund, with a doctorate from Leipzig, and formerly professor of German at the University of Belfast, for the German position at Rice, and by May the *Thresher* was publicizing his acquisition. Lovett also located Marcel Moraud, an associate professor of French at the University of Toronto, and convinced him to move to Rice as professor of French, replacing the beloved Guerard.

Every year during the decade of the 1920s Lovett succeeded in enlarging the faculty—most of the appointments being at a very junior level—in order to meet the teaching needs of a student enrollment that had exceeded 1,200 students. (It was often difficult, as Guerard had told the trustees as late as 1924, to persuade even junior faculty to come to Houston. For example, one prospective hire had written a current member of the engineering faculty in 1919, "Yes, a favorable opening in teaching would interest me. . . . The climate would probably be bearable, unless it is actually enervating and produces a languor and drawl so characteristic of the South. Perhaps you can tell me a bit more about that.") And with the specter of the departure of Guerard fresh in the minds of the trustees, when Griffith C. Evans received repeated offers of a full professorship from Harvard, Lovett was able to convince the trustees at their January 8, 1926, meeting to raise his salary very significantly to $9,000 annually to prevent his leaving Rice. Evans had already made Rice an internationally known center for mathematical research. Similarly, when longtime philosophy professor Radoslav A. Tsanoff—a popular lecturer and prolific scholar—received an attractive offer from the University of Southern California in June 1928, the trustees followed Lovett's recommendation and gave Tsanoff a raise of better than 50 percent in order to retain him. At last the hemorrhaging of faculty was stopped, at least for the time. Lovett may well have thought that problem was solved, and other positive developments might have offered him a glimmer of hope that the original vision of institutional greatness could be achieved.

That promise was provided by a series of new buildings that became available to Rice faculty and students. In the fall of 1920 a utilitarian field house was completed near the corner of Main Street and University Avenue, just to the south of the football stands. This was not the grand gymnasium called for in the original plans, and it was assumed to be a temporary facility, but it did allow basketball games on campus and other kinds of athletic activities. That same year, just across Main Street from the three residence halls, Autry House opened, and although it belonged to the Diocese of Texas, it served as the de facto student center of the university. Mrs. James L. Autry had donated the funds in honor of her husband (both their children had attended Rice) to build the center, which had been envisaged by the Reverend Harris Masterson, Jr., to serve the needs of Rice students. The handsome structure, designed by Rice architectural professor William Ward Watkin, would be central to student life for the next thirty-five years: plays were performed here, various student groups held meetings there, meals were provided, and the comfortable lounges (Autry House was styled "the fireside of Rice") were especially beneficial to women students, who had no housing on campus.

In 1925 another, even larger, laboratory building was constructed. The original architectural firm, Cram and Goodhue, made preliminary drawings, but William Ward Watkin (a former Cram and Goodhue employee), who had been discussing programmatic needs in consultation with chemistry professor Harry B. Weiser, revised those plans. The result was an *E*-shaped structure, clearly respectful of the design traditions established by the original campus buildings. It offered laboratories as well as substantial office and classroom space not only for chemistry but a variety of other departments, and it provided a handsome lecture hall that opened directly onto the street. Reminiscent of the tiles and carvings adorning the administration building, the chemistry building had tiles reproducing alchemical symbols and a set of cartoonish carvings depicting campus personalities Dean Caldwell, registrar McCann, chemist Weiser (shown as a winged monster crushing a piteous student), and an amazingly spindly William Ward Watkin himself. The placement of this building suggested an expansive future for campus construction—no one could have known in 1925 that it would be more than two decades before another academic building would be constructed.

Yet another Watkin-designed building opened in 1927, this one dedicated to the creature comforts of the Rice faculty. In the first major act of philanthropy to the Rice Institute since its founding, merchant George S. Cohen (he was president of Foley's, the city's leading department store) gave funds in honor of his parents, Robert and Agnes Cohen, to underwrite the construction of Cohen House to provide lounge facilities, meeting and game rooms, and a dining room for faculty, with several additional rooms provided upstairs for the use of guests of the university. The building attractively complemented the original academic buildings, and the beautiful wood-beamed ceiling of the lounge, the tile work, the reliefs of many early faculty, and the courtyard and gardens gave Cohen House a feeling of warmth and grandeur that made it an extraordinary enhancement of the quality of faculty life.

This stream of buildings in the 1920s may have helped insulate Lovett from full recognition of the impact of the shortage of funds, and this shortage needs to be understood in context. The Rice Institute was still munificently funded compared to most private and even state universities in the South: its campus was widely admired for its beauty, and its faculty, most of whom held Ph.D.s, was far more distinguished than that of most southern universities. And of course, all students attended tuition-free! The term *shortage* is applicable, however, when one compares the state of the Rice Institute in the 1920s with the ambitious vision proclaimed in 1912. Rice was intended not merely to be good but to become great, and remembering the spectacular promise exhibited during the formal opening ceremonies in October 1912, the university now seemed to be in a holding pattern.

Given the size of the initial endowment, more than $6.7 million, soon augmented with the timber sales from the Louisiana lands, why weren't more funds available? The trustees were cautious lawyers, bankers, and businessmen, and acting under the restraints of their interpretation of the legal principle called the prudent investor rule, which held that fiduciaries of trusts should never make investments that carried risk, they avoided investing the Rice endowment funds in stocks. Instead, they invested only in the safest bonds and in secured loans to local builders, businesses, churches, and private individuals. But neither bonds nor secured notes brought high returns although such a conservative investment strategy was safe (no substantial losses in the stock market crash of 1929, for example) and did result in steady if decidedly unspectacular growth. The Rice trustees left all academic matters to the discretion of President Lovett, approving every recommendation and request he made, but in the same way that they expected him to guide the academic aspects of the institute, they expected to make all the decisions regarding investment policy and disbursements. Lovett seemed to accept without question this arrangement of responsibilities. Consequently, the trustee meetings show practically no discussion of any academic matters and instead read more like the minutes of a small-town savings and loan. Short paragraph after short paragraph indicates the discussion and usual approval of small loans (usually in the $5,000–$10,000 range). When Lovett made a special request, such as a salary increase to retain an Evans or Tsanoff, the recommendations seem to have been approved automatically.

Why did Lovett not push the trustees more aggressively for additional funding? Perhaps he shared their attitudes toward investments. Certainly he believed that the university should not in any year spend beyond its income, but the records show that every year the university reinvested surplus funds. Perhaps he was just too much of a "gentleman of the old school" to advocate monetary matters vigorously—perhaps he felt it unseemly? Lovett had been named as one of the trustees in 1910; since he was one of the group and not, as it were, an independent advisor or advocate, he may have felt uneasy about breaking with the group consensus. Often people find it difficult to disagree strongly with the other members of a group with whom they have worked and shared hopes and concerns, and the fact that the trustees so trustingly backed Lovett's academic recommendations would have intensified the desire on his part not to buck them in other matters. (Often children of a stern, judgmental parent learn to be conflict adverse, and this tendency of Lovett's might have been reinforced by his irenic relationship with his prominent father-in-law, Colonel Hale.) Lovett from the very beginning demonstrated great loyalty to Captain Baker, and the Lovett and Baker families grew closer over the years together in Houston, sharing their devotion to the institute. Lovett's daughter Adelaide's marriage to Baker's son Walter Browne in 1923 probably made it even more personally difficult for Lovett to pressure his respected elder.

The Rice trustees, elder statesmen of the community, saw their role to be careful fiduciaries of the funds on hand; they did not see themselves as active fundraisers in the community. The public widely shared a belief that Rice was fabulously wealthy, and its absence of tuition seemed to back up that perception as did the stately marble-and-granite buildings in the middle of a large campus. The records of the trustees reveal no fundraising efforts for any academic initiative, no attempt to augment the endowment (and hence the available funds)

in any way other than the following of their regular investment policies. Had the Rice Institute had a religious affiliation, the trustees or
president could have appealed to the denominational authorities or individual churches, but of course that avenue was closed off. At the time
there existed no broad spectrum of philanthropic foundations, and the
two largest, the Rockefeller Foundation and the Carnegie Foundation,
gave to a narrow range of causes and supported mainly a small handful
of privileged research universities—and none in the South.* State funds
were certainly unavailable to a private university. The only way to generate additional funds for a university that did not have recourse to
tuition was to solicit the public or special audiences for contributions.
Unlike modern university presidents, Edgar Odell Lovett seldom made
such appeals. Despite the charisma he had evidently demonstrated so
abundantly when attracting faculty in the earliest phases of the university and articulating his vision for the institution, Lovett was at heart
a reserved, even shy person, more scholarly in demeanor than demon-
strative, and a man of cultivated dignity. Unlike present-day university
presidents, he never understood his role to be primarily a solicitor of
funds. Nor did the board. At a time in the early 1920s when other
major universities—for example, Johns Hopkins, Princeton, and Harvard—were mounting modern-style fundraising campaigns replete with
professional fundraisers and public relations experts, campaigns that
netted millions of dollars, Rice (as it would again in the 1970s) forwent
the opportunity and consequently lost momentum. Even had Lovett
stepped down in protest of board policies, it is inconceivable that the
trustees would have replaced him with a more aggressive—more modern—fundraising president.

On rare occasions, usually in the form of a public address, Lovett,
after first acknowledging that the university was "thoroughly solvent,
and its solvency will be maintained," made low-key pleas for additional
funds. For example, addressing the Houston Kiwanis Club luncheon
meeting on September 22, 1926, Lovett told the members that the Rice

---

*The Carnegie Foundation, for example, in the 1920s and 1930s gave most of its aca-
demic funding to only seven universities: Harvard, Yale, Princeton, Johns Hopkins, Chicago, the California Institute of Technology, and Stanford.

Institute needed "men [faculty] and money," and he pointed out that each year "interest rates are declining and expenses mounting." He said that the university had the ability to "administer wisely tomorrow a gift of ten million," and could in fact over the next decade benefit from four times that amount. Appealing to the competitive spirit and pride of the Houstonians, he pointed out that in the previous year alone Harvard, Yale, and Princeton had received in gifts a combined total more than the entire assets—including campus buildings—of Rice. If these New Englanders could contribute $15 million in one year, he said, "why cannot the friends of education in Houston pledge one million a year to Rice for the next fifteen years?" He then went on to say that this region—in the Rice Institute—ought to have a great graduate school, a law school, and a medical school equal to those at such places as Harvard and Johns Hopkins, indeed, first-rate training in "all the manifold brain-working professions of our time." He clinched his argument with this line, "If Boston, New York, Baltimore, and Chicago can promote such undertakings successfully, why not Houston, Texas?"

But apparently there was no follow-up to this plea for funds. Nevertheless, Lovett remained relentlessly optimistic. In an interview with the *Houston Chronicle* published December 30, 1928, he "made it known informally that he is taking steps to establish a law department at Rice within the next few years. This will later be followed by a school of medicine if the plans mature." Along those hopeful lines, the following spring, in April 1929, civics professor John W. Slaughter wrote financier Jesse Jones to make the case that "the Rice Institute if provided with means . . . can be for the Southwest what Harvard is for New England."

But the means were not forthcoming. For one thing, Houston was a far smaller city in the 1920s than were Boston, New York, Baltimore, and Chicago. And Rice was so much younger than the major universities in those cities, and so much smaller, that it did not have an alumni base sufficient to support significant fundraising. In 1926, for example, there were fewer than nine hundred living Rice alumni, and almost all of them were under thirty years of age—not the age when individuals typically have the ability and inclination to make major philanthropic gifts. The Rice Institute had nothing remotely similar to a modern university development office: there was no organized fundraising, no identification of possible donors, nothing of what today is termed *cultivation*. Lovett did not make fundraising calls on anyone. Perhaps even more important, the members of the board of trustees were almost totally uninvolved in fundraising and did not see that part of their own role should be the providing of additional funds through acts of philanthropy on their part. Again, they believed that their role in this regard was confined to the cautious investment and expenditure of the funds on hand. If someone voluntarily came forward to make a contribution, they accepted the gift and acknowledged their appreciation, but their role was completely reactive.

In fact, the board of trustees was passive on every issue facing the university except intercollegiate athletics. The university had joined the Southwest Conference in 1914 to promote and organize intercollegiate competition in a variety of sports, and while Rice fielded teams in basketball, baseball, track, and tennis (there were no intercollegiate teams for women athletes), it was football that attracted the most attention. Student interest was high, attendance at contests was good, and on occasion a train was chartered to take students to and from gridiron battles at such places at Austin, Baton Rouge, and College Station. Athletics was overseen by a Committee on Outdoor Sports, a committee whose mission was based on that of a similarly named committee at Princeton, and the longtime chair of the committee was architect William Ward Watkin. (Watkin had been Rice's delegate at the formation of the Southwest Conference and served as the conference's vice president and then president in 1918–1919 and 1920–1921.) From the beginning there were concerns that too many football players flunked out and that the team was insufficiently competitive—and that sports lost money. The Committee on Outdoor Sports was the only university committee that regularly presented reports to the trustees, and athletic issues were the only aspect of university life that was not conveyed to the trustees by Lovett.

As the Rice board of trustees became increasingly interested in promoting intercollegiate sports, Lovett seems to have been somewhat converted to the cause, though perhaps this was more the result of his reading the political realities of life in a region where football was supported with religious-like fervor. When he first began planning Rice after his hiring in January 1908, Lovett's views were colored by his experience of football at Princeton and in the Northeast. Intercollegiate football began in the Northeast—in fact, the Princeton-Rutgers contest in 1869 is called the first football game between two colleges, although the game played bears slight resemblance to the sport today—and the great football powers were what today would be called the Ivy League teams, along with several other universities in the Northeast such as Army, Rutgers, and Temple. By the early twentieth century the sport had gotten out of control: so-called tramp players would play for several teams in succession during a season; players would play for five or more years because there were no agreed-upon eligibility rules; the games was marked by excessive, even brutal violence. The result became a national scandal, with lurid stories in muckraking magazines fanning the outrage; university presidents, sportswriters, even President Theodore Roosevelt began to insist that the sport be cleaned up. A series of meetings and conferences were held in 1906 and the next few years, gradually resulting in rule changes and reforms that began to produce a game that would be recognizable today, although the forward pass did not gain widespread acceptance until 1912.

When Lovett outlined his vision of the Rice Institute in that same year, his discussion of campus sports reflected the bad repute that overorganized, hypercompetitive football had earned for itself—it was yet to be seen what the results of the recent reforms would be. Lovett believed that exercise was essential for healthy life, although his preference was for solo sports that individuals could pursue throughout life. His personal preference was what he termed "meadow-running across country," and for most of his life he remained an inveterate walker. When he first came to Rice he often walked from his downtown hotel out to the campus, and until he was in his seventies he continued to walk from the Plaza Hotel to the campus and back. (In his September 1932 matriculation address Lovett told the students that "I walk a great deal, chiefly for physical exercise in the open air, but quite as much, I think, to compose my temper and to calm my spirit." Later, students would occasionally join him for his walk to campus, but they and others came to recognize by how he handled his cane if he welcomed companions that day or wanted to be left alone as he worked through the day's problems in his mind.) But he recognized that universities had to offer a wider palate of sports, with ideally every student being able to find some form of "systematic and regular physical exercise" to balance their intellectual pursuits. Yet how to provide sports and avoid excesses was the problem. "No feature of organized college life," he said in his formal speech, "The Meaning of the New Institution," that opened the university, "has been the subject of greater criticism than the organized devotion to athletic sports, both in the colleges and among the colleges." While he made clear that he fully believed in the value of outdoor sports, he recognized that "The dangers lie in over-training, in high specialization, in professional tendencies in the highly developed team, making sport for the few and spectators of the many." What he hoped to do was to get the students "off the bleachers" and into intramural sports and into "class, club, and college competitions, by fostering the sportsman's spirit of amateur sports."

From this idealized conception of college sport Lovett began to evolve his position almost immediately, although he seems never to have accepted what he initially termed the "professionalizing tendencies." He reported in 1932 that his views began to change that very fall of 1912 when he witnessed the University of Texas-Texas A&M game; he was surprised (and perhaps somewhat dismayed) to discover the high level of the sport in the Southwest. "But on that day I was persuaded that the new university then still ahead of us ought to make some provision for taking part in intercollegiate football games." As he said in his talk to the "R" Association dinner honoring the football players in 1932, "The rest is history." He went on to explain that "In the face of some disappointment, discouragement, and defeat I have from time to time reviewed that decision with misgiving, but despite disappointment, discouragement, and defeat I have never revised the judgment." What else could he have said to that audience? But his words suggest that while his initial ideals had been sorely tested, the compromises made were necessary given the demands of the alumni, the public, and the students themselves to have competitive teams—compromises in fact that nearly every university president has made over the last century. As Lovett said in his matriculation address of 1923 praising the university's offering enough intramural sports for all students to participate if they desired, it was noteworthy that the "capital contests" with specialized players attracted the attention and support of a wide cross-section of the citizenry of Houston, and this was to the good of the university. Certainly the board of trustees shared that rationalization. And Lovett himself clearly enjoyed attending Rice football games.

The trustees in the early 1920s wanted to improve the football fortunes (and hence increase both attendance and revenues), a desire that the Committee on Outdoor Sports responded to. In 1912 Lovett along with William Ward Watkin had recruited as the first coach a graduate of the University of Chicago, Philip Arbuckle, to oversee all athletics, including not only coaching football but handling the one-year course in physical activities required of all the men students. In its first year of competition, the Rice squad had even played high school teams, but the competition grew stronger after Rice in 1914 became a charter member of the Southwest Conference. And as Arbuckle took on more responsibilities, the football team became even less competitive, so he was reassigned in 1921 to professor of physical education and director of athletics (he resigned from Rice in late 1923), and others were brought in to coach football. After two young coaches failed to improve the team's fortunes, Watkin argued for and got permission from the trustees to seek a high-profile coach. He settled on the already legendary John W. Heisman, a graduate of Brown and the University of Pennsylvania and former coach of Auburn, Clemson, and Georgia Tech (where one of his teams had beaten a hapless Cumberland College eleven by the score of 222–0) who had helped popularize the forward pass.

On February 12, 1924, Watkin brought the high-powered Heisman to meet the trustees, and after some discussion they agreed to hire him at the then extraordinary salary of $9,000 for the year, with the understanding that he would have to be present only for three or four months following September and then about a month in the spring. This was a salary thousands of dollars more than that of any professor, and for less than six months' service per year. All the negotiations with the board appear to have been handled by Watkin. What did Lovett think of this? Did he think it futile to resist the trustees' desire to achieve prowess on the football field as well as in the halls of academe?

A little over a month later, when trustees and other athletic supporters officially welcomed Heisman to the city with a banquet at the Rice Hotel, Lovett sent Watkin a telegram asking him to present his "confident good wishes to the guest of honour at this evening's dinner and express my regret that earlier engagements prevent my personal participation in the hail and acclaim to health, happiness, and high achievement citizens and collegians are extending to John W. Heisman." Given Lovett's normal prose, that reads as a rather lukewarm welcome. The faculty, whose salaries had not been keeping up with inflation and were seeing some of their stars like Guerard leave, could not have been happy with this turn of events.

Although the Heisman-coached team beat the University of Texas that fall, Heisman did not inaugurate a winning era in Rice football. His first year the team went 4–4, stayed practically the same at 4–4–1 the next two seasons, and then fell to a disappointing 2–6–1 in 1927, after which Heisman resigned to take over the directorship of the New York Downtown Athletic Club. Heisman had not been a good match for Rice. Lovett, Watkin, and ultimately even the trustees were unwilling to make the kinds of compromises with academic quality that Heisman wanted. He urged aggressive recruitment of players, providing them with generous scholarships (at Rice, football players were awarded campus jobs but not given "athletic" scholarships, though the line between the two would blur in the late 1930s and 1940s), and reducing the academic rigor expected of them. While Watkin and Lovett (and certainly the trustees) were willing to bend their scholarly standards, they were unwilling to do away with them completely.

In December 1927, in response to a query from Captain Baker about what could be done to both attract more football players and keep them from failing out, Watkin wrote a long letter making a number of suggestions (He sent a copy of the letter to Lovett.). Perhaps Rice should admit not thirty but seventy "freshman football possibilities" each fall, but the problem was preventing their flunking out. Ideally a "first-class preparatory school for boys" could be established in the city that could turn out athletic boys who had better academic preparation. As it was now, "The most capable high school athletes are frequently the poorest prepared students entering college," and at Rice typically half of them failed after their first year. Perhaps a much-expanded tutoring system could be established. But Rice with its small alumni base would always be at a disadvantage given the size of the dominant Southwest Conference universities. Enlarging the number of incoming athletes and providing them with adequate tutoring seemed at present the only recourse. "I don't believe we should consider any modification of the standards to permit any indulgence to an athlete which is not equally true to the nonathletic student." As if the point needed to be emphasized, Watkin stated that "I don't believe the Institute faculty will be sympathetic in any policy that would tend to assure the incoming athlete the promise of passing his courses relatively easily." When the faculty in December 1928 discussed a committee recommendation that a degree program in physical education be developed, it passed but elicited spirited opposition. Griffith C. Evans and Radoslav A. Tsanoff spoke against the proposal, and although Stockton Axson could not be present, he let his disapproval be known. Yet because the existing degree programs (majors) at Rice clearly did not facilitate the development of a consistently winning football program, the trustees decided to address this issue.

The trustees met in January 1929 at James Baker's residence, "The Oaks," and began to discuss among themselves the formation of a new academic program at Rice, one in physical education, that would be more conducive to attracting and retaining better athletes. Lovett must have told the trustees that in order to avoid faculty opposition, such a program would have to be separately funded outside the normal endowment income, for he made that point when asked to make a presentation to a group of community leaders attending a dinner the trustees hosted at the Houston Club on the evening of February 16, 1929. There Lovett told the audience that he had been all his life "an ardent believer in athletic sports." He then outlined some of the life lessons he believed organized sports could teach: teamwork, discipline, courage, fortitude. Because he valued sports and the attributes they promoted, he valued the training of coaches for the public schools. (Since there would be coaches, wouldn't it be better for Rice to educate its share of them?) Toward that end, he said, Rice was proposing a new degree program in physical education to help attract to Rice and graduate an additional forty male students a year who would benefit the football team and provide a needed public service afterward in the schools. These would be "men of the same caliber as are those who have already invested their lives in the Rice Institute." This program could not be allowed to starve any existing programs at Rice, so new funds to the order of $20,000 annually would have to be raised. After Lovett spoke, the trustees made a plea to the well-heeled audience members to pledge five-year annual gifts sufficient to underwrite the proposed new physical education program at Rice. Such prominent citizens as Jesse Jones, William S. Farish, Harry C. Wiess, William L. Clayton, and Walter W. Fondren made pledges.

One prominent citizen, Lamar Fleming, Jr., was unable to attend the dinner but took the liberty of writing Baker that he was not sympathetic "with the suggestion of any change in the curriculum whose major objective is the attraction of young men as athletic material." In fact, Fleming wrote, he was "astonished that many serious people consider that the victory or defeat of a Rice athletic team is a matter of serious importance to the undergraduates, the institution itself, or the community." Perhaps Fleming, the cosmopolitan president of the huge Anderson, Clayton cotton firm, had lived so long in Europe as director of the company's European operations that he had grown out of touch with the local infatuation with winning football teams. But he was a man of such substance and importance that Baker enlisted Lovett's assistance in writing a joint reply. They wrote that they shared the surprise that many "serious people" so valued team success, "but the stubborn fact remains that such is the case." They fully agreed with another point Fleming made, that "the conduct of athletics should serve the purpose of giving athletic enjoyment and development to a maximum number of undergraduates." But they went on to state their belief "that athletic sports are an indispensable adjunct to academic life." They agreed with the importance of maintaining academic integrity but argued for the value of intercollegiate competition. In order to support such competition but not sacrifice standards, they proposed to follow the example of universities like Stanford, Wisconsin, and Berkeley in establishing a department of physical education. It would offer one course per year in a student's program, and the remainder of the courses would be drawn from the regular curriculum (including sciences and foreign languages);

the department "would be directed by men of first-rate academic training, who will do no coaching." To prevent any harmful effect on existing programs, the physical education department would be separately supported by specially raised funds. While this letter did not convince Fleming, it does suggest the rationale that motivated both Lovett and the trustees. That the letter read at times like an apology for the program was probably the result of Lovett's input; that it nevertheless stated university policy no doubt reflected the controlling decision of Baker and the other trustees.

Subsequently, as the student newspaper the *Thresher* reported on September 19, 1929, a department of physical education opened that fall semester. Harry A. Scott, who had earned his doctorate at Columbia University in 1921, joined the faculty after having chaired the physical education program at the University of Oregon for eight years. He was a man of principle and standards, and he wanted to develop physical education programs that involved and benefited the entire student body. The department's courses would also result, after four years, in a B.S. degree in physical education and, the trustees believed, greater success on the football field.

Lovett may well have felt quite optimistic about the university's prospects as the 1929 fall semester opened. He could hope that the troublesome athletic issue was settled or at least on the way to being settled, and at no cost to the academic programs central to the university. At the beginning of the year mathematician Griffith C. Evans had written Lovett a persuasive letter about the importance of additional funding so that the already prestigious math department could be enlarged, funding for travel to professional meetings provided, and generous leaves of absence be instituted. Perhaps Lovett returned to thinking about how to respond to that request in the early fall. Also, over the past two years there had been discussion of at last providing a library building, and Cram and Goodhue in 1927 had prepared some preliminary sketches. Watkin himself had asked Lovett's permission in 1926 to begin thinking about the design and placement of a fine arts group, and in 1928 the Association of Rice Alumni had begun considering a fundraising campaign to construct a three-story building (mirroring the physics lab) that would be in honor of William M. Rice. And in

December 1928 Lovett himself had, as we have seen, mentioned to a newspaper reporter that Rice was contemplating in the not too distant future developing both a law and a medical school. Lovett's focus was decidedly academic, on intellectual training. "It is not our business to tell you what to think," he told the incoming class in his matriculation address on September 25, 1929. "It is our business to teach you how to think, to transform you, as far as that may be possible, into independent thinkers." This was the chief function of a university.

Lovett may well have believed that the relative doldrums of the 1920s were to be followed by a resumption of academic momentum and the promise so memorably expressed in October 1912. But on October 24, 1929, Black Thursday as it came to be called, the stock market collapsed, buyers panicked, and then after a feeble rally on Friday, the bottom fell out on Tuesday, October 29. A record for the time of 16 million stocks were sold in frantic trading, and billions of dollars in stock value were lost. Within months the U.S. stock market lost over 80 percent of its total value. The grim decade of the Great Depression had begun. At Rice, as throughout the nation, sunny optimism died that fateful October.

# CHAPTER SEVEN

# CONFRONTING THE GREAT DEPRESSION

PERHAPS THE DEFINING CHARACTER TRAIT of Edgar Odell Lovett was his steadfast optimism, a conviction—not just a hope—that his life-defining goal would be achieved. Given the opportunity entrusted to him in 1908 to take William Marsh Rice's vague charter and, backed with a substantial endowment, build a university, he had developed a comprehensive vision of an institution that would begin with a carefully limited range of activities but that would—it was confidently expected—over time, and with additional funding, mature into a full, rounded university. When the endowment failed to acquire significant augmentation in the 1920s, Lovett nevertheless constantly held that ambitious vision before the board of trustees and the faculty both to keep the ideal alive and to maintain high academic standings even in the midst of an era of generally lowered expectations. That undaunted optimism served Lovett—and the Rice Institute—particularly well during the dreary years of the Great Depression. Again Lovett had to bend, to tack against the winds of economic adversity, but he never lost sight of his original vision or his certitude that it would be realized. Another sign of his constancy was his loyal devotion to Mary Hale Lovett, his wife of more than thirty years. Totally bedridden now, she no longer could take long walks with him or even visit the university, but Lovett's love and attention to her never faltered. Whether or not he knew Shakespeare's line from Sonnet CXVI, "Love is not love which alters when it alteration finds," Lovett embodied the sentiment. In 1965 mathematician Hubert Bray reminisced about an occasion thirty years before when he had driven Lovett in his Model A Ford to College Station to address the local chapter of the American Association of University Professors. On the way back to Houston—it was mid-April—Lovett noted bluebonnets growing along the roadway. He had Bray stop the car, and they both got out and picked an armful of bluebonnets to take home to Mary. As Bray recalled, "It was a bit illegal, but nobody caught us, and after all, he was thinking of Mrs. Lovett." It was his optimism and steadfastness in the face of disappointment and loss that made Lovett such an effective and beloved university president.

The overwhelming and perennial problem of the 1930s for the university was financial. Several months before the 1929 crash, A. B. Cohn, the longtime assistant secretary to the board of trustees who primarily oversaw investments, warned the trustees that the bond market, especially overseas bonds, was increasingly shaky and was not producing the desired level of returns. But of course that early warning did not foresee what happened to the U.S. economy after the stock market collapse. The university had practically no investments in the stock market, but the falling revenues from the investments in bonds provided little cushion. The largest portion of the investment portfolio was in local secured notes. The falling economy meant that the rate of return on these small loans fell precipitously, many of them soon bringing no more than a 3 percent annual income. Moreover, with the falling economy, local debtors found themselves unable to meet their payment obligations. Rice found itself possessing worthless loans, and foreclosures on property brought little or no financial returns. The result was a sharp drop in income. Total income from investments fell from $733,890 in 1929–1930 to $652,500 in 1932–1933, and of course the board did not know how much farther it might fall. In truth the university's financial situation was nowhere near as fragile as the trustees feared. Even in the 1932–1933 academic year, income exceeded total expenses by $174,976; the university followed the excessively cautious practice of subtracting from available income a substantial sum that was called a depreciation allowance on the fixed assets of the university. This depreciation allowance—really a paper expense—amounted to $94,743 in that year, still leaving a surplus of $80,233 to which should be added another $34,300 garnered from various student fees. Yet the very cautious trustees interpreted this as an emergency situation and began to press President Lovett to make draconian cuts in the university budget.

This was the first genuine crisis to face Lovett; he had dealt over the past decade with financial restraints that had slowed the university's ascent, but cuts such as those proposed threatened the long-range prospects of the whole enterprise. After all, Rice as Lovett envisioned it was not to be merely a small, teaching-only local or southern college but had a higher destiny: to become a major university player on the world academic stage. Lovett did not reply to but was no doubt worried by a series of brief notes trustee chair Baker had begun sending him in early 1932 enclosing clippings about other universities cutting their faculty salaries and overall budgets—Southern Methodist University, for example, according to one clipping had just announced that it was reducing faculty salaries by 20 percent. Then the other shoe dropped. On March 26, 1932, Baker wrote Lovett that the trustees expected the university's income to fall another $50,000 in the coming year and they wanted Lovett to consider "economies and reductions of expenses" that would "remedy this situation." They meant remedy not in the sense of exploring ways to raise the revenue but rather in ways to cut the budget "without," Baker explained, "impairing the efficiency of the Institute." But of course efficiency and quality were different matters. Baker said that "Some of the trustees are inclined to think that there should be a substantial reduction in the number of students being enrolled this fall and subsequent years, that the number of instructors may be reduced, and also a reduction in salaries paid." Such cuts, of course, went to the heart of the issue of trying to sustain the university's aspirations.

Lovett replied three days later. "For the last six months," he wrote, "I have thought of little else than these matters of grave concern." He reported that he had been considering every kind of approach to the budgetary problem, "hoping, perhaps against hope, that harm to the prestige of the institution might still be avoided"; he asked for an extension of several more weeks before responding with a proposed budget. (Lovett was responsible for developing the entire academic budget; the athletic budget was developed by the business manager of athletics and handled directly by the board, without Lovett's input.) Yet given the declining revenues and the institution's charter prohibition against borrowing money and the commitment to live within its means, the trustees demanded a budgetary reduction. Since the university by virtue of the precise wording of its charter charged no tuition, there appeared to be at the time no ability to raise additional funds by that means. At the board meeting on June 2, 1932, which Lovett was unable to attend, the trustees voted to reduce the salaries of all faculty and staff (who made more than $100 per month) by 10 percent effective July 1, 1932. Those whose salaries were just above $100 per month would have theirs reduced to no less than $100. Within days the faculty began to implore Lovett to try to limit the impact of the salary reduction on the lower-paid married faculty (many of whom of course had children). Lovett took the proposal of many of the faculty back to the board, urging that those married men making less than $3,750 annually be exempted from the 10 percent salary cut. This time Lovett was at the board meeting, strongly representing the cause of the faculty. After extensive discussion the board compromised: it decreed that men making less than that amount would receive only a 5 percent reduction, effective not on July 1, 1932, but rather at the beginning of the next academic year. The total expenditure for faculty salaries fell from $280,805 in 1931–1932 to $253,304 the following academic year and continued to decline until it reached a low point in 1935–1936 of $208,008, representing a total reduction of monies to be paid in faculty salaries by 26 percent. The total educational budget in that same period fell more than 24 percent.

Lovett tried to limit the effect on the more or less permanent faculty members at the rank of assistant professor and above by letting go some instructors and lecturers. Tenure did not yet exist at Rice, and though those at any professorial rank were considered permanent employees, the appointments of instructors and lecturers were considered temporary and contingent on need and available resources. (In 1935 Baker would request Lovett to examine the existence and practice of tenure at other institutions. Lovett then wrote to a number of universities, but tenure was far less common then than today and more varied in its application, so his poll was inconclusive. At any event, the board did not take action—tenure would not be instituted at Rice until 1962.) Accordingly, the total teaching staff declined from a high in 1930 of 73 to a low in 1936–1938 of only 58. Although enrollment dropped from 1,375 in 1931–1932 to a low of 1,201 in 1934–1935 (with a corresponding drop in graduate enrollment from 98 to 69, and it would fall farther to 46 in 1938–1939), the student-to-teacher ratio increased, reaching 21:6 in 1936. These were unhappy developments, but Lovett was responding to the demands of the budget given him by the trustees and trying to retain the core of his faculty. These of course were frustrating times for many of the faculty. Even though the cost of living fell, they found themselves struggling to make ends meet and having to teach larger classes. And where was the prospect of the university's reacquiring the sense of movement toward increased stature?

Probably in anticipation of the kinds of questions faculty would have of the board and would direct to President Lovett, trustee chairman Baker wrote Lovett a long letter explaining the board's actions, a letter that sounds as though Baker had the faculty more in mind than Lovett himself. After discussing the severity of the worldwide depression and the fact that many businesses had had to cut the number of their employees and reduce their salaries, he suggested that "No one could reasonably expect the Institute to escape the common misfortune of all." He emphasized that the trustees had taken this step reluctantly and only after having considered all other options, and saying that they knew the "high character, broadminded and generous spirit" of the faculty and therefore were confident that in such a crisis, "when every government in the world seems tottering to its fall, that they will cheerfully make this sacrifice for the good of the Institute, which lies so close to the hearts of all." In other words, to complain was to be small-minded.

Of course no sensible faculty member could blame Lovett for this turn of events and reduction in prospects, but some did wish that he would develop a more consultative relationship with the faculty, a complaint expressed several times over his tenure. For example, only three days after Baker's letter to Lovett laying out the rationale for budget constraints, physicist Harold A. Wilson—while volunteering to contribute 10 percent of his salary to the physics department (with the assurance that his recently renegotiated salary would not be cut)—went on after this token of generosity to say pointedly to Lovett that "I believe that it would be a good thing for the Institute if meetings of the faculty were held from time to time say 4 or 5 times a year and if at these meetings you were to make statements as to the policy of the Institute in matters of general interest, the future prospects, the financial situation, and so forth and invite discussion." The faculty should be kept informed and not be blindsided by such announcements as the recent salary reductions. Taking the faculty into his confidence, Wilson argued to Lovett, "promotes the idea among members of the faculty that they are a permanent part of the institution and that their cooperation in all matters pertaining to its welfare is regarded of value." What Wilson, who greatly respected Lovett (there would eventually be a tiny minority of disaffected faculty who considered him dictatorial), exactly had in mind is unclear. There were monthly faculty meetings, chaired by Lovett, that dealt with most aspects of university life, though usually this consisted of consideration of matters forwarded by the various standing committees for faculty action. Lovett did not use the faculty meetings as a forum to discuss his plans of actions vis-à-vis the board.

Perhaps such a policy of more openness on Lovett's part would have prevented a great disappointment, the departure of Griffith C. Evans at the end of the 1933–1934 academic year to join the faculty of the University of California, Berkeley, as professor of mathematics and chairman of the department. Evans had been one of the original Rice faculty and had quickly been promoted to full professor. He had built up the mathematics department, he had just been elected to membership in the National Academy of Sciences, and in no one on the faculty did Lovett place more trust and respect. Lovett had gone to the board in 1926 to get a large raise for Evans to keep him from accepting an offer from Harvard. In 1929 Evans had written Lovett a letter requesting the kind of support required to allow him to build a great mathematics department, and of course no funds were forthcoming, but the board did find the funds to develop a department of physical education for the avowed purpose of improving the athletic teams, an action Evans deplored—he voted against the plan in a faculty meeting. Additional funding of the football program in the early 1930s and enlargement of the stadium apparently convinced Evans that the trustees valued sports over academics, and that conviction, along with the considerable academic attraction of Berkeley, convinced a reluctant Evans to make the "painful" decision to resign from Rice and accept the Berkeley offer. (Berkeley had carefully analyzed the universities that had most successfully trained graduates who won National Research Council fellowships in math and, on a per capita basis, Rice was in the top two of American universities. So Berkeley decided to "raid" Rice to bring Griffith Evans to California.) Although Evans made a special effort to assure Lovett of his respect and affection for Lovett himself and for the Rice Institute (Evans had even married a 1917 graduate of the university, Isabel Mary John), Evans's departure was a real blow to Lovett and the university. The faculty resolution of good wishes to him, adopted on June 2, 1934, as he was leaving, expressed "a deep sense of the loss which his going brings to all here." Evans would later write of being homesick for Rice and of how there was "no greater inspiration" than being involved in the creation of a university. Still, he was gone, and his leaving had left a void that Lovett never filled. (The following year, 1935, came another great loss to the institute and to Lovett personally, the death of Stockton Axson. Axson's death was a profound shock to Lovett, for they had been especially close since Princeton days together. Lovett responded to Evans's note of condolence by saying that when he first got the word of Axson's passing he had been on a trip to the Northeast and that night he "took a long walk in a blinding snowstorm to pull myself together, but to this day I have great difficulty in accepting the fact.") Though reserved in personality, Lovett was very empathetic in his attitude toward the problems of others, and he kept a tight rein on his emotions in all relationships with faculty and students.

Before economic hard times really hit the university, one piece of unfinished business from the past had finally been completed on June 8, 1930, when a seated bronze statue of founder William Marsh Rice was unveiled. In November 1909 the board had arranged to have his ashes sent by a New York City undertaking establishment back to Houston, where they were placed in the institute's "fire proof vault" until suitable arrangements could be made for them. After a long delay, in 1922 the board formed a committee consisting of Lovett, Will Rice, and Benjamin B. Rice to plan the proper disposition of the ashes. This led to a prominent sculptor, John Angel, being commissioned to sculpt a statue, which would be placed over a granite pedestal in the center of the Academic Quadrangle. Rice's ashes were interred at the base of this pedestal on May 22, 1930. With appropriate ceremony—including an address by Ralph Adams Cram—the statue itself was formally unveiled some two weeks later. Lovett of course had never met William Marsh Rice, but he greatly respected his signal act of benevolence. Still, this welcome act of reverence on behalf of the university's founder could not hide the economic crises of the 1930s that brought painful choices to both the board and President Lovett, and led to the loss of Griffith Evans.

It was clear that intercollegiate athletics, at least its financing, was under the sole control of the board. Lovett and faculty committees had little input, and the board even hired an outside accounting firm to try to ascertain expenditures and budget needs. But the effort begun in 1929 by the trustees to raise sufficient monies by pledges to underwrite the physical education program failed, despite repeated efforts in the early 1930s to get persons to fulfill their pledged commitments. Athletic business manager Dr. Gaylord Johnson tried mightily to run an efficient and honest operation, and did so, but still the athletic department lost money. The trustees tried everything imaginable, and with good coaches, Rice did have excellent teams, winning the Southwest Conference championship in football in 1934 and 1937 and beating the University of Colorado in the Cotton Bowl in January 1938. Funds were raised by subscription—and this time the board members made contributions, along with dedicating the profits from the Cotton Bowl appearance to the project—to more than double the size of the stadium so that it held 30,000 fans by the end of the decade. (And following the hiring of Jess Neely as head football coach in 1939, the Rice football program would garner additional championships and bowl appearances over the next quarter century.) Similar success in the 1930s was achieved in other sports such as basketball and track. But economic success did not follow, with the result that the increasing losses in the athletic department put more pressure on the university budget.

In the midst of the Great Depression ever more numbers of local men students decided to live at home to save money, resulting in unfilled dormitory rooms and hence lost revenue. The board responded by requiring men students to live on campus for at least one year, no doubt a severe burden on many males "of slender means." Almost two hundred students had part-time jobs on campus funded by the National Youth Administration (NYA), a New Deal program ably administered in Texas by a young Lyndon B. Johnson. (Later, at the direct suggestion of Johnson, Lovett had a blue and gray pennant of Rice sent to

Washington, D.C., so that it could be carried in the January 20, 1937, inaugural parade for Franklin D. Roosevelt along with the pennants of the other eighty-six Texas colleges participating in the NYA college aid program.) Despite the impecunious status of many students, in February 1933 trustee chairman Baker wrote Lovett proposing that in order to help generate additional funds to spend on athletics, the students could be charged a mandatory "student athletic fee of perhaps $10 annually." It is noteworthy that the board members, rather than make additional contributions themselves, would attempt to raise the additional monies from the students, many of whom were struggling to stay in school because of the desperate economic times. After all, the most the proposed fee could raise would be less than $13,000 annually. But with the surprising support of student leaders, a reduced student athletic fee was approved that produced $4.20 annually per student for the athletic department.

What was Lovett's position in these matters? Lovett had long made it clear that he enjoyed outdoor sports as a spectator, and he believed that students should both cheer for the university's intercollegiate teams and participate themselves in fully amateur sports. Lovett often spoke to alumni groups and others on behalf of Rice sports, and although he often made pleas for greater attendance at games (which would result in greater revenues), he hesitated to make out-and-out appeals for funds, considering that unseemly for the university president. Lovett of course was not blind to the unique popularity of football to the students, the alumni, the Rice trustees, and the greater Houston community—this was before the existence of major league professional teams in Houston, and the University of Houston did not yet field big-time teams. To have taken a rigidly principled stand against intercollegiate athletics would have jeopardized his presidency. Lovett was in his sixties, his wife was completely bedridden, and he was not independently wealthy—he needed to hold on to his position. But far more important to him than these concerns was his steady devotion to the vision he had originally laid out for the Rice Institute. He had internalized his role as the leader of the university so completely that he could not imagine turning it over to anyone else as long as the ultimate achievement of the founding goal was questionable in any way. Better for him to bend to local pressure for prowess on the football field than to resign in protest or, alternatively, protest so strongly as to lose influence with the trustees on other issues.

In today's political environment, compromise is often equated with "sell out," but for Lovett, it represented something like a strategic maneuver. His ultimate principle was the furtherance of the Rice Institute, and that took precedence over his commitment to totally amateur intercollegiate football. Consequently Lovett continued to speak favorably about football but he always did so in such a way as to hold up the ideal of amateur sports and student-athletes. That is, his remarks on football were intended to describe the sport in its Platonic ideal rather than the actual activities with literal accuracy. This way he could support Rice sports—and he loved attending the games* and even on occasion was seen watching practices—but talk about them in such a way as to hold the coaches to the absolutely highest standards in an implicit caution about going too far in the pursuit of athletic success. It was not a case of reform from within—Rice was never guilty of the kind of recruiting excesses and underhanded payment of athletes that occurred at some other institutions—but a determination to do athletics right (after all, the situation demanded at least moderately successful football teams) and not lose sight of the higher goals of the university. In the same way that the Rice Institute stood for academic rigor and excellence, Lovett wanted its athletic programs—insofar as possible—to serve as a model for true amateur sports played by student-athletes.

Lovett turned to these themes again and again when speaking at such venues as the Rice football banquet, the "R" Association, local alumni clubs, and the athletic committee of the Houston Chamber of Commerce. He often quoted the old adage about "a sound mind in a sound body," and while, for example, he urged the members of the Rice alumni club in Port Arthur to send Rice good students "with aptitudes

---

* At a memorable game in Waco in 1934 at which Rice clinched the Southwest Conference championship, Lovett was asked to give the players a pre-game pep talk. Lovett did so with an elaborate analogy to the Greek myth of Jason and the Golden Fleece. Almost certainly the players were puzzled by the story, but Lovett loved to apply classical examples to present-day events.

at games," he urged them to keep themselves physically fit and vigorous. He continued even into the 1930s to now and then warn against
the abuses often associated with football, but on the whole he lauded
the skills it taught in teamwork and discipline. Addressing the Houston
Chamber of Commerce, he insisted that he was not there "to pass the
hat," but he suggested the members should support Rice football by
better attendance at the games. In 1931 he told the members of the
"R" Association, an athletic support club, that it was essential to keep
things in balance, the "things of the spirit and mind and those of the
body and muscle." Speaking again five years later to the same group,
he once more emphasized how important it was to maintain "college
football as an amateur game among gentlemen," and, within the Rice
context, he said the players had "to take to their books as well as their
boots [cleats]." In the spring of 1933 eight football players had been
suspended for Honor Code violations that occurred in the fall semester final exams, and though they were declared ineligible for the next
season, Lovett always implied that such problems were anomalous. The
degree program in physical education reduced the high flunk-out rate
of athletes, but Lovett and the faculty in general insisted that there be
no athletic dorm and that athletes generally be treated as regular students. Of course, most of them were "regular" students and pursued
regular degree programs—this was before the era of aggressive athletic
recruitment and exclusively athletic scholarships. So, cognizant of the
board support for football and the immense appeal it had for the general public—football attendance at Rice games in the 1930s was substantially greater than it was in the early 2000s—Lovett steered his
way amid conflicting forces always with his eye on the goal of shep-
herding the Rice Institute toward fulfillment of the destiny he had outlined in 1912.

Despite the economic cutbacks, academic life at Rice in the 1930s
was not without excitement, accomplishment, and high ambition.
Again, one must remember that even with the financial restraints imposed on the university, the Rice Institute was significantly better off
than most southern (or national) universities. Students paid no tuition;
the campus buildings were comparative new, well designed, and well

equipped; most of the faculty held their doctorates and faculty research was still supported (for example, the physics department in 1937 began constructing a 2.5 million volt linear accelerator in a green frame building adjacent to the biology department's animal house); the library continued to purchase books, though at a reduced level; and in large part through Lovett's influence and example, there was a sense among the faculty that Rice was a genuine center of learning and scholarship. There was no summer school; instead, faculty members were expected to focus on their research—often in cooler climes—during the summer months. And many faculty members in fact did travel, conduct research, and write during the summer. The result was a steady progression of books and articles, gaining individual faculty academic renown and bringing prestige to the university. The absence of a large graduate program limited faculty scholarship to a degree, but the Rice Institute maintained a reputation for research and high standards that made it exemplary for the region.

Even with some financial straits, most faculty appreciated the ethos of academic excellence and freedom that Lovett had worked to establish from the beginning. For example, as history instructor Floyd S. Lear, a newly minted Harvard Ph.D., explained in December 1925 while turning down an offer to go elsewhere at a higher rank: "I have complete autonomy in all my teaching, and every plan or suggestion that I have advanced has been accepted without question. This very liberal attitude combined with only nine teaching hours weekly makes my Instructorship a thing not to be resigned without much consideration. I have never had more delightful students to work with, and the class of people with whom I am associated at the Institute is most pleasant." Clearly, there were other rewards besides salary at Lovett's university.

Perhaps Lovett's greatest contribution to the Rice Institute was his inculcation of the special nature of the place, a view that was shared by most faculty and students. Dean Caldwell, for example, authored a piece on Rice for a special Texas supplement to the *London Times* in 1925. "There is," he wrote, "something more than brick and stone and mortar about the Rice Institute. There is a spirit here which in every detail is given expression. It is the spirit of Rice, the spirit of unending

patience and endeavour in striving for the best, whatever be the goal."
Lovett had planted the goal of excellence in the ethos of the university.
And the faculty projected to the students that they were enrolled at a
first-class institution. In no way did Lovett or the faculty scale back
their ambitions because of Rice's location in the South. Rather than
have a self-conscious identification with the region and a defensive adjustment of its aspirations as a result, the Rice Institute, under Lovett's
leadership, always envisioned itself as a national university sited in
Texas, which seemed more western, more future oriented, more optimistic than the traditional states of the South.

Lovett's travels and correspondence meant that his contacts throughout the American and European academic worlds were extensive. He
used his networking skills to arrange and support a steady stream of
eminent visiting scholars to campus to present lectures or to accept
one- or two-semester temporary appointments. This constant contact
with leading scientists, humanists, and university leaders gave the Rice
faculty a consciousness of self-identity with the larger academic world,
minimizing much of the sense of intellectual isolation that afflicted
most southern university campuses. From the opening, Lovett had
funded such visits, and over the years Rice faculty and students had the
opportunity to see and hear such luminaries as Sir Arthur Shipley of
Cambridge, Princeton astrophysicist Henry N. Russell, composer Maurice Ravel, Shakespearean scholar George Lyman Kittredge of Harvard,
University of Paris literary scholar Louis Cazamian, mathematicians
T. Levi-Civita from Rome and Karl Menger from Notre Dame, educator John Dewey, and historians Ulrich B. Phillips, W. E. Dodd, and
Samuel E. Morrison. These lectures were widely publicized on campus,
they were reported on by the *Thresher*, and they provided the source of
much faculty discussion. And even during the times of most stringent
budgetary constraints, Lovett insisted on continuing to provide funds
for visiting lecturers.

Often these lectures were reprinted in the *Rice Institute Pamphlet*,
a quarterly serial publication begun in 1915 by Lovett to "facilitate the
prompt publication and distribution of the products of [the university's]
library, laboratory, and lecture activities." These pamphlets, in truth
a scholarly journal, were sent to many hundreds of academic libraries

around the world, and in an era when there were far fewer venues for publishing the results of research, they were an important part of Rice's commitment to scholarship and publication. Two of the main purposes of a university, Lovett had stated in 1912, were "the discovery and distribution of knowledge." Dozens of Rice faculty—Stockton Axson, Asa Chandler, Griffith C. Evans, Floyd S. Lear, Alan D. McKillop, Marcel Moraud, Radoslav A. Tsanoff, Harold A. Wilson, and many others—published significant articles and monographs in the pamphlets, and not only did they provide faculty with a publication outlet but they served to keep the university's name in the minds of academicians throughout the world. The *Rice Institute Pamphlet* was a constant symbol that the university had ambitions beyond its time and place. There is no doubt that Lovett's reputation and his efforts to promote Rice and its ideals gave the institute a fame that belied its small size and limited programs. In the same way that the University of Chicago and Stanford University stimulated and inspired the state universities of the Midwest and California to become excellent, Rice's example—albeit on primarily the undergraduate level—of research and well-trained faculty helped improve the burgeoning state universities of the Southwest. When in 1935 the leaders of the far larger southern universities (Duke, Vanderbilt, University of North Carolina, University of Texas, and others) organized a Southern University Conference "for considering matters pertaining to the upper division of college work and college study," of course Rice was invited to join, and at its third meeting in 1937 Lovett was appointed to the Committee on the Improvement of Graduate Education, a reflection of the respect with which the other leaders viewed both Lovett and the Rice Institute.

From the very beginning President Lovett had promoted a synergistic relationship between the faculty of the Rice Institute and the business and professional leaders of the city of Houston. Remember, in 1912 he had told his audience of faculty and visiting educators and scholars at the opening ceremonies of the university that amid the bustling commercial world of the city they would "learn to talk about lumber and cotton and railroads and oil, but you will also find," he pointed out, "every ear turned ready to listen to you if you really have anything to say about literature or science or art." Of course it was this insight into the nature of the local environment that led Lovett to develop in the first years of the university an extensive set of free public lectures. And this understanding of the relationship of the university and the city, fully shared by many of the original faculty, led in January 1920 to the organization of the Houston Philosophical Society. Meeting at the University Club in downtown Houston, a group of committed faculty (many of the usual suspects: Harold A. Wilson, Griffith C. Evans, Claude W. Heaps, Harry B. Weiser, Radoslav A. Tsanoff) founded the society to promote town-gown discussion, to "stimulate interest in modern developments in science and philosophy," with philosophy used in the sense of all learning except narrow technical and practical precepts and skills. The membership would be open to all members of the faculty and to a wide cross section of the city's legal, medical, and other professional leaders. The meetings, which usually consisted of a dinner before the formal talk and then discussion, soon moved to the newly opened Cohen House faculty club on campus. The Houston Philosophical Society almost immediately became a beloved, respected arena for university and civic leaders to interchange ideas and perspectives, and it remains today an active organization. Particularly in its first three decades, when Houston was a much smaller city than today, the society performed a significant role in bridging the gap between the groves of academe and the office towers of a rapidly growing city.

The faculty that Lovett had played such a major role in recruiting to Rice, with the full support of the president, also took steps among themselves to invigorate and sustain a spirit of intellectual excitement and engagement with important issues. In addition to their individual research and publication, several Rice faculty, mainly from what at the time were called the academic disciplines (as opposed to the science and engineering disciplines), had organized the Historical Society in 1922 "for free exchange of opinions, for criticism of articles and books of common interest, and for the reading and discussing of original papers by members of the society." Rice's physical isolation from other major universities made it particularly important to create local opportunities to test ideas and propositions through interaction with critical minds. The society, whose eligible membership was composed of "all faculty members of the Departments of English, German, and the Romance Languages, of Philosophy, Psychology, and Education, and of History, Politics, and Economics," met on the second Wednesday of each month, usually in the private home of one of the participating faculty. The handwritten minute books demonstrate the impressively wide range of papers given, and the presenters were drawn from across the academic disciplines. Many of the better-known faculty gave multiple papers over the years, and President Lovett himself found time in October of the society's founding year to give "an instructive and inspiring address on the 'Fellowship of Learning.'" That the Historical Society continued to meet into the 1960s suggests the vital role it played in the intellectual life of the Rice faculty.

Of course President Lovett was not solely responsible for the vibrancy of research, teaching, and intellectual exchange on the Rice campus even during the years of the Great Depression, but he did embody the optimism and catholicity of interests that created and sustained a nurturing environment. The able faculty in an era of limited university budgets may have turned even more intensively to their own internal intellectual and creative resources to help keep alive the promise that the Rice Institute had been founded upon. The students too, closely limited in number by the available dormitory facilities and number of faculty, were unusually talented. These were the days before standardized Scholastic Aptitude Tests (and test preparation courses), but Rice students were among the most able from the region, carefully selected and on the whole serious and hardworking—the rigor of the curriculum demanded that. Lovett thought of himself primarily as an educator, and he always kept the best interests of students in mind. For example, in his 1930 matriculation address he advised them, almost parentally, to get "plenty of work, some play, and all the sleep you need. . . . On your schedule I think you should always have at least one subject that affords you great delight, and one at least that gives you great difficulty. . . . Finally, breakfast required, luncheon elective, evening meal light." Yet then as now, able, hardworking students could also be immensely creative and multitalented, as alert to humor and pranks and youthful excesses as to hard work in the library and laboratory.

Rice students in the 1920s and 1930s did their part to uphold the words Lovett had had inscribed on one of the initial dormitory buildings: "the freedom of sound learning and the fellowship of youth." Rice students regularly won admission to the best graduate, medical, and law schools of the nation to continue their education; they won major national fellowships and research awards. Beginning in 1929 each year the engineering students held an Engineering Show to which the general public was invited to see equipment, student research projects, demonstrations, and other evidences of engineering advances, and these annual events became hugely popular. Approximately 48,000 people attended the 1938 Engineering Show. This was exactly the kind of university-city interaction that Lovett desired, and he took great pride in the event. Rice's application for a chapter of Phi Beta Kappa (PBK) had been approved in 1928. (Six years earlier the national secretary of the honorary organization had written Lovett that there was no concern about the academic quality of Rice's programs but rather a question about its title of institute—normally PBK chapters were only established at colleges and universities, and even the Massachusetts Institute of Technology [MIT] had been turned down for this reason a few years before.) The imprimatur the PBK chapter bestowed upon Rice also pleased Lovett immensely, as did the news in January 1931 that a Rice student, Samuel Rhodes Dunlap, had won a Rhodes Scholarship, additional evidence of the university's maturing reputation as "a real seat of learning."

Student publications provide a valuable index not only to student activities but also the publications and awards of faculty, the steady stream of guest speakers who made presentations, the fortunes of the athletic teams, and the varied issues and concerns that arose to occupy and at times roil the campus. The weekly *Thresher* was surprisingly balanced over the decades, and its pages reveal much of the character and ethos of the university. Its editorials and articles are almost uniformly respectful of President Lovett and supportive of his policies. Although by the 1930s he was older, busier, and seemed more remote from students—he was basically a reserved man, and, ensconced in his fourth-floor office in the administration building high above the Sallyport, he now tended to leave most of the day-to-day mechanics of running the university to the dean, bursar, and registrar—he maintained his great interest in students in the abstract. The student impression of Lovett's aloofness was captured in a limerick:

> A great man is Edgar O. Lovett
> His office has nothing above it.
> It is four stories high
> As close to the sky
> As William Ward Watkin could shove it.

Even so, Lovett actually remained more interested in student welfare and activities than his personal reserve suggested to students. At the beginning of each academic year he wrote a piece for the *Thresher* welcoming the students and preparing them for the challenge and excitement of university life.

But if the *Thresher* seemed sedate and responsible, the student humor magazine, the *Rice Owl*, which began publication in December 1922, is a stunning reminder that Rice was not a typical southern university. Lovett had long promoted and praised the maturity of the student body; he advocated student self-governance in a variety of ways, but especially so in matters of residential life and the operation of the honor system, and for that reason he had helped create the tone and environment that led the faculty in 1920 and then more formally in 1922 to outlaw fraternities and sororities, along with hazing, precisely because such organizations and behavior were antithetical to the sense of democratic community Lovett wanted to promote on campus— probably a carryover from his experience with the elitist eating clubs at Princeton. The board of trustees accepted Lovett's stewardship of the university in all respects. The trustees had been upset in 1926 by a slightly ribald serialized story in the *Thresher,* but they had sufficient confidence in Lovett to ask Dean Caldwell to handle all aspects of the controversy and not enter the fray themselves in some heavy-handed manner. Still, that Lovett and the administration allowed the publication of the *Rice Owl*—despite scattered protests about its "low literary standards"—without attempting to censor its pages is vivid testimony to Lovett's respect for the students and the Rice community. It also is a reflection of the freedom of action allowed a private university not sub-

ject to potentially narrow religious or state control. And it might well
have reflected attitudes Lovett had developed when, as an undergraduate at Bethany College, he had edited the college literary magazine that
also contained humorous and wry comments about fellow students and
society at large. Lovett was a careful wordsmith and especially appreciated limericks.

The *Rice Owl* in physical appearance reminds one of the *New Yorker*
magazine, with sleek, handsomely drawn covers. It was filled with car-
toons and jokes, but unlike the *New Yorker,* the *Rice Owl* contained no
long articles and only the briefest of editorial comments. But its humor
was witty, smart, filled with word play, puns, and double entendres.
Much of the humor made references to sex and alcohol, but in contrast
to some modern campus humor, it was not vulgar. The humor was fast-
paced, modern, edgy, and on the whole had an almost breathlessly ir-
reverent tone—a kind of sublimated rebellion that really accepted the
leadership of the university but poked fun at contemporary mores and
suggested that the students were on the cutting edge of societal change.
As the magazine itself said, "a college comic is not printed primarily
for mothers, but for big red-blooded college boys and girls who 'know
their onions.' " Satire, tongue-in-check comments, and disrespect for
stuffed-shirted authority became a hallmark of Rice student attitudes.

Such an outlook shaped the response of the Rice Dramatic Club
when spirited if not hysterical opposition developed among members
of the United Daughters of the Confederacy (UDC) after they learned
that the Rice thespians were planning to produce *Uncle Tom's Cabin* in
the fall of 1933. The city newspapers reported that leaders of the UDC
thought it outrageous that such a play would be staged on a southern college campus, and the UDC even filed a court suit, which the
judge promptly and sensibly threw out. The determined UDC then approached university officials, but Dean Caldwell—showing the respect
he and Lovett had for the students' sense of responsibility—without
applying any pressure, allowed the members of the Rice Dramatic Club
to decide how to respond. They decided to drop plans to perform *Uncle
Tom's Cabin* and instead performed Marion Short's now long-forgotten
*Rose of the Southland, or, the Spirit of Robert E. Lee,* a mocking cari-
cature of southern devotion to the Lost Cause. The UDC should have

left well enough alone! The *Thresher* praised the new production and considered it quite amazing given the short time the players had to prepare for it. "A club of this caliber," the *Thresher* editorialized, "is decidedly an asset to Rice Institute."

The Rice Dramatic Club was capable of far more than satire; it could also show unusual social awareness on the international level. This might be considered surprising on a southern university campus, but not for Rice. From the internationalism represented on its initial board of trustees (one of the six was from Switzerland and another from England) to the round-the-world trip of Lovett that enabled him to recruit an initial faculty that was thoroughly international in background, the Rice Institute had never been a provincial or even regional university. Lovett constantly talked about intellectual and scholarly matters in an international perspective, and he made sure that in addition to a cosmopolitan faculty, the mostly southern-born students would have access to a procession of visiting speakers who spoke with foreign accents and brought viewpoints from beyond the United States. The Rice Institute was located in the South, but it was intentionally not a *southern* university. Lovett articulated his internationalist position in 1927 while addressing the First Annual Conference on International Relations and American Diplomacy held at Louisiana State University in February 1927. "To me a very striking thing about the educated mind today," he said on that occasion, "is that almost without exception it begins as an individual mind and ends as an international mind. It thinks in terms of the planet, all the people that were and are and are to be. . . . It expands patriotism into a passion for humankind." That broad perspective he took pains to cultivate on the Rice campus.

Related to this, Lovett promoted religious tolerance in the context of the region. In a broader culture that was openly Christian, Lovett from the beginning had welcomed Jewish students (there were no Muslim or Hindu students in the South, so religious diversity primarily meant openness to Jewish students as well as those from various Christian backgrounds). We have already seen that one of the first trustees, and one of the most important at that, Emanuel Raphael, was a respected Jewish leader, and Lovett had invited Rabbi Henry Barnston of Congregation Beth Israel to give the 1926 baccalaureate sermon. Lovett spoke at local Jewish meetings as well, and it was largely as a response to his obvious respect for the Hebrew religion that Rice soon attracted a goodly number of Jewish students, who organized a Menorah Society within the first few years of the university's existence. Rice as early as the 1920s had a student body of whom approximately 4 percent were Jewish—not much compared to today, but given the size of the regional Jewish population, quite substantial; for example, when Lovett had been at Princeton, Jewish students had made up only about one percent of the student body, and that from a region in which the Jewish population was proportionately much larger. Unlike at many prestigious universities where Jewish students were banned from debating and literary societies, they fully participated in campus life at Rice.*

The visible presence of Jewish students, along with the presence after the mid-1920s of at least some Jewish faculty—at a time when there was still shocking prejudice again Jews in most of the northeastern universities—no doubt helps explains why the Rice Dramatic Club in 1937 presented a play entitled *Blood on the Moon*, a realistic portrayal of Nazi persecution of a Jewish family in Germany. The play was an effective "protest against political and religious intolerance," and the students had had the script read and approved in advance by two prominent Jewish civic leaders, physician Louis Daily and his ophthalmologist wife Ray K. Daily, who was also a member of the Houston school board. The play was also endorsed by the local chapter of the National Committee of Jews and Christians, whose local chairman was Rice trustee John T. Scott. Some fifteen months later the *Thresher* carried a news item concerning Nazi atrocities in Germany and a report that the faculty of the City College of New York had voted to drape a black flag over the German flag in "sympathy for the real Germany and faith in her early restoration."

In retrospect it is surprising to see how aware the campus community was of the emerging problem in Germany, and to see how very limited anti-Semitism seemed to be on this southern campus. The only

---

* At this time, anti-Jewish sentiment was especially strong at such northeastern institutions as Princeton, Dartmouth, Amherst, and Williams. The students at Williams in 1910 actually protested against the admission of any Jewish students.

firm indication of that malady occurs in the writing of two of the early English scholars, reflecting the anti-Semitism that existed in elite circles of English society. In July 1920 former professor Julian Huxley wrote to a former student inquiring: "I heard indirectly the other day that Rice is very full of Jews rather to the exclusion of other people, these days. Is this a fact?" The student's reply is missing. And on July 31, 1928, Huxley's former British assistant, Joseph Davies, wrote to the same student that "last year a Jew [underlined three times] gave the money to build a faculty club." But on the basis of available evidence, these appear to have been isolated prejudices at Rice, although for a short while in the early 1940s some conservative engineering faculty apparently discouraged Jewish students from taking engineering ostensibly because it was difficult to place them after graduation. There is no indication that Lovett knew of this before some Jewish citizens called attention to the practice, and the board instantly acted to prohibit such discouragement to would-be Jewish engineers.

In the late 1930s a young professor of German, Heinrich Meyer, a native and very nationalistic German scholar, gave several talks to campus organizations in which he justified Germany's need to expand and take over land in Czechoslovakia. Then in April 1938 he published a letter in the *Houston Press* attacking Jewish influence in Germany, arguing that it was the German people, not Hitler, who desired anti-Jewish legislation, and claiming that the Austrians wanted a Nazi government. A prominent Jewish layperson sent trustee chairman Baker a copy of the clipping and raised the issue of whether it was proper to have a faculty member advocate such anti-American and pro-fascist causes, but the correspondent made clear that he was only bringing up the issue for Baker to consider and did not want to make a "public issue" of it.

But a week later, the *Thresher* on April 29, 1938, published a strongly worded editorial condemning Meyer's pro-Hitler comments and his insinuations against German Jews. Ironically the first Rice student to die in what became World War II was Kurt Von Johnson, who had moved back to Germany in 1931 before finishing Rice and, as a German officer, had been killed in the Nazi invasion of Poland in September 1939. Meyer published an article in the next issue of the *Rice*

*Owl,* which earlier that year had morphed into the alumni magazine, again defending Germany's expansionism, and he dedicated the article to "the memory of my former student and friend, Kurt Von Johnson." This in-your-face defiance rankled many faculty, especially French professor Marcel Moraud, whose son John had been killed a few weeks earlier in France en route to the Western Front. Almost certainly Lovett disapproved of Meyer's views, though for the time he apparently respected the German professor's academic freedom to articulate even unsavory opinions. But Lovett's attitudes toward German excesses and Nazism were clear, a conviction reinforced by a letter he received from English professor Alan McKillop, an internationally renowned expert on eighteenth-century British literature, written on September 5, 1938, from London after a recent sixteen-day trip to Germany. McKillop reported that they returned with "deepest misgivings about the future. Up the Rhine and through the Black Forest we scarcely heard a single 'Heil Hitler,' but by the time we got to Berlin they had fairly turned on the heat. It was at Nuremberg that we felt the change; there we happened upon Herr Streicher [Julius Streicher was the founder and editor of the anti-Semitic newspaper *Der Stürmer,* which popularized vicious rat-like caricatures of Jews] addressing a great crowd in front of a synagogue that was being demolished with pomp and circumstance."

In less than two years Lovett would be approaching the U.S. War Department about establishing a Reserved Officers' Training Corp (ROTC) unit at Rice and making other preparations for the war he foresaw the nation soon to be engaged in. But for the meantime Lovett urged students to remain neutral. In his annual message printed in the first fall issue of the *Thresher* on September 14, 1939, Lovett stated that "what you think or should think about the war are questions we cannot answer for you." But the university's stance had to be neutral because the government had declared neutrality as the official policy of the nation, and "such neutrality can be preserved only through the strictest observance of it on the part of all of us." Still, Lovett understood that students could not "avoid hearing about the war, nor can you possibly banish it from your thinking, but you can resolve to go forward with the business that brings you here as though there was no war, and thereby become better equipped to serve the country with all your might in peace, and, if you must, in war." Lovett had no doubt, even in 1939, that a time would soon come when students would have to serve their nation in war.

Paradoxically, although Rice students and faculty in general were quite progressive on the issue of religious tolerance and not indifferent to international issues, southern racial prejudices went unchallenged on campus. As an outgrowth of the national Student Volunteer Movement, the Cranmer Club (an Episcopal organization) in the spring of 1932 sponsored a forum to "study the interracial hatred question," which was labeled a "very pertinent problem." But little came of this discussion. William Marsh Rice's charter in 1891 prescribed that the institute would be "for the white inhabitants of the City of Houston, and State of Texas," and no person in authority at Rice questioned that racial proscription. Segregation seemed a totally unexamined given of southern life, and the acquiescence to southern racial mores was the only significant indication of Rice's regional location. On several occasions the *Rice Owl,* the humor magazine, reprinted what at the time were called "darkey jokes," but, while demeaning, the humor did not involve vicious stereotypes. Lovett himself never addressed the issue but employed neither racist language nor racist stereotypes. German professor Lindsey Blayney had publicly protested the reemergence just after World War I of the Ku Klux Klan movement in Houston, but other than that, the issue of race appears not to have arisen on campus, an indication of the almost total pervasiveness among students, faculty, staff, and board members of the prevailing southern assumptions about the correctness of racial separation. It is instructive, for example, that while the faculty Committee on Examinations and Standings recommended to the board in 1927 and 1928 that there should not "be a rigid rule for the exclusion of" "students of special promise . . . from outside the state," the exclusion of blacks was not mentioned. The committee justified such a policy of accepting out-of-state students in contradistinction to the charter prescription on the grounds that such students are "of a direct benefit to the great majority who are and must continue to be local residents. The college is thus differentiated in a very real way from the public school system and its standing as a national institution, won with so great expense and difficulty, is not sacrificed." If that did not make the point, the committee concluded that "Such a policy can be defended as adding something of real value to the degree of every Houston boy and girl, and seems to the Committee not inconsistent with the purpose of the charter." In other words, the geographical limitation was secondary to the larger purpose of proving a quality education. (In 1930, for instance, there were seventy-seven students from eighteen other states and six students hailing from Mexico.) But no one on the committee or in any position of authority at Rice argued at the time that the proscription against admitting black students should be ignored for exactly the same reasons.*

The educational budget of the university fell to its Depression-era low in the academic year 1935–1936, then slowly began to improve. The income trend was positive but only gradually so over the next few years, and this, along with budget cuts, helped the board to realize that finances were less critical than they had originally thought. The entire university community had been buoyed at the end of 1934 when the trustees were surprised to learn that Eugene L. Bender, who had been a wealthy Houston capitalist (he had owned the Bender Hotel, where the Lovett family had once resided) and lumberman with no previously known relationship to Rice, left a bequest to the institute of $200,000. It took almost four years for the will to be probated, so the funds did not materialize until 1938; university officials decided to use the monies to help build a stand-alone library building, a project delayed by the beginning of the war. But when, in 1947, construction finally began on what became the Fondren Library, the Bender bequest funded what was at the time called the Science Reference Room. So even though the infusion of Bender money did not affect the annual educational budget, it was seen as a harbinger of things to come.

This renewal of economic optimism, combined with the financial restraint that Lovett had exercised, led the board in June 1936 to make a very positive decision. As Captain Baker explained it in a letter to

---

* The Rice board in 1963 initiated a legal procedure with the state attorney general to remove the formal restriction in the university charter against admitting nonwhite students, and after defeating in the courts a countersuit filed by a tiny group of disgruntled alumni, Rice admitted its first African American students in the fall of 1965.

President Lovett, "While conditions as they existed at the time of the reduction [of faculty salaries in 1932] have not improved as much as we all hoped for, yet notwithstanding this fact, I am happy to say that the Trustees at their meeting yesterday afternoon unanimously passed a resolution restoring these reductions, effective July 1, 1936." One can almost hear the collective sigh of relief; at a general meeting on June 24 the faculty unanimously passed a resolution "gratefully and sincerely thank[ing] the Board of Trustees for their very generous action in restoring the salary reductions." Now Lovett and the faculty could dare hope that progress would again soon be in the offing, although they could not know that another great World War lay between their time and the recovery of institutional momentum. Even so, the Bender gift along with the salary restoration, raised spirits. Then in 1936 came the first significant act of generosity to the university by a trustee. In that year William M. Rice, Jr., gave the institution stock in the Reed Roller Bit Company (an oil well equipment manufacturer) worth $330,000, and this gift resulted in an annual augmentation of the university's available funds of from $8000 to $12,000. In 1938 Arthur B. Cohn, who had been founder William M. Rice's secretary and, following the establishment of the actual university, had served as the assistant secretary to the board, in which capacity he oversaw the university's investment portfolio, died, and at his death Mr. Cohn willed the Rice Institute some $100,000. In 1939 the Association of Rice Alumni once more began a program to raise funds to build a much-needed classroom building on campus, a campaign that had begun in 1929 but soon stalled. (The alumni also in 1939 urged the university to begin an aggressive public relations department to raise the visibility of Rice—its promise and its needs—both locally and beyond.)

Yet still these much-needed gifts did not really solve the university's long-term income problem, although they lessened the sense of crisis. Captain Baker still hoped to find ways to bring in more funds. On April 16, 1941, he sent a letter to the other trustees informing them that he had asked lawyers to see if there was a way to go to the courts to get permission so to amend the university charter that tuition might be charged. The rationale for the charter revision was that "the general object of the trust will be greatly hampered and in part defeated unless the change is made." But as in the case of several other issues, this proposal was soon overtaken by the course of the war and unforeseen enhancements of the university endowment that made the issue moot for more than a decade afterward. Actually, a faculty committee in 1928 had recommended that most students should pay tuition, with generous scholarships for those less affluent, but this recommendation went nowhere. Philanthropist and civic promoter Will Hogg had even suggested to the board in May and June 1929 that it appeal to the city for funds. The board never acted on his idea.

President Lovett's family seemed to be thriving in the Depression decade. Of course Mrs. Lovett was still bedridden, but she maintained her positive outlook, and every evening Dr. Lovett came home to have dinner with her in her bedroom and discuss the events of the day. Their daughter Adelaide Baker was now a mother and active in social and intellectual circles, playing a prominent and progressive role in the life of the city. She often served as hostess when President Lovett needed one for university functions. Older son Malcolm had graduated from Harvard Law School in 1924 (and that same year joined the law firm then named Baker, Botts, Parker & Garwood), married Martha Wicks at Christ Episcopal Church on June 4, 1929, and in 1938 become a partner in the prestigious firm today known as BakerBotts.

By this time both Adelaide and Malcolm were parents themselves, and grandchildren brought a special joy to the Lovett suite in the Plaza Hotel. When the children came to visit and rapped the door knocker, Dr. Lovett would open the door with a slight bow and say, "Come in, my dears." Mrs. Lovett, confined to her bed, especially enjoyed having the grandchildren bring their energy and laughter into her bedroom. The grandchildren, decades later, recalled "Mother Lovett's" sense of humor and the gentle, patient nature of "Father Lovett," who intently watched them play, had a robust laugh, and, indulgent grandfather that he was, gave them nickels to buy chewing gum. He loved ingenuous mechanical toys, showed them puzzles, did tricks with string—cat's cradle was a favorite. On occasion he would take a grandchild up on the roof of the Plaza Hotel and point out the constellations. In a few years the older grandchildren, gathered at the apartment for a Saturday lunch with their grandparents, were expected to converse in French, and "Father Lovett" assigned them poems and literary snippets to memorize and recite. Later, when the grandchildren themselves became college students, "Father Lovett" was deeply interested in their studies, their opinions, and their life plans.

The apartment in the Plaza, in addition to thousands of books, contained many artifacts from the round-the-world trip and reproductions of famous artworks on the walls, like the *Winged Victory of Samothrace*, a reminder of Dr. Lovett's love of ancient Greek language and art. On Sunday afternoons both elder Lovetts enjoyed listening to the opera broadcasts on their large radio, a handsome set made of dark wood, with an arched top, and with the front speaker covered with a brown and golden woven material. Theirs was a cultured and gentle life.*

But warning signs soon began to develop with the Lovetts' son Alex, although no one recognized them at the time. Alex always admired his older brother and sought to emulate him, but Alex was neither the student nor athlete that Malcolm was. Impulsive, temperamental, difficult to discipline, this younger son often had trouble staying focused on a single task or project, and he was easily frustrated. Alex's academic record at The Hill School, a prestigious college preparatory private school in Pottstown, Pennsylvania, was mediocre at best, but he insisted that he wanted to go to Harvard as Malcolm had done. Even at The Hill School, Alex often grew impatient when learning came hard, and this impatience soon left him discouraged and tempted him to drink too much. Already he felt oppressed by the success of the Lovett men in his family—father, uncle, and brother—and by what he assumed to be parental expectations for him, though in truth it was in his own expectations that he would fail. In August 1931, when he was twenty, Alex wrote revealingly to his sister Adelaide about having visited his Grandmother Lovett in Cleveland, where her other son, Guy D., a prominent dentist, practiced. "I often wonder what she thinks about having two such fine men who excel in their professions; she must be proud of them. Malcolm and I shall have to be big successes to make Mother & Dad happy in their old age. In the past few months," Alex confessed,

* Although it would be hard to imagine today, Dr. Lovett's private home telephone number (Hadley 4644, or H-4644) was then listed in the city telephone book.

"this thought has taken a firmer hold on me, and has made me work harder. Despite my mental heritage, learning comes hard for me." Alex was already putting almost unbearable pressure upon himself.

That desire to excel, to match the achievements of his brother, ill-advisedly drove him to apply to Harvard. Again he found the academic work extremely demanding, and although he did moderately well in his classes and in football his first year, in his second year his grades fell, he was demoted to the third team, and he injured his knee. College remained a struggle, and then after graduation, ignoring the advice of his teachers, friends, and his parents, Alex insisted on going to law school and subsequently graduated from the University of Colorado. Coming back to Houston determined to emulate his brother's success, he met another disappointing failure—he could not obtain a position at Malcolm's firm, now called Baker, Botts, Andrews & Wharton. Stubbornly unwilling to practice at another firm—and apparently unwilling to accept what one of his doctors later termed his "lack of capacity"—Alex then began a partnership with a friend and tried his hand in the oil business. This too resulted in failure, and in his disappointment Alex sought escape by excessive socializing and drink. Soon he was living beyond his means, was depending on $150 monthly provided by his father, and found himself reduced to having to board with his parents. Then his life came crashing during the week on May 29, 1939, when he effectively had a nervous breakdown, marked by nonstop talking, inability to either concentrate or sleep, and striking out angrily at those around him. Something had to be done, so older brother Malcolm and brother-in-law Walter Browne Baker took him by train to Baltimore. The trip was an ordeal, as Malcolm described in a letter to President Lovett on June 3. Along the way Alex was extremely talkative and excitable, uncooperative, and at times wanted to fight Browne and then others. After talking to doctors at the University of Maryland hospital and finding out that they did not have the proper facilities, they took Alex to the well-known Sheppard and Enoch Pratt Hospital in Towson, a suburb just to the north of Baltimore. This facility, established in 1891 and situated on a former 340-acre farm of rolling hills and trees, was one of the most highly respected psychiatric hospitals in the nation.

It must have been excruciatingly difficult for Dr. and Mrs. Lovett to read each week the detailed letters that came from Dr. Ross McC. Chapman, the superintendent of the hospital. In clinical language Dr. Chapman described the status of Alex, and his accounts would have upset any parent, especially when it was the youngest child and the one who had been born with such hope for good health in 1911. Imagine the worry and heartache that a letter such as Dr. Chapman wrote on June 13, 1939, must have caused his elderly parents: "Your son . . . has been exceedingly confused. He is pretty much out of contact a good deal of the time. He hears voices constantly. He is not able to refrain from giving himself over completely to this experience so that his grasp on reality is rather tenuous. He does not show any particular interest in anything which goes on about him, spends much of his time in his own room and becomes quite upset when we make any effort to get him interested in things outside. He refuses to keep his clothing on a fair share of the time, becomes quite upset when we try to get him to do so. He frequently waves his arms around forcefully and in a rather threatening fashion. . . . He frequently strikes himself, particularly on the legs." The hospital doctors diagnosed Alex as manic-depressive (today the more common term is *bipolar*), a disorder heavily biological in origin usually, but in about 20 percent of the cases more a result of psychological stresses that are a response to one's social-cultural situation. Alex may well have inherited from his mother a biological vulnerability that was triggered by the pressure he felt to measure up to the prominence of his father and older brother.

Treatment at Sheppard Pratt followed the best practice at the time: Alex's routine consisted of hearty meals, plenty of sleep, and exercise. There were then no drugs tailored to address the underlying physiochemical imbalances that produced manic-depressive behavior. Slowly he began to improve, came to enjoy strolling along the attractively rolling hills of the hospital campus, and even got to the point where he was allowed to go into nearby Towson to attend movies. By early 1941 Dr. Chapman's letters reveal that Alex was making good progress; he still exhibited resentment toward his family, felt insecure, feared that tensions would arise should he go home, but understood that his family would be helpful and supportive in every way they could. He acknowledged that he himself was the cause of all his problems and felt badly that he had let his family down, but he increasingly came to look forward to returning to Houston. He did not want to live in the Plaza Hotel with his parents anymore and thought it best that he not live with his brother's or sister's families; instead, he wanted to get a little apartment on his own and slowly return to productive life, although he had an uneasy feeling that he might get sick again. Dr. Chapman's last letter to Dr. Lovett, on April 14, 1941, reported that Alex was eager to go home and understood that his apprehensions in the past had not turned out so badly as he feared, hence he was quite hopeful about going home.*

As in those years at the beginning of the century when Lovett had dealt stoically with the death of his daughter and the breakdown of his wife and found relief in burying himself in his work, so too here as the nation and university again approached World War, Lovett remained almost totally engaged in the affairs of his office. Apparently much earlier in life he had learned to focus on his work and distance or isolate himself from his emotions while so engaged. Perhaps this is why many people thought Lovett reserved or aloof—only an emotional flatness enabled him to function so effectively as university president while his wife was bedridden and now his son was hospitalized. Nothing that he said or did—or did not do—hinted at the family difficulties that rent the contentment of his personal life. Most people knew nothing of these personal problems. It is probable that Lovett's religious faith also helped sustain him through these trying times. As he said in reference to another issue in his 1933 matriculation address to the class of 1937, "The great issues of life bring men to their knees." Lovett's apparent inner peace was noticed and noted by others. A Presbyterian minister from San Antonio commented to him that "You are an intellectually and spiritually wealthy person," while an old acquaintance from Princeton wrote him in 1948 that he was glad Lovett was still alive "in spirit and in body." Whatever the source of his inner peace, religious conviction or what psychiatrists call isolation of affect—essentially compart-

---

* Alex did subsequently return to Houston and eventually became quite prosperous running a bail-bonding company. He proved to be a shrewd investor as well, but he chose to essentially isolate himself from his prominent Houston family.

mentalizing his emotional life apart from his professional life—Lovett maintained his equanimity throughout the stresses he faced.

There remained severe budgetary worries at the university, although the situation had improved over that at the beginning of the decade. At a far slower pace new faculty were still being hired to replace retirements, with fresh faces such as physicist Tom Bonner and historian David Potter enlivening classes and campus discussion. The alumni were discussing ways of raising additional funds, a new high-profile football coach, Jess Neely, promised greater athletic successes in the future, and the university, under Lovett's direction, was slowly but surely shifting to a wartime mode. In March 1941 Lovett informed the board that an official of the federal government had inspected the campus and recommended that the trustees "install a Naval Officers Training Corps." This would require that a small, rather Spartan building be constructed for the exclusive use of the ROTC students. Lovett requested and the board appropriated $18,000 to build and furnish the facility, and Lovett proceeded to file an official application for the ROTC unit.

Shortly thereafter Lovett made official something he had privately broached with the trustees. On May 14, 1941, Lovett addressed a letter to Captain Baker in his capacity as president of the board of trustees. "I was born in the spring of 1871," began Lovett. "That date affords sufficient reason for the action I hereby take in earnestly requesting you and your associates . . . of the Board of trustees of Rice Institute, to relieve me of the duties of the office to which I was called in late autumn of 1907." Lovett continued, "If it should meet the pleasure of the trustees, I should be glad to continue in the discharge of my administrative responsibilities until they shall have selected a successor." When Lovett's letter was made public, it had the effect of a bombshell. The end of a memorable era in the life of the university was near.

# CHAPTER EIGHT

# WAR, STRESS, CHANGE, AND PROMISE

ONLY EDGAR ODELL LOVETT truly understood how difficult it had
been for him, in May 1941, to offer his resignation, effective upon the
choice of a successor, of the presidency of the Rice Institute. For thirty-
four years, almost half his life, he had dedicated his considerable energies and intellect to planning, administering, and leading the university through good times and bad, and it must have been hard for him
to contemplate life without Rice at the forefront of his mind. He confessed as much to former Harvard president A. Lawrence Lowell, who
had written Lovett on June 24 to say that he was "sorry to hear that
you are retiring, although I do not question the wisdom of doing so.
You have so much to be proud of," Lowell continued, "that you ought
not to regret leaving the position, & yet it is very hard not to when one
has made it, as you have." Lovett much appreciated Lowell's words and
admitted to him that resigning "was a hard [step] to take." In a reflective mood, Lovett confided that "Although I have never doubted the
wisdom of it, yet I thought the mere thought of giving up would kill
me, but I am already well over the worst of it, and now my one desire is
to help find the next man, give him as good a running start as possible,
and then get completely out of his way if such a course should seem
best." In his letter resigning the presidency he had requested that he be
allowed to retain his membership on the board of trustees "so long as I
may be of service."

Lovett's letter recalled his initial appointment and those glorious days
in the fall of 1912, when they had all been involved in founding and
"dedicating the institution to the purposes of the founder," though of
course it was Lovett far more than William Marsh Rice who developed
the purpose of the Rice Institute. "I had great faith then," stated Lovett,
"and I have abiding and absolute confidence now, in the ability and determination of the trustees to carry on single-heartedly the building of

this house of learning in the memory of the founder, for the welfare of mankind, and to the greater glory of God." As was typical of Lovett, that generous characterization of the trustees' activities was meant less to be taken as a description of past behavior and more to be understood as an implicit exhortation for exemplary action in the future. Captain James A. Baker replied to Lovett's letter on behalf of all the trustees, expressing their reluctant acceptance of his retirement and their happiness that he would continue on the board itself and in fact in the presidency until his successor could be found. "Your wise counsel and sage advice so frankly and freely given to your associate trustees especially in the early days of the institute, were of inestimable value to your associates. They are delighted that . . . your advice and counsel will not cease upon your retirement." Then Baker quoted remarks that the president of Princeton had presented at Rice in 1922, upon the anniversary of the university's first decade, at which he fulsomely praised Dr. Lovett. Baker closed his letter by saying that "It is with a feeling of pride and pleasure that we cordially endorse this estimate of your accomplishments, which in our judgment is as true now as it was when originally uttered, and is a true measure of our sense of obligation and gratitude, and our devotion to you." Whatever tensions that might have arisen between Lovett and the board during the financially trying days of the 1930s were papered over in these parting words. Lovett tended always to look at future potential rather than dwell on past failure.

Everyone was vaguely aware of Lovett's age, but for most it was simply impossible to think of the Rice Institute without Dr. Lovett. And though his resignation was ultimately inevitable, it—like the death of an elderly parent—still caught people by surprise. Most people in the Rice community were thunderstruck by the announcement of his resignation. The *Houston Chronicle* and the *Houston Post* carried front-page articles on the announcement, and both sketched Lovett's long history with the university since from before its opening. Both articles were respectful, their tone represented by a comment attributed to bursar John McCants. "No one knows better than his colleagues how completely [Lovett] has devoted his life to the development of the institution. His achievements speak for themselves." The *Thresher*, the student newspaper, dismissed what it labeled "the unthinking few who criticized the president for his seeming isolation" and said that even they realized "the great loss" when Lovett decided to step down. "He is the life force of a great university," the student paper concluded. The faculty at their next scheduled meeting on May 23, 1941, unanimously passed a resolution expressing "their high appreciation of his services to the Rice Institute." From individual faculty came a number of heartfelt encomiums. No one had known Lovett longer than architect William Ward Watkin, who wrote Lovett the morning the daily papers published the news. "Your decision announced today comes with intense regret to each of us," wrote the man who had been sent by Ralph Adams Cram to supervise the construction of the initial campus buildings and remained to teach architecture and practice the craft the rest of his life. "Out of the marsh and swamps of this campus you have brought beauty and fineness at every step along the way. Into its building you have woven your life with all its clearness and kindliness. All that we see about us is yours in every sense, creative, nurturing, and fulfilling toward an enduring meaning."

Prickly and self-important Marcel Moraud of the French department also wrote Lovett that morning, having heard the decision reported on the radio the night before. Moraud recalled his first meeting with Lovett in Paris at the Hotel de Saint Péres years before and said that he had never regretted his decision "to come and cast my lot with the Rice Institute. It has always been with the greatest pleasure and confidence that I have gone up to your 'tower' to ask your advice and discuss whatever problems which might have arisen. I have always appreciated your frankness and your courtesy and also your personal interest in all of us." Here was the voice of an older member of the faculty who had developed a relationship with the president much earlier in the institution's history. Unfortunately, some of the younger faculty and most of the students knew Lovett only as a soft-spoken, dignified, courtly, remote "great man," who almost always wore a three-piece suit and a hat, sometimes with colored or striped shirts, high-topped shoes with hooks for the laces, and stood and walked with uncommon erectness, his shoulders thrown back. Usually in his lapel he wore his Légion d'honneur rosette from the French government. One student from the time remarked that she had never seen the president smile, and there were stories about him coming to campus one day after a vaunted football victory only to find that the students had locked the gates in order to give themselves a holiday. Lovett neither scolded nor smiled but, ever proper, and holding his bowler hat with his hand, he slipped through the hedges and continued his stately stride to his office above the Sallyport.

One of the most eloquent tributes came from English professor Alan D. McKillop. The famed specialist in eighteenth-century British literature lamented that in the rush of daily life few of us acknowledge "personal relationships too valuable and too significant to be carelessly taken for granted," but the news of Lovett's resignation, which he had just read in the morning paper, brought McKillop up straight. The shocking news "set him to thinking anew of the great premises on which our daily life at the Rice Institute is founded—your unflinching adherence, through good days and through bad, to the highest standards of academic life, and your generous confidence—generous, but never, I think, blindly or lightly given—in those whom you trusted to uphold those standards. . . . The twenty years I have spent here have put me greatly in your debt professionally and personally." Lovett appreciated these words, replying to McKillop that his letter "had brought me great joy, at a time of sore need, if any measure of equilibrium between resolution and emotion were to be maintained." Lovett revealed his close identification with the faculty with whom he had worked for all those years, admitting to McKillop that "At the moment I don't see how I could ever live away from my present associates." For Lovett and the handful of senior faculty, the Rice Institute was a close community of deep common commitment.

Other letters came from civic leaders. Miss Ima Hogg, philanthropist, public citizen, and cultural leader extraordinaire, who had been the anonymous donor making possible the appearance of Maurice Ravel as a Rice lecturer and performer, wrote Lovett that "as a citizen of Houston and Texas I have observed with pride and appreciation the development of the Institute into its present distinguished phase. While we are aware of your wise and splendid leadership, only time, I think, will reveal the true significance of your great contribution to our community and state." Somewhat later financier Jesse H. Jones, at the moment serving as the U.S. secretary of commerce, sent his appreciative remarks: "By your work in creating and building Rice, and by the great dignity of your personal life, you have given Houston an atmosphere of culture in which we can all take pride." Surely this avalanche of praise made Lovett feel good about his life work, but he well knew that much yet remained to be done, especially as the threat of war loomed ever larger. The string of accolades reached a highpoint for Lovett on November 7, 1941, when he was presented the Rice Alumni Medal for Distinguished Service. In remarks read on that occasion for either the deceased James Baker or perhaps William M. Rice, Jr., the writer—who had obviously known and worked with Lovett since the establishment of the university—stated that "During all the years I have been closely associated with Dr. Lovett, and I have known no man with higher ideals nor have known one more conscientious about his work [on a similar occasion financier Jesse Jones called Lovett the most rigid self-disciplinarian he had ever known] . . . he has striven at all times for what would enhance the value of our Institution. I hope the next statue on the Rice campus will be one of this great and good man." There is now (2007) one being planned.

In 1941 there was no doubt in Lovett's mind of the responsibility of the university and all its members to stand ready to serve the nation; his attitudes toward national service had not changed since his earliest days at Princeton and later during the crisis of World War I. While in his 1939 matriculation address Lovett had admonished the students to maintain a stance of neutrality and devotedly go about their studies, by the fall of 1940 in his matriculation address he was preparing the students for almost certain future involvement in war. Lovett told the incoming students that "We are not forsaking our ideals of the good, the beautiful, and the true. Indeed, we are proposing to pursue these ideals with greater zeal than ever. But we wish to make them immediately effective in the service of the government. And this is our strong desire, because we have not the slightest doubt of the national emergency in which we find ourselves." For this reason Lovett explained that he had made application to establish a Reserve Officers Training Corps (ROTC) infantry unit at Rice and stood ready to assist the cause in any way appropriate. "It is not of our own choosing," he explained, "but we are obliged, every one of us, obliged to get ready for service to the national defense. To that end, we mean, as rapidly as the government can make use of our facilities, to offer supplementary training. This determination is dominated by the idea that he who is unwilling to do his part in the service of his country is utterly unworthy of his country." In May 1941 the ROTC unit was established at Rice, and by that fall 107 first- and second-year male students had been accepted into the program.

The catalogue for the 1942–1943 academic year (which came out in the early spring of 1942) had a special note added at the beginning that explained a variety of "war emergency changes." Among other things, the commencement exercises for that year were moved one week earlier, to May 31–June 1, 1942, both to facilitate those who needed summer jobs and to make it easier to attend summer school. The actual academic year would end on May 2 for senior engineering and architecture students so those graduates would be able to "enter the national service" somewhat earlier. But for the academic year beginning in the fall of 1942, senior courses in engineering and architecture would be accelerated so that those students could complete all coursework by April 3; their diplomas would be granted approximately two months later at the regular commencement. Provisions were made for both rising seniors and juniors to receive credit for two courses taken at an "approved summer school" that would allow even earlier graduation, and rising seniors were to be allowed to register for an additional course at Rice. Juniors who left before their senior year to enroll in dental, law, or medical schools would have their Rice bachelor's degrees granted after they had earned their professional degrees. Other students, including all freshmen and sophomore students, would have their schedules unaltered, although the catalogue did state that future events might require yet unforeseen changes in subsequent years. No other Rice catalogue was published during the duration of the war.

In addition to the Rice students who were in the ROTC program (and their numbers swelled to 188 in 1943), President Lovett was notified in the spring of 1943 that Rice had been chosen to host a Navy V-12 program that trained previously enlisted men to become naval engineers.

These 342 men had not applied to Rice initially; they were already in the Navy and were assigned to Rice for accelerated, around-the-calendar-training in specially designed classes. These men were given all the campus housing (civilian men students now, like the women, had either to live at home or find board elsewhere), were paid, wore uniforms, and followed strict military routine, although they were permitted to participate in every aspect of college life, including intramural sports. The school year was divided into three sixteen-week semesters, and the Navy dictated the curriculum of the V-12 students, although regular Rice students were allowed to enroll in the naval engineering classes if they wished. Many of the V-12 students were not as academically able as the regular Rice students, and this caused some tension on campus, but most of them worked extremely hard and completed their programs (which actually required fewer credits than a Rice degree called for). Speaking at the first commissioning ceremony for naval students in October 1944, Lovett acknowledged that they had "had to bend cheerfully to duty, discipline, and drudgery day in and day out, the whole year round." Many of these students returned after the war to take several more courses and thereby earned their Rice diplomas.

Lovett seems to have learned a lot from his disastrous experience with wartime academics in 1917–1918, and during World War II none of the difficulties of adapting the campus to military needs led to protest as it had during World War I. Perhaps it was to forestall any such discontent as had arisen in 1917 that he prepared students for potential problems in his September 16, 1942, matriculation address: "I have understanding and sympathy with you in these difficulties that you face this autumn. We face the same difficulties individually and as an institution. We must see them through, perhaps only day by day, but see them through we will. To that end, by and large, we are trying to steer a middle course. In your interests and in the interests of this institution we are trying to steer a course between living and working as though there were no war, and working and living as though there were nothing but war." Two desires motivated them all, he said, both "to serve humanity, the country, and the United Nations" in winning the war and to then see that freedom and justice triumphed in the peace to follow. And in patriotic language that reflected the moral intensity of the era,

Lovett apparently spoke for himself and most of the Rice community when he said that "we are ready and willing, every man and woman of us, willing and ready to die to the last one of us to win this war." By September 1943 this rhetoric had risen to the level of Lovett's seeing the students' role in winning the war as part of a divine mission. "For my own part," Lovett wrote in the *Thresher*, "I believe in the Providential ordering of all this war business. You, the students of this institution, are to be individual instruments in shaping the destiny of your country and of the freedom-loving nations of the world. It is a higher mission than most men have had." Such language sounds over the top in an academic setting today, but it was common as men of good will faced German and Japanese aggression in the midst of World War II.

There were a number of minor adjustments and developments on campus during the war. The *Thresher* reported in its January 16, 1942, issue that O. D. Wyatt, Jr., of Fort Worth, who had earned his B.A. from Rice in 1939, was killed in the Philippines, the first Rice graduate casualty of the war. Of lesser moment, in March 1942 it was announced that in order to meet the requirements of the sugar rationing program, the cooks in the dining hall kitchen would start serving only presweetened tea because it took less sugar to sweeten warm tea. The university participated in the development of a citywide civil defense plan that would go into effect in the advent of an air raid. A target range was established on campus for the use of the naval students, and faculty and staff struggled to meet the increased curricular needs that resulted from the presence on campus of the naval personnel. The U.S. Office of Education sponsored evening vocational courses at Rice open to the public in such areas as industrial drafting, electronics and radio, and shop mathematics, obviously intended to assist the war effort. On June 1, 1944, Lovett announced to the student body that the Spiritual Preparedness Committee of the Office of Civilian Defense had sent out a request to all colleges and universities that they have a moment of prayer for the Allied military forces on the day the soon-expected invasion of the European Continent began. Seven days later Lovett praised the students for the "promptness, earnestness, simplicity, and decision" demonstrated by the "response of the students—Navy and civilian alike—to the bugler's summons" at 11:00 a.m. on June 7, the beginning of D-Day.

President Lovett was constantly corresponding with various government offices to try to get academic deferments for graduate students and faculty, but on occasion his statements as to the special qualifications of faculty in particular only made them sound better candidates for one or more government/military research laboratories. A number of faculty did leave for wartime research appointments, and, in response to increased federal funding—through the Office of Scientific Research and Development—for military-related research on university campuses, faculty like physicist Harold A. Wilson received grants for research that had to be kept secret. Similar developments were occurring at research universities across the nation, and federal funding would grow in subsequent decades to eventually dominate the support of scientific research on university campuses. Rice faculty like Wilson and Claude Heaps did research related to the development of the atomic bomb. The Rice connection to that weapon came full circle on August 9, 1945, at 11:02 a.m. when an atomic bomb—nicknamed "Fat Man"—was dropped on the coastal city of Nagasaki at the far eastern end of the Japanese archipelago. The bombardier was Rice graduate Kermit K. Beahan, class of 1940, who had been a member of the Rice football team.

Of course world events dominated the news and the experiences of everyone in the Rice community in the first half of the decade of the 1940s, but at the local level there were deaths, developments, and decisions—some of which were beyond the notice of students and alumni—that were to have a major impact on the future history of the Rice Institute. One technical legal issue was easily taken care of. The Rice Institute had been chartered on May 18, 1891, for a fifty-year period. In anticipation of the end of this term, the trustees on April 23, 1941, called a special meeting to propose extension of the charter for another half century, and this proposal was filed in the Texas attorney general's office on May 19, 1941, just in time to preserve the legal existence of the Rice Institute. Of course, over everything hung the eminent departure of Dr. Lovett, as soon as a successor could be chosen, but the trustees found that practically every distinguished scientist (and it was assumed that the next president would also be a scientist) was too engaged in important wartime research work to contemplate assuming a presidency, so the search was in effect put on hold.

Then on August 2, 1941, eighty-four-year-old James A. Baker, who had been chairman of the Rice trustees since the beginning, died after more than fifty years of service on behalf of Rice. The next most senior trustee, William M. Rice, Jr. (Will Rice), who had served since 1899, was named to replace Baker without any apparent discussion or objection—it just seemed automatically the thing for the cautious board to do. At the same board meeting Benjamin Botts Rice, who had been on the board since 1901, was elevated to replace Will Rice as vice president of the board. But of course this left a vacancy, and at the subsequent October board meeting Will Rice suggested that each of the remaining trustees provide a list of about six names to be considered. Finally at the May 1942 meeting the board unanimously selected Harry C. Hanszen to become a trustee. Hanszen, who at age fifty-eight was fifteen years younger than the trustee average, had spent two years at the University of Chicago and was considered a brilliant oilman. His comparative youth and vision began the remaking of the Rice board of trustees.

In addition to the membership changes on the board, the financial outlook began to improve. Captain Baker by his will left his stately home, "The Oaks," to Rice, with the understanding that the proceeds from its sale would underwrite scholarships, fellowships, and prizes and be used to augment faculty salaries. The home had been built in 1910 in the style of Frank Lloyd Wright, and it sat on a ten-acre site (at 2310 Baldwin, occupying the whole block between Baldwin and Bagby just west of the intersection with Hadley) surrounded by eighty live oaks. In May 1942 the board finalized the sale of the large and stately home for $62,500 to the M. D. Anderson Foundation, which would soon begin its cancer hospital there, later to become a preeminent institution within the just emerging Texas Medical Center across Main Street from Rice. Far more important than the Baker bequest was an idea hatched in the mind of Judge Roy Hofheinz, a Rice graduate, who in his court had the complicated disposition of the estate of oilman W. R. Davis, involving the Rincon oil field in Starr County, Texas. Indebtedness and high corporate taxes meant that no company wanted to purchase the property, and Hofheinz realized that if a nonprofit institution—exempt from corporate taxes—bought it, the potential payoff could be enormous. Hofheinz—who his entire life fit the Texas stereotype of the wheeler-dealer and later built the Astrodome—contacted another legendary Texas wheeler-dealer, construction magnate George R. Brown (who had attended Rice for two years) and Humble Oil Company president Harry C. Wiess and proposed to them that they persuade the conservative Rice board to purchase the oilfield. Their proposal included the idea that several friends of Rice would contribute $500,000 toward the purchase, but after the banks insisted on a minimum price of $1 million, the board was convinced of the reasonableness of the university itself using $500,000 of its own funds—it went to the district court to get approval from the Texas attorney general to spend from its endowment the necessary amount. The proposal was extraordinarily complex and involved out-of-town banks, the Internal Revenue Service, and teams of lawyers, but finally it was done. The oil field was so productive that Rice's share of its income paid back the original investment and the debts by 1946 and over the next few decades brought tens of millions of dollars to Rice.

Lovett's involvement in this transaction is unknown, although as a member of the board he was obviously involved in the decision. The board was clearly impressed with the vision and competence of George Brown, and after trustee Robert Lee Blaffer died (on October 22) in the midst of the Rincon deal, the board moved quickly to name Brown a trustee in January 1943. Blaffer had been the youngest member of the board when appointed, but on June 25, 1944, came another death, eighty-six-year-old trustee chairman William M. Rice, Jr. The trustees quickly appointed Harry Wiess, who had, like Brown, impressed them with the sagacity of his advice. Lovett may well have played an important role in the choice of Wiess, a native of Beaumont, Texas, for he had taught Wiess years before at Princeton. In fact, when one December Wiess was delayed a day or two returning to Princeton following Christmas vacation because of a bad snowstorm in the South, Lovett had not reported his absence, knowing that, according to a faculty decision in 1904, students were supposed to sign in on the day the Christmas break ended or be subject to disciplinary action. After coming to Rice, Lovett in 1912 received a letter from Wiess in which the former student first wished his old professor success in his "hope for the establishment of a new Princeton" in Texas and then assured

Lovett that "I shall never forget your convenient 'lapse' of memory on one occasion which meant a great deal to me at that time." Lovett in subsequent years could not have been ignorant of Wiess's rise to the presidency of Humble Oil and must have been gratified by his leadership in the Rincon enterprise. Lovett certainly knew that Wiess was already a charter trustee of Princeton and a term member of the Corporation of the Massachusetts Institute of Technology (MIT)—evidence of his distinction. But Lovett could not have known in 1944 how substantially the leadership of the three new board members—Hanszen, Brown, and Wiess—would affect the affairs of the university in the decades to come.

One dramatic development was clear, however, and that was the generosity of former board member Will Rice. When his will was probated, the trustees were flabbergasted to learn that he had given the Rice Institute some $2 million, by far the largest gift in the university's history and the first really significant gift by a trustee. This gift alone brought an annual income of $100,000 to the university, and almost simultaneously the discovery of oil on university lands in Louisiana resulted in royalty payments of another $100,000 annually. These new sources of income, along with that of the Rincon field, meant that by early 1945 the disposable income of the university had increased by 50 percent over the past few years. The energetic new board members, along with Lovett, were fully aware that a new era was opening up for Rice, heralding a resumption after two comparatively stagnant decades of the original ambitious trajectory toward academic distinction.

Though in ways President Lovett must have been wearied by his stewardship of the university and the continued infirmity of his wife, there must also have been moments of real exhilaration in the fall of 1942 and then 1943. But seldom do periods of unalloyed joy last for long, and in that very autumn when the promise of the Rincon property began to be understood, an ugly faculty dispute arose. Its origins, ironically, lay in the very cosmopolitanism of the Rice faculty. Heinrich Meyer, a German national with his doctorate from the University of Freiberg, had been appointed instructor of German in 1930, and he had proven to be an energetic member of the faculty, publishing widely and participating actively in such local organizations as the faculty's

Historical Society (to which he presented at least five papers and served a term as secretary) and the Houston Philosophical Society. He published in Germany a long novel about a German immigrant to antebellum Texas, and he organized a German conversation club and led the students in singing German songs. But he had as well an irritating aspect of his personality. He enjoyed poking at people verbally, needling them, making "cracks" as he called them just to see how people would respond. Some faculty enjoyed bantering with him, others found him more than annoying. He took a critical stance toward many things and often commented acerbically on aspects of life in America that failed to meet his standards. Staunchly conservative in politics, he despised Franklin Roosevelt and the New Deal and never hesitated to voice his opinions. A highly nationalistic German, he often defended Germany's "need" to take over additional land from weaker European nations, defended (in 1933 to the Kiwanis Club in downtown Houston) Hitler for being "a man of convictions, [who] can make the people think that it is not so bad to be a German," and disparaged the influence of the Jews in Germany. Such comments brought local notoriety, as we have seen (he was even the subject of a scolding editorial in the *Thresher* in 1938), and earned him the enmity of colleagues Marcel Moraud from France and Radoslav Tsanoff from Bulgaria—Moraud lost a son in the French army in 1939, and Tsanoff's dislike of Germany had even been noted by Julian Huxley in 1915. Meyer's combative personality meant that he seldom hesitated from making caustic comments and thereby provoked his enemies to speak sharply to him. By 1940 Meyer felt that many of his colleagues disliked him, regarded him with suspicion, somehow almost blamed him for the German raids on London, and he began to feel depressed. At this moment he temporarily considered expatriation back to Germany but never followed through with his application. He heard rumors that the Rice administration wanted him to desist from ever discussing politics in class or with students, but he later said he went to bursar John McCants and received no such advice; he was, however, asked to stop leading the students in German folksongs. Clearly Meyer was an unhappy, conflicted, tormented man—people who knew him recalled decades later that he was "an odd duck"—who was becoming a man without a country, because by now he was disillusioned with the virulent anti-Semitism in Germany and other aspects of German political and cultural life. And it was in this context that the Federal Bureau of Investigation (FBI) began to question Meyer's colleagues and acquaintances about his activities and attitudes.

Because of what then happened, it is important to consider how Meyer had been treated by the Rice administration—read Lovett—before the United States entered World War II and before the FBI investigation began the unraveling of Meyer's career. There is no evidence that Lovett ever criticized Meyer for any of his controversial remarks, and despite Meyer's acrimonious personality, Lovett tapped him to present public lectures on such topics as Goethe and the historian Leopold von Ranke. Meyer wrote Lovett on August 12, 1939, saying that he had been using the library at Dartmouth College but when someone there asked if he would like to teach at Dartmouth, Meyer reported that he had said "that I did not think I would fit in as well as at Rice." Almost two years later, when Meyer heard the news of Lovett's retirement (subject to a successor being found), Meyer had written that "It is with profound regret that I am reading your letter of resignation. I feel that it will be a personal loss as well as a loss for the German department." He hoped that Lovett would now have time for such things as the faculty's Historical Society meetings and concluded that "I want to assure you of my continued loyalty and gratitude." Doubtless Lovett's long and often expressed support of academic freedom was the basis of his apparent acquiescence in behavior and views not at all to his personal liking. From the beginning of his tenure Lovett had proclaimed that one of Rice's advantages was the freedom that resulted from not being subject to either religious or state support. He stated in 1912 that the university's "greatest strength . . . is its freedom," by which, he made explicit, he meant the freedom of its faculty "to teach and search—each man a freeman to teach the truth as he finds it, each man a freeman to seek the truth wherever truth may lead." Lovett essentially repeated this principle over the years, and it undergirded his support for faculty to explore issues and hold controversial views in the fields of religion and science, for example.

However, in wartime, Lovett may have felt that total freedom of expression was unacceptable, though he never explicitly stated such a position at this time. He did say, in a statement written in April 1942 for inclusion in that year's yearbook, that "for the entire duration of the conflict, whatever its length, your rights of individual mastery you will renounce to the mandates of your country." For him, the war was about the survival of Western civilization, freedom, fair play, and everything that made life worth living; in such a conflict, temporary suspension of such things as individual expression and personal choice had to be endured for the greater cause. And Lovett never doubted the nobility of that cause. But Lovett's response to Meyer may also have been colored by a public relations disaster on the Rice campus more than two decades before that had resulted in the board's sacrifice of the academic freedom of a controversial professor in order to protect the local reputation of the university.

Today the principle of academic freedom is absolute and total, but in the past, faculty freedom of expression was often considered contingent, and university boards tended to think that external events could justify restriction of faculty freedom. Behavior or language that might bring controversy or public disapproval to a university, much less actions that could conceivably threaten the security of the nation, were subject to university restraint or dismissal of offending faculty. For example, during World War I, there were from today's perspective shocking restrictions of basic academic freedom at such institutions as the University of Virginia, the University of Minnesota, and Columbia University, with faculty being dismissed simply for expressing less than enthusiastic support for the war against Germany. Columbia president Nicholas Murray Butler defended these actions, declaring to alumni in 1917 that "What had been tolerated before becomes intolerable now. What had been wrongheaded was now sedition. What had been folly was now treason." Even the most innocuous comment could result in a faculty member being severely reprimanded or fired. And no sooner had the war ended than the so-called Red Menace erupted. The Russian Revolution had resulted in a Bolshevik takeover, followed by announcement in the spring of 1919 of a policy advocating worldwide revolution that raised the specter of communist uprisings throughout the Western world. In January 1919 there was a massive strike of shipworkers in Seattle, then in September a strike of over 300,000 workers at U.S. Steel, followed by a near simultaneous strike by the policemen of Boston.

Were Communists and anarchists on the march in the United States? In April a bomb was sent to the home of the Seattle mayor, the next day a bomb exploded in the hand of a maid to a U.S. senator, and other bombings occurred, including one that destroyed the front portion of the home of the U.S. attorney general. Public opinion exaggerated the fear of the Russian threat, and the result was a period of repression and severe reprisals against any expression that could be considered insufficiently patriotic or even mildly pro-Russian. Universities across the nation were attacked for being "hotbeds of bolshevism," with faculty from such institutions as Harvard, Columbia, Yale, and many others accused of being "pink" and "Soviet defenders."

It was against this backdrop that a young instructor of sociology at Rice, Lyford Paterson Edwards, found himself in trouble in May 1919 after he made some remarks to a Sunday School class on Nikolai Lenin and Russia—and the university's ultimate response to this flare-up would shape Lovett's reaction more than twenty years later to Heinrich Meyer. Hence a flashback to an earlier age is necessary. Speaking to an adult class at the First Congregational Church on May 11 that was meeting in the pastor's residence (but who was not present), Dr. Edwards's topic was "Russia and the Soviet Government." Although there is no transcript of exactly what Edwards said, apparently he praised the idealism of Lenin and said that *if* the Russian experiment in government worked out, he might go down in history as the greatest statesmen of all, even including George Washington. One visitor to the class, J. H. Hawley, took great objection to these comments and left the class in a huff, after which he complained to the press that Edwards was praising "the bolshevik head" and claiming that Lenin was "destined to become the greatest figure in history." No one else but Hawley and his host complained, and later other class members said that had Hawley attended the previous lecture and stayed to the end of this one, he would have understood that Edwards was talking in abstract and theoretical terms and explicitly stated that he was not advocating the philosophy of Lenin. But any praise of Lenin and the Bolshevik revolution, however carefully stated, was explosive in the context of May 1919, and the Houston papers for the next several days turned this rather academic Sunday School lecture into a cause célèbre.

Inch after column inch of hyperbolic newstype followed, with Ed-

wards transformed into a radical who was attempting to foment a Bolshevik cult on the Rice campus and in the city. The *Houston Post* opined
on May 16 that it did "not believe that Rice Institute will be permitted
by the wise and patriotic men who direct its destinies to harbor such an
incubator of bolshevism as this professor. It would not have been tolerated in war, and it surely will not be tolerated in peace." It is difficult
to imagine today how such a minor, private lecture could have ignited
such rampaging coverage. That same day Mayor A. E. Amerman announced that he was ordering Kenneth Krahl, public service commis-
sioner, to undertake a formal investigation of the lecture by Edwards
(whom the mayor accurately understood to be a Canadian), including
the taking of signed affidavits from people in the class and people (including students) at Rice who might have heard him speak in other
contexts. The press reported that President Lovett of Rice and most of
the board members were out of town, while trustee John T. Scott, who
was present, stated that he wanted to apprise himself of the situation
before giving a statement. Three days later the mayor reported that on
the basis of the hurried investigation, he understood Rice to be a "home
of 'isms,' where dangerous doctrines are taught to the youth of the city
and where student socialists find a haven." The mayor understood that
most Rice students were not socialists, but he believed nonetheless that
if the Rice board looked into the matter, they would find that "these
freak doctrines, including socialism, have many champions amongst
the boys on campus." Actually, according to the *Houston Chronicle*,
"from all available sources, it appeared that the student body at the
institute warmly backs the professor, declaring that he has never taught
anything but strongly pro-American and pro-ally doctrines." Still the
papers were filled with sensationalist reporting on the "Lenine [*sic*]
eulogist," and both papers in their editorials and letters-to-the-editor
section had comments worrying about the damage done to Rice by the
reportedly unpatriotic views of Dr. Edwards. Both papers were calling
for the dismissal of the offending professor.

By now Dr. Lovett was back in town and surveying the situation; he
announced on Sunday evening, May 18, that the trustees would carefully examine Dr. Edwards's comments. One women's literary group,
the Axson Club (completely unaffiliated with the university despite

its name), was publicly calling for the dismissal of Edwards, as was the Dick Dowling Camp of the United Confederate Veterans and the Oran M. Roberts chapter of the United Daughters of the Confederacy. The presiding elder of the Houston district of the Methodist Episcopal Church, South, also called for his dismissal, adding that this was not the first time the Rice faculty had been charged with teaching freak (he meant Darwinian) doctrines.

On Friday, May 24, the Rice trustees released the results of their inquiry, based not only on the affidavits and letters gathered by the mayor's investigation but an extensive conversation with Dr. Edwards himself. They concluded that nothing he said in his Sunday School lecture should have upset anyone, as indeed they did not to those who listened to all his remarks. The trustees also concluded that Edwards, a British subject, had been unusually active during the war giving patriotic addresses at Camp Logan, Ellington Field, high school commencements, and elsewhere—his patriotism had never before been questioned. (Lovett earlier released a signed statement attesting to Edwards's wartime loyalty and exemplary service.) Yet despite this, based on their frank conversations with him, the trustees decided that

> While asserting and maintaining great loyalty to his own as well as to this country, he possesses certain views in respect to the political conditions in Russia, the character of Lenine [sic], and some of the principles underlying the soviet government of Russia so at variance with the prevailing sentiment of the people of this and the Allied countries, and so contrary to the fundamental principles of our government, as, in the opinion of the Trustees, to utterly destroy his further usefulness to the Institute.

Stating that of course neither the trustees nor the president had previously known the tenor of his beliefs, but now that they had ascertained them, "The trustees have therefore requested his resignation, which has been tendered and accepted." Realizing perhaps that they were caving in to public opinion and outside pressure, the trustees took care to explain their commitment—despite appearances—to the principle of freedom of speech.

They pointed out—in words that suggest the hand of Lovett—that they had "not been unmindful of the freedom of speech that should always be permitted to the teacher and researcher after truth." They said that they believed "in the fullest academic freedom, but in times like these indiscrete persons, while perhaps violating no law, may so conduct themselves as to impair their influence and destroy their usefulness." Exactly what they meant by this was made clear in the next sentence: "Under no circumstances will the Trustees engage, or continue in the service of the Institute, any one, however capable, who does not measure up fully to the highest standard of American citizenship and unquestioned loyalty to our country, its laws and fundamental policies." In saying this the Rice trustees reflected the actions of similar boards elsewhere: no other orthodoxy, neither in religion nor economic theory, was defended so carefully as political loyalty to the American government.

The trustees evidently felt that the public hysteria had forced their hand, for the next several pages of their report criticized the way the incident had been handled by "complaining members of Dr. Edwards's audience, by the local press, by his Honor, the Mayor, by some of the literary and patriotic societies and by some of the citizenship at large." Outrageous charges and ill-founded rumors had damaged the reputation of Rice, perhaps "the greatest asset of Houston." It would have been better for everyone if the person who took offense at Edwards's lecture had simply brought the matter to the attention of Rice officials, who could have investigated the issue in a calm and deliberative manner. But no, the criticism was made public and subject to sensationalism: "as in the days of Rome, the depraved taste of the populace demanded the sacrifices of the lives of the gladiators to quicken the zest of a Roman holiday." As a result, "the good name and reputation of our great institution must suffer and pay the penalty." (The trustees did not mention the damage to the career of Dr. Edwards.) They pointed out that the trustees, all but one, lived in Houston and met weekly as a board; critics of the institute should simply bring their complaints and suggestions to the board in an orderly fashion, respectful of the fairness and responsible nature of the university. The trustees, including President Lovett, signed this document and released it to the press on May 23, 1919. (A draft of a statement about the case, in Lovett's handwriting, says, after defending Edward's character and patriotism, that "he can no longer be either happy or useful as an instructor at the Rice Institute.") The dismissal of Edwards, not the board discussion of the process, gained nationwide publicity, including condemnation by *The Nation* magazine but widespread regional newspaper support.

The Rice faculty strongly supported Edwards and lamented his release. Although the faculty protest was confined to a unanimously passed resolution on May 26, 1919, in defense of the principle of academic freedom, the resolution remained respectful of administrative authority. Still, considering the temper of the times, it made an unambiguous stand for academic freedom:

> On account of certain possible implications in recent resolutions of the Board of Trustees, the faculty of the Rice Institute desires to go on record as follows:
>
> We believe that every Instructor should be responsible for ability, character, and conduct, and not for personal beliefs. We recognize the duty of every Instructor to remember always the dignity of his position, and to refrain from unwise and indiscrete public remarks which may bring the good name of the University into disrepute. But we also feel that any action which seems to limit the freedom of thought or to check the proper expression of beliefs is opposed to the dignity and best interests of the University. Such action necessarily tends to cast doubt on the honesty of teaching, especially conservative teaching. When taken in answer to newspaper stories, it compromises seriously the independence of the University.
>
> We believe as strongly as any one that one of the chief functions of a university is to promote good citizenship and an intelligent love of country. The record of patriotism in great universities is one of the most remarkable by products of the present war, and is attested by the way in which university men in every country have risen to a great occasion. We are convinced that the truest patriotism must always be based on the broadest freedom. These sentiments appear in familiar language in the First Amendment to the Constitution of the United States, in the Constitution of each of the forty-eight American states, and in the writings of almost every American Statesman. We claim no privilege which we do not ask for every citizen. These principles seem to us to be of the very essence of true Americanism.
>
> In spreading these resolutions on our minutes and in communicat-

ing them to the Board of Trustees, we are not unmindful of the many difficult problems which they must solve as the Administrators of a great public trust. And we desire to pledge to the President of the University and to the Board of Trustees our loyal desire to cooperate with them fully in service to this community and to the broader cause of education.

Lovett no doubt shared these sentiments.*

Lovett most likely regretted the way the university handled the Edwards case in 1919, and this probably led Lovett to bend over backward to put up with behavior and statements by Heinrich Meyer in the 1930s that Lovett found personably distasteful. But Meyer's comments came to the attention of the FBI, and as they began questioning people who knew Meyer, subtly but noticeably the hostility and suspicions about the beleaguered German professor began to rise. Meyer himself noted in his later trial testimony that the mere fact that the FBI was investigating him caused acquaintances to think there must be some basis for their interrogations: Meyer testified that even Dr. Lovett suspected that " 'something was in back of it' as soon as he learned that the FBI was on his trail." There was a blow-up at a normally sedate meeting of the Houston Philosophical Society in February 1941. Meyer said, in response to a positive portrayal of Franklin D. Roosevelt by speaker George Williams of the English department (and a New Deal Democrat), that the New Deal and FDR were no different than Hitler, to which philosopher Tsanoff replied to Meyer, "Hitler—he's your man." The resulting commotion broke up the meeting.† Later that year, in June, Meyer admitted to bursar McCants that "I may hit hard at times, especially when someone unjustly treads upon my sensibilities," but he

---

* In July 1919 Lovett received a request from mathematician William Caspar Graustein, who had just left Rice for a position at Harvard, asking if Lovett could vouch for Graustein's patriotism. Because of his father's German ancestry, and because Graustein had had scholarly communication with a German mathematician, some U.S. officials had questioned his loyalty. Lovett (and board chairman Baker) quickly responded with statements attesting to Graustein's good character and loyalty to the United States.

† The minutes of the Houston Philosophical Society simply give the title of Williams's paper, "The Democratic Fallacy," with no indication of the controversy that ensued.

wrote pointedly that "I should not like to have again the term 'Nazi' applied to myself, since it does not apply." Obviously tensions were rising in the faculty.

Matters came to a head on September 17, 1942, when the federal government asked that the U.S. citizenship of Meyer, granted in November 1935, be revoked on the grounds that he had been disingenuous in applying for it, had not really renounced allegiance to Germany, had gotten it simply for convenience sake, had disparaged America and Americans, and had tried to return to Germany. Shortly afterward Meyer sent a carefully worded letter to President Lovett on September 20 in which Meyer replied to either a previous letter or conversation with Lovett. Referring to Lovett's comment that even should Meyer win his case, he might "be forced to leave town for reasons of public opinion," Meyer said he assumed such a move would not affect his salary. He agreed with Lovett's request that he refrain from meeting his classes for the moment, but he did so with the expectation that this would not be permanent. He also said he could not completely comply with Lovett's request that he not come to campus because he had materials in his office necessary for preparing his defense. But there was no other contact with Lovett, who played no role whatsoever in the subsequent trial.

After a number of preliminary skirmishes (in a completely separate development, Meyer's wife successfully filed for divorce in December 1942), the trial got under way in federal district court on February 14, 1943. Days of testimony followed, covered in excruciating detail by the Houston papers, with people like Marcel Moraud testifying against Meyer, along with various former students and a professor or two from elsewhere: Meyer clearly said things that the thin-skinned Moraud found offensive, although it seems to a reader today that Meyer was simply blunt or insensitive and often too quick with a caustic retort. Meyer then testified at length, saying that he liked America and American institutions, that he had been so favorably impressed with two Rice faculty, Stockton Axson and Griffith C. Evans, that he had decided to apply for citizenship, that he had at various times thought about building a house here, that on several trips to Germany he had been repulsed by aspects of the society there and was only too glad to return to America. A number of Rice faculty testified on his behalf—New

Dealer English professor George Williams, rock-ribbed Republican history professor Floyd S. Lear, mathematician Hubert Bray, psychologist Frank A. Pattie, known for practical jokes he had deployed at Meyer's expense—along with faculty from elsewhere, including a fellow Germanist from the University of Texas, and several Rice students. Even Meyer's estranged wife returned to testify on his behalf.

The testimony was by turns intellectually exciting, moving, humorous, sad—Meyer was noticed to be softly crying when some of his old letters were read in which he described how he felt alone and isolated. The audience was largely made up of Rice students. But when it was all over, Judge Allen B. Hannay—considered a "hanging judge"—announced the verdict on February 23: guilty, and Meyer's citizenship was revoked. Within days he was sent to a barbed-wire enclosed alien concentration camp in Kenedy, Texas. Following the conviction, the Rice board met on February 24 and instructed President Lovett to inform Meyer that the trustees had "terminated his services as Instructor in German and to enclose with his letter a check carrying Dr. Meyer's salary through June 30, 1943." Lovett complied with this directive the next day, and Meyer acknowledged the letter—both letters were formally polite.

With support from a number of his faculty friends, especially George Williams, Meyer decided in April to appeal his conviction to the Fifth Circuit Court of Appeals in New Orleans. Friends had raised money to help pay for lawyers, George Williams assisted Meyer in preparing written documents, and finally, on April 5, 1944, the Fifth Circuit Court reversed the lower court decision, dismissed the complaints against Meyer, and set aside the citizenship cancellation order. The appeal court decision, written by Judge Joseph C. Hutcheson, Jr., of Houston, was harshly critical of Judge Hannay's handling of the case. "Born of war hysteria and ideological conflicts," the appeal decision stated, "this is another of those fortunately rare proceedings in which an un-American intolerance of opinions not acceptable to the majority, puts our adherence to the American constitutional principles not only of tolerance but of justice to the test lest, done mere lip service to, they become a byword and a hissing." The next day both Meyer and Lovett declined to make comments to the press, and indeed Lovett apparently never mentioned the case again.

Lovett's role in the case remains vague; he seems, by the record, simply to have been a bystander, writing Meyer the termination letter at the command of the board only after Meyer's initial conviction. But four months later Meyer sent Lovett an angry letter, charging that Lovett had been deceived by gossiping underlings, that he had dismissed Meyer on the basis of faulty evidence, and that he had failed to appreciate fully all that Meyer had done for the university. After a number of aspersions on Lovett's character and honor, Meyer concluded that he hoped in the future Lovett could find God's forgiveness; Meyer's valediction read "Very sincerely, your brother in Christ, Heinrich Meyer." Maybe Meyer expected or wanted Rice to reappoint him, but that never happened. (In the fall of 1946 Andrew Louis, with a doctorate from Cornell, joined the faculty to replace Meyer.) About 1945 Meyer moved to rural Pennsylvania and for several years helped edit a gardening magazine, but then he was appointed to the faculty of Muhlenberg College, where he taught German until 1962 before moving to Vanderbilt University to finish his career. He maintained a correspondence with several Rice friends, especially George Williams, and occasionally wrote positively of much of his experience at Houston.

How does Lovett himself emerge from this event? While this was not his finest hour, his even-handed treatment of Meyer before 1941 or so testifies to Lovett's commitment to academic freedom. Apparently Meyer did not feel that the president in any way pressured him or infringed upon his rights before that date, and although Meyer later said that Lovett cautioned him that he "said too much," that seems to have been intended by Lovett as avuncular advice. Once the investigation and trial began, Lovett remained punctiliously neutral, not rushing to Meyer's defense. Lovett took no move against Meyer until, following his conviction in 1943, the trustees instructed Lovett to send Meyer a letter of termination. Lovett did not protest the board's instruction, but whether this implied weakness in the face of board pressure, a response to expected public outrage if he did not so act, a principled distaste of Meyer's habit of caustic and cutting remarks and record of at least borderline anti-Semitic remarks before the war, or a heartfelt belief that— in time of warfare—faculty should be held to a higher standard of uncritical patriotism is unclear. Perhaps it was a complicated combination of them all. Certainly some faculty who did not consider Meyer guilty as charged found him an unlikable fellow, a troublemaker, difficult. Others who knew him well enjoyed his wit, his sardonic attitude, his quick intelligence and almost Mencken-like willingness to attack sacred cows. Lovett was too removed from this degree of camaraderie with faculty at this time in his career to have appreciated the more favorable aspects of Meyer's personality. In the midst of wartime, he likely saw Meyer as a distraction, one whose published remarks defending Germany's right to expand its territory and disparaging Germany's Jewish population could only bring disrepute to the university, and one whose skepticism was out of step with Lovett's wholehearted commitment to the Allied cause. In truth, it is difficult for many today—following the cynicism with which most Americans have come to regard U.S. military engagements in Vietnam and Iraq—to appreciate the depth and near universality of support for the war effort that Lovett exemplified.

For Lovett, with his extensive educational experiences and academic friendships in pre–World War I Europe, the rise of Nazism and the resulting German aggression against England and France and the near destruction of the open tradition of German universities made the war seem to him more than to most a war to save civilization—not only in Europe but in the world at large. He had told the incoming Rice students in September 1940 that "you who have known ["freedom," "democratic fellowship," "respect for the rights of all the sons and daughters of men to life, liberty, and the pursuit of happiness"] will spend yourselves to the uttermost to preserve such conditions of self-government, freedom, and self-realization for all the people of our country against every agency of aggression." For the next three academic years, Lovett was almost totally absorbed with putting Rice on a wartime footing: developing the ROTC program and then the V-12 program, adjusting the curriculum accordingly, putting in place the necessary facilities, dealing with the problem of maintaining enough faculty to support the needed courses, and struggling to maintain the size of the civilian student body. These pressing practical issues, combined with the great cause to defeat German and Japanese aggression, likely meant that to Lovett the Meyer case was more an annoyance than a central concern. Certainly in the context of the war effort, Meyer's plight seemed a minor issue.

For almost forty years Lovett had motivated men largely by the power of his vision and words, and it was his rhetorical skills that he employed most personally in support of the war. Rice students from this era recall more than a half century later how they had been moved and inspired by Lovett's written and oral words in the course of their years on campus and beyond. Lovett continued to greet new students each fall with a letter in the *Thresher;* he opened the fall semester with a matriculation address; and he prepared a message to be published in each year's edition of the *Campanile.* Perhaps for students the yearbook statements were seen as the more permanent representations of Lovett's thoughts. Even before active American involvement in the war he wished for the class of 1940 "years of youth and years and years of usefulness in thwarting the powers of darkness and in making a new world of light for all the individual sons and daughters of men." Always optimistic, Lovett told the class of 1941 that even in those dark days he was confident the graduates had "the reverence, sincerity, and vision, to make beauty, to know truth, and to attain to humane and righteous ways of living. And these are the only issues that really matter." His faith in the graduates, and in the "wonder" of mankind, were the grounds of his hope for the future.

After Pearl Harbor, Lovett's commitment to the cause became even more passionate. Writing in April 1942 for that year's graduating class, he praised the university's contribution to the graduates' moral fiber: "I know that the freedom we have given you to think and speak and argue and seek truth fortifies you to fight to the bitter end for the victory of freedom." Arguing that all the nation's institutions were threatened "by aggressive force of enemies' arms," he rested confident in the knowledge that Rice students would "stand to the last man and woman of you, even unto death, until the rights of all men to think, to work, to worship, and to serve their fellows be restored to humankind upon this planet." That captured his sense of the importance of the struggle. By November 1942, when he was writing the message for the 1943 *Campanile,* he well understood that most of the male graduates at least would be destined to serve their country, which would entail danger and hardship. But such dedicated service also brought a profound happiness and sense of purpose. Lovett, normally a gentle man, spoke frankly of the moment when there was no time to reason with one's enemies. "You cannot reason with a rattlesnake ready to strike or a tiger to spring. You must kill him or he will kill you. Nor have you much choice in answering your country's call. But if doing your duty to God, kin, country, and kind, by giving all you are, have, and hope to be, is not happiness, then I have little or no understanding of what happiness is or why we are here." Thus Lovett sought both to laud and to fortify the members of the class of 1943. As he told next year's class, your lives "have been joined at their very start to large issues." And he summarized what to him was their lives' purpose: "to banish hate and deceit and cruelty from the face of the earth, and to bring back honesty and integrity, love and loyalty, pity and laughter, friendship, fidelity, and hope, to the common ways of women and men all over the world." Lovett had not actually personally experienced the terrible savagery of World War I with its horrors of trench warfare and astronomical casualties, and this may have made it easier for him to see such heroic purpose in the present conflict.

Two classes graduated in 1944, and there were two separate *Campaniles;* in the second one Lovett was already beginning to anticipate the successful conclusion of the war: "Your immediate objective and ours is victory over the aggressor. And our next nearest objective is to prevent the recurrence of such aggression." He spoke of "our horror at the betrayal of western civilization, our irrevocable determination to recover that civilization, and our zeal for restoring conscience and moral law to the common ways of men and women on this planet." By the time he was composing the message for the 1945 yearbook, victory was on the horizon. In a line that could have been the credo for his life, Lovett wrote: "In the exercise of the will to work strong men find their strength." He could foresee in the decades to come that the graduates would, in diverse ways, be working "for the welfare of humankind the world over," and to Lovett, the elderly university president, that was a "most moving prospect." And in his final *Campanile* message, published shortly after he had stepped down from the Rice presidency and was entering retirement, Lovett counseled the students one last time that "the task we set ourselves is an excursion of faith that what is true and what is right shall prevail in the belief and conduct of men." From the beginning to the very end of his tenure at Rice, Edgar Odell Lovett was an indomitable optimist.

The years from 1941 to 1945 were eventful ones for the world, the nation, and the Rice Institute, but now World War II was over (V-E Day, May 8; V-J Day, August 15, 1945). Although President Lovett had asked to step down before the United States entered the conflict, he ended up leading the university through those tumultuous years. The Rice board of trustees was probably right in its conclusion, shortly after the announcement of Lovett's conditional resignation in May 1941, that practically every important science administrator was too involved in nationally significant war research to be attracted to the presidency of the Rice Institute. For that reason, no serious effort to mount a search for a new leader was made at the time because it was simply assumed that the next president should have a scientific background. It would be four years before an organized effort to seek the next leader of the Rice Institute would begin, so Lovett understood that his tenure would not end soon. How must he have felt, at that moment when he offered his resignation, as he contemplated further service? No doubt he was tired, but he could—despite years of wartime and then the Great Depression and now another war—look with considerable pride on what had been accomplished since 1912.

In the present academic year, 1940–1941, Rice enrolled a still mostly local 1,401 undergraduate students and 54 graduate students; of these, 6.9 percent of the undergraduates were from states other than Texas, while one-third of the graduate students hailed from other states. A disproportionate percentage of the undergraduates were native Houstonians (57 percent of the males, 89 percent of the women—there was no on-campus housing for women students), but this helped to increase the sense of community, for many students had known each other for years. In contrast to 1912 when there were 77 total students and a dozen faculty, now the faculty totaled 69, 36 of whom held doctorates and from such distinguished universities as Harvard, Yale, Princeton, Cornell, Columbia, Chicago, Michigan, and Berkeley, along with four European universities. Of the 69 faculty, 18 (or 26 percent) held the rank of professor, although only 2 departments had more than one full

professor. In part because of the more than a decade of financial stringency, Lovett had tried to stretch the size of the teaching faculty as the
student population grew by emphasizing faculty hires at the lower-paid
ranks of lecturer, instructor, and assistant professor—almost no one
was promoted during the 1930s. Yet all the while Lovett kept alive on
campus the sense that the Rice Institute was, though small and limited in programs, a real university with high standards. Faculty bought
into this concept, and students were told and believed that they were
at a genuine seat of learning and research, and the regular parade of
distinguished visiting lecturers seemed to validate the assertion. Academicians throughout the nation as well as laypeople locally held the university in highest repute. Everyone knew that the university maintained
high standards and that its students were bright. Houstonians, in fact,
viewed the Rice Institute with a combination of awe and pride.

Despite the obvious accomplishments that he could look back on as
he contemplated retirement in the spring of 1941, Lovett at the same
time understood that the rapid ascent of the young Rice Institute into
the uppermost ranks of academic standing had been stymied by the limitations in size of the initial endowment since its growth did not keep
pace with the needs of a maturing university. The financial problems
were only exacerbated by the restraints forced by the Great Depression.
Now, in early 1941, with another World War looming on the horizon,
Lovett might have been excused for a sense of thwarted ambition as
he composed his letter of resignation. He could not foresee that over
the next couple of years—even as the university shifted into wartime
mode and adjusted its curriculum and the makeup of its student population accordingly—changes would occur and new developments arise
that forecast a brighter future. Significant additional funds became
available, the board of trustees was transformed by new appointments,
and the overall economy could be expected to improve with the return
of peace. President Edgar Odell Lovett by the end of the war began
to see that the Rice Institute's best days lay before it, building on the
foundation Lovett himself had so carefully constructed. With a sense of
exhilaration and his congenital hopefulness and optimism, he pledged
himself to do everything within his power to continue to advance the
prospects of the university to which he had dedicated his life.

# CHAPTER NINE

# FULL CIRCLE
## RETIREMENT, TRANSITION, RENEWED MOMENTUM

THE WORLD WAR II YEARS were a period of sustained boom for Houston. Shipyards and plants for the production of high-octane aviation fuel, artificial rubber, and a smorgasbord of other petrochemical derivatives fueled population and employment growth, and it was during these years that Houston overtook New Orleans to become the largest city in the South, with a population that grew from about 500,000 in 1945 to 600,000 by 1950. Perhaps because the city had become a major seaport in 1914 as a result of dredging the sleepy Buffalo Bayou into the ship channel, there was a can-do spirit about Houston that created a confidence that great things could be accomplished there. During the first years of the war the seeds of the Texas Medical Center were planted, ultimately to become far and away the largest medical complex in the world. Downtown skyscrapers pushed upward as housing sprawled to the south and west: Houston impressed visitors as an unfinished city, a city on the make. In this heady atmosphere the trustees of the Rice Institute, with its financial resources on the mend and energized by vigorous new board members, began to strategize for another period of growth and improvement as the city's leading university. More than four decades earlier Edgar Odell Lovett had spoken about the synergistic relationship between great cities and great universities, so no one could have more quickly than he grasped the importance of Houston's spectacular growth and maturity for the future prospects of Rice Institute.

By the summer of 1944 Lovett submitted a brief report—in response to a request from trustees Harry C. Hanszen and George R. Brown—reprising the history of the university and highlighting the strategic choices that had been made in the beginning. These two trustees, joined just a month previously by Harry C. Wiess, did not intend to be passive caretakers of either the endowment or the direction of the university, and both of them understood that Lovett would be their best ally as they contemplated enhancement. Alumni leaders too had been urging that the university embark on a public relations effort to increase awareness of the importance of the university to the community and the need for systematic fundraising, and even the student editors of the *Thresher* were advocating that the university augment its physical facilities and offerings in "liberal learning" to balance the traditional emphasis on science and engineering. The *Thresher*'s lead editorial for February 1, 1945, urged trustee Harry Wiess to write an article for the newspaper on how the trustees envisioned Rice's future, and the paper indicated strong disapproval of any plans that might constrict the university's offerings and transform the university into "the Rice Institute of Technology." A few weeks later the *Thresher* published Wiess's response. He was studying every aspect of Rice's past and its present in order to better understand what should be done next, and he pointed out that "The formulation of a sound long-range program . . . requires careful consideration of the needs of the community and area, the interests of present and prospective students, and the faculty that is available or can be secured." Such analysis was necessarily time-consuming, but he did point out that "The broad concept established by the founder and others who have contributed to the endowment of the Institute provides an opportunity and imposes a responsibility on the Trustees to do everything they can to make Rice an outstanding educational institution."

To further this analysis, the board established three special committees, the first of which was the Survey Committee to "make a survey and report on past development, present status, and future outlook of the Institute's financial and educational affairs," and to this key committee were appointed trustees Wiess, George Brown, Benjamin Botts Rice, and Edgar Odell Lovett. The Finance Committee, consisting of Brown, Hanszen, and Alexander S. Cleveland, would recommend the purchase of securities for the endowment. The Loan Committee, consisting of John T. Scott, Rice, Cleveland, and Lovett, would analyze and approve secured loans that would be made. The first two committees were clearly the more important, and they were dominated by younger board members. No longer would affairs be handled as in the past; there would be more open analysis, reporting, and discussion. The invigorated board would proactively help shape future development of the university. And by late spring 1945 the trustees were ready to begin announcing the changes they anticipated.

The Rice faculty must have been filled with excitement and hopeful curiosity as they gathered for a dinner hosted for them at the Faculty Club by the trustees on the night of April 10, 1945. This was the first time the board had ever made an effort to reach out so that they "could have an opportunity to visit with [the faculty] and become better acquainted." After dinner John T. Scott, chairman of the board of trustees, offered remarks that clearly gladdened the hearts of those members of the faculty who were of a progressive bent, and certainly Scott's words reflected the ambitions of President Lovett. Scott expressed appreciation for Lovett's leadership over the years, explained the causes of the fall in endowment revenue after about 1930, then explained the several significant new sources of revenue that had developed over the last few years. After this review of finances, Scott told the assembled faculty that "there are some bright prospects ahead for Rice." Then he got as specific as he could: "While we cannot make any commitments in advance, it appears to us at this time that it may be possible to increase the budget for educational purposes by some 50 per cent above the level of recent years. This will enable the Board to do some things it has wanted to. . . . More adequate compensation to the faculty, an increase in faculty personnel, construction of new buildings, and other improvements are all contemplated for the next ten-year period." Of great importance, given these positive prospects, was the choice of a new president. The trustees assumed he should be a "man of excellent character, with an established reputation." Second, "He should have experience in teaching, the ability to lead and inspire confidence, and the personality to deal with people." And third, while he should have scientific training, they wanted a person of "sufficiently broad background and attitude to give appreciation to all of the needs of a well-balanced educational program." And to help them select such a man, the trustees asked the faculty to elect three of its members to a temporary committee that would both suggest names and vet the names that came in otherwise. This degree of consultation with the board had never happened at Rice before. The faculty must have felt elated by the evening.

The faculty subsequently elected English professor Alan D. McKillop, chemist George Holmes Richter, and civil engineer Lewis B. Ryon to the advisory committee. When the committee met with the board on April 25, the committee discussed "their views with reference to the type of man who should be considered," views that apparently closely matched those of the board itself, and the committee thanked the board "for the confidence that was bestowed on them." At that same meeting the trustees heard a recommendation from an alumni committee urging that funds be raised for a library, though the board hesitated until plans for more systematic building needs and fundraising potential were worked out. But beyond doubt, the board was very actively analyzing the situation and beginning to formulate plans. On May 7 a very detailed report on the university—covering enrollment, degrees earned, number of faculty, endowment income, educational expenses, and other pertinent data for the period 1929–1943—was prepared by the Survey Committee (including President Lovett) for the board of trustees. This was the kind of compendium necessary for long-range planning, and given the paucity of administrative help on campus (essentially the only administrators were the bursar and the registrar), Lovett must have played a large role in the preparation of this report, both the retrospective section and the concluding page entitled "Future Outlook—Educational Program." The report had already indicated the rosy financial outlook. In this final section it addressed what now needed to be done.

"The Institute has reached a point," the committee argued, "where it must expand in order to make continued progress and to serve the needs of this area. The increase in population and the rapid development of industry in Texas, particularly in the area surrounding Houston, creates an educational problem which Rice Institute can help to solve by improving its course of studies." This 1945 statement reflected the rationale of 1912, when President Lovett had initially argued that, given the time and place, the Rice Institute should begin its development "at the science end," with enhancement of other areas to come as circumstances allowed. The times now seemed to permit such further development. "A well rounded and balanced program will require some expansion in existing departments, development of new courses, and the construction of additional buildings." The board understood these enhancements would require growing financial support, and it indicated its willingness to undertake such fundraising as would be necessary. The anticipated changes would not mean a sharp turn away from the plans initially laid down but rather a fulfillment of them. "It is the recommendation of this committee [on May 7, 1945] that Rice Institute continue the basic program that it has developed since 1912. The emphasis originally placed on engineering and science is believed to be sound, and these studies should continue to be the center of a broad program. The work in liberal arts, however, must keep pace with technical branches if the Institute is to serve its most useful purpose. Sound training in arts and letters is essential in itself for the good of the community, as well as for the development of a satisfactory technical program." The Rice Institute should begin to move toward becoming a university in modern terms. Originally the title *institute,* at least in Lovett's understanding, suggested the research and scholarly function that should complement the teaching function, but now the term *university* suggested breadth of offerings as well as research and teaching.

It was becoming clear that the Rice Institute was entering a period of rapid change and improved prospects, in effect a new beginning. After almost two decades of slowed development and dampened progress, the onrush of decisions and announcements now underway suggested the unclogging of a river. At times the torrent of plans and programs must have seemed almost breathtaking to the seventy-four-year-old Lovett. On July 30 the board unanimously adopted a twelve-point long-range program for further development of the Rice Institute, and although Lovett was by no means solely responsible—no doubt the primary proponents of the far-reaching program were the trio of younger, more far-sighted trustees, Hanszen, Brown, and Wiess—his educational philosophy and influence were most evident. The trustees authorized the plan to be distributed to the three major city newspapers along with the *Thresher* and the *Rice Owl* (now the alumni magazine). Here the future of the Rice Institute was spelled out.

The first point was quintessentially Rice: "to provide especially good training for a limited number of students . . . provide a broad and sound basic program with a well developed and strong curriculum in arts and letters and with the emphasis on science and research that is required to meet challenging circumstances." True to Lovett's initial plans, the university would "set a high standard of scholarship and provide leadership in higher education." Then in order to improve the efficiency of the board, the trustees set up a number of standing committees and began to plan for an emeritus board position for those over a certain age. The board called for a close relationship between university administrators and faculty, with administrative officers teaching an occasional class. To address severe overcrowding, the board expected to build a new library and several other classroom and laboratory buildings, including additional residential facilities and, at long last, a president's house.

Recognizing that the student-to-professor ratio at Rice was scandalously high compared to the best American universities (where it was "generally less than seven to one"), the trustees set themselves the goal of hiring enough additional faculty to drop the ratio from its present 20:1 ratio to approximately 10:1. In part this faculty enlargement would allow the university to broaden its course offerings for undergraduates and for "graduate and research work." In a significant departure from the past, and made possible by the improving prospects, the board acknowledged that "The realization of the high objectives and standards envisioned for the Institute will require additional emphasis on graduate and research work." Both had, of course, been present from the beginning, but Rice had until now been overwhelmingly undergraduate and, with the exception of one history doctorate in 1933, all doctorates had been offered in only four fields: biology, chemistry, mathematics, and physics. This would change in the future, and for the very near future, the trustees expected to grow the student population back to its pre-1941 levels. Finally, and very important, the trustees recognized that achievement of these various programs would require substantially more endowment and income than even recently improved conditions could provide, but they were confident that as Rice grew and improved, it would attract these necessary funds. These were ambitious plans for sure, plans that harkened back to the ambition of the beginning. Edgar Odell Lovett must have been extraordinarily gratified by this turn of events after years of what he later called "halting and warping of plans by war and depression and war."

All these plans were eloquently explained to the Rice community on November 9 when trustee Harry C. Wiess addressed a meeting of the Association of Rice Alumni on the topic of "Rice Looks Forward." The trustees had already acted, at a board meeting on October 11, to give all the faculty members substantial raises, along with a bonus, and announced fourteen faculty promotions (usually from instructor to assistant professor, although four were from assistant to associate and one to full professor)—here was clear evidence that the trustees were serious about regaining academic momentum. Wiess essentially summarized the twelve-point program earlier approved by the trustees, and he restated the older traditional view (classically expressed by Woodrow Wilson and underlying Lovett's thinking from the beginning) of universities' responsibility toward serving their society in the new context of the Atomic Age. Speaking just three months after the dropping of an atom bomb on Nagasaki, Wiess said that "We stand today at a critical point in world history and in the tide of human affairs. The war, so recently concluded, has brought about far-reaching changes in the world, changes which may either cause the downfall of our civilization or the dawn of a better world." Aware that nothing about a university—its size, its outreach, the spectrum of its programs—was fixed for all time but rather that viable universities were living, evolving institutions, he said that "It is necessary and appropriate that institutions of higher learning take stock of their role in the community and set forth on a course that will add to the progress and welfare of humanity."

Wiess reminded his alumni audience of how the institute's financial outlook had recently brightened, and then he emphasized that Rice had "reached the point where it must expand in order to make continued progress and to serve the needs of this area." While the basic objective of the university was unchanged—"to maintain the high standards of the school and to provide exceptionally good training for a limited number of students"—an expansion in the number of students and faculty and a "substantial building program" were necessary for the future. With greater numbers of faculty, "it will be possible to broaden the course of study, strengthen the undergraduate program, and increase the proportion of graduate and research work." Holding true to President Lovett's bedrock beliefs, the trustees also understood that there was a positive, fruitful relationship between research, graduate training, and undergraduate teaching. Wiess concluded by saying how important it was to choose a new president wisely, that much progress was being made on that front, and that "Rice Institute is definitely looking forward to the next few decades as a period of substantial achievement and public service." The university was again on an upward trajectory in pursuit of Lovett's founding vision, according to which the destiny of Rice was not meant to be the small, largely undergraduate, mostly local, almost entirely technical institute at which it had plateaued in the decade of the 1930s.

Meanwhile, during the fall months of 1945 the board, with the assistance of the special faculty committee, was making good headway in identifying a candidate for the presidency, with Lovett favorably impressed by the ever-shortening list of names. On December 7 the trustees voted unanimously to offer the position to physicist William Vermillion Houston of the California Institute of Technology. Houston and his wife had just visited the Rice campus, and the two parties were mutually impressed. There were several issues that Houston was concerned about. He wanted to be able to maintain a laboratory and continue research and teaching at least to some extent; he wanted to expand the faculty, institute a compulsory retirement plan for faculty, provide faculty ample funds to travel to scholarly meetings, and continue the tradition of having a steady stream of visiting speakers. After expressing some concerns about the appropriateness of big-time football at a small research university, he reluctantly agreed to accept the athletic program with the understanding that it would be limited in size. He stated a desire to expand the graduate programs particularly in the sciences and engineering and expand the undergraduate offerings in other fields. After a telephone conversation on December 27, Houston sent his acceptance letter the next day. Confirmatory letters were then exchanged, with the formal announcement of his acceptance of the Rice presidency made on January 3, 1946. His formal inauguration would come later in the spring.

The very next day the Rice board met and approved a carefully considered amendment to the bylaws of the university that proved to be extraordinarily important. This change, whose purpose was graciously stated to be "to permit any Trustee who has attained the age of seventy

(70) to be relieved of the burdens imposed by the duties and responsibilities of such office," allowed such board members to resign and
become trustees emeriti. As emeriti they would still have the privilege
of attending board meetings and could still be able to offer the university "counsel, advice, and guidance," but they would no longer have
a vote in the resulting deliberations. This bylaw passed unanimously,
whereupon B. B. Rice and A. S. Cleveland promptly offered their resignations and were replaced by William Alexander Kirkland and Gus
Sessions Wortham. Then President Lovett "tendered his resignation
as a Trustee, and on motion made and seconded, the resignation was
accepted with great reluctance by the Board." (All other resignations
were recorded without comment.) Lovett was replaced by Frederick
Rice Lummis, M.D., who, as a member of the faculty of the Baylor
University College of Medicine,* became the first academic to serve
on the Rice board. Then the remaining older trustee, John T. Scott,
resigned, and was replaced by Lamar Fleming, Jr., who almost two decades before had expressed strong disapproval of the attention the Rice
board paid to athletics but whose obvious cosmopolitanism and acu-
men recommended him—despite his iconoclastic temperament—to the
completely new board of trustees.

These changes to the board were more substantial than might be
apparent. The oldest member of the trustees now was younger than
the youngest member had been in 1940, when the board had been led
by two octogenarians, James Baker and William M. Rice, Jr. The new
trustees had been educated at such institutions as Chicago, Princeton,
and Harvard and several headed larger, more complex, more international companies than had earlier trustees. Gus Wortham, founder
of American General Insurance Co., was extremely skilled in the field
of investments and emphatically pushed the university to change its investment strategy and move toward flexible securities such as common
stocks; William A. Kirkland, a prominent banker, along with Harry
Wiess was a charter trustee of Princeton; George Brown had helped
found the huge construction firm of Brown and Root largely on the

---

*In 1969 the name was changed to Baylor College of Medicine when the medical school
separated from Baylor University to become an independent institution.

basis of federal grants, so he appreciated this potential funding source that would be instrumental in the development of modern science research; and Fleming had extensive European business experience and had held major consultative appointments with the U.S. government. So this younger, better-educated, more aggressive board was more worldly than the previous Rice board had been and had an understanding not only of government and finance but also significant experience with other major universities. A strong, proactive group of trustees is essential if a university is to be enhanced, and these trustees must be able to work hand in hand with the institution's president. The new board was prepared to provide the leadership, the funds, and the cooperative spirit necessary for advancing the Rice Institute to the next level of academic accomplishment.

The Rice faculty at their March 2, 1946, meeting adopted two resolutions, one welcoming William V. Houston and expressing gratification at his selection as the new president, and a heartfelt acknowledgment to Dr. and Mrs. Lovett. This resolution stated that the faculty felt "that the traditions of the Rice Institute, as a place of education, learning, and research, built up under President Lovett's guidance, are its greatest asset and insure its future as a great university." Lovett's long and distinguished tenure was finally drawing to a close, with his last major contribution to be the introduction of President Houston to the Rice community at the March 4, 1946, commencement exercises. What must have been going through Lovett's mind as he composed these remarks? Surely it was a combination of both pride in what had been accomplished and a sense of vindication as the new board made ever more clear its program for the future. Lovett also saw William V. Houston as a worthy successor; there seemed to be no trace of proprietorship on Lovett's part as he prepared to welcome the new president, no sense of defensiveness, no touchiness at all but rather an admirable graciousness toward the new president. In 1928 while on a Guggenheim leave Houston had studied at the University of Leipzig, and that might have served as an unexpected bond between them. Lovett was careful to say or do nothing that might restrict Houston's freedom of action or foreclose any possibilities. Lovett knew that the development of a great university was a process of marathon proportions; he knew too that he had run a good race, and now it was time to hand off the baton. Nowhere was this more evident than in the words Lovett used to introduce Houston at the commencement.

This would be Lovett's final official act as president of the Rice Institute, and his emotions were surely stretched to the utmost as he looked out over the audience of robed graduates, family, and friends, with the faculty and trustees behind him on the stage. "Rice is in a state of transition," he immediately announced to his listeners. "It is in a transition from good to better. Facing extraordinary opportunity, the institution is about to become braver, stronger, sounder, more beautiful." One of the best measures of an institution-builder's achievement and character is the nature of his handling over the reins to new leadership, and Lovett passed this test with high colors. Lovett in his introductory remarks briefly mentioned the lean days in the past but said that despite that travail, "good fortune has attended the Rice Institute all the way." By this he specified the founder and the founding trustees, the initial faculty, the adventurous students who chose to come to a new university, and the continuing support of the larger community. "These circumstances inspire hope and confidence in the new day already dawned," he said. With that background established he praised the "new board of seven, . . . highly resolved and competent," the recent augmentations of the endowment, current plans for new buildings and especially a new library, and he summed up his recitation of progress by saying that "the most significant of all these events was the final achievement of the trustees' survey and faculty committees in bringing to a successful conclusion the comprehensive search for a president." Lovett warmly sketched Houston's background and accomplishments, quoting Cicero to the effect that "You have no rival but the extraordinary expectations you have raised." And with that, he concluded, "Ladies and Gentlemen of Rice and Houston, the President of the Rice Institute." Lovett's tenure ended with those final six words.

How Lovett had handled himself on that occasion moved many in the audience. As one of the most respected of the senior faculty, Alan D. McKillop, wrote Lovett that very afternoon, "Since I didn't have an opportunity to speak to you after the exercises this morning, I feel prompted to set it down simply that you have conducted today the most perfect and gracious academic ceremonial I have ever seen. Never have the high standards you have set for the Rice Institute been more fully met or more brilliantly illustrated. The dignity of your bearing and the felicity of your words will always remain in my memory, and, I am sure, in the memories of all who heard you." But it was the long letter from Harry Wiess, the trustee to whom Lovett was closest and had known since a class at Princeton, that most moved Lovett, bringing tears to his eyes. As Lovett wrote in acknowledgment, "your wonderful letter of the 9th is the most beautiful letter I have ever read . . . . It was all blur before I got through the first lines, but I can recite every word of it this morning. It is a benediction that will wear to the end of my days."

Wiess had written Lovett on March 8 to complement him on "the outstanding and successful manner in which you conducted the Commencement Exercises. . . . It seems to me," stated the trustee, "that this could not have been done so beautifully but for the inspiration derived from the great accomplishment in your thirty-eight years of devotion to Rice." In a vein common to many of the tributes that Lovett had first received in 1941, when announcing his conditional retirement, and again now, Wiess wrote that the "Rice Institute is, and will continue to be, a monument to and reflection of your ability, character, and leadership. You have dedicated your life, with unusual singleness of purpose, to the advancement of Rice Institute." The success of that endeavor was marked by the esteem in which the university was held. "Your task has been a difficult one," acknowledged Wiess, "and your problems were not always fully appreciated. Nevertheless, you have persevered consistently in carrying out the high objectives established under your leadership at the time of the inaugural ceremonies. You have led Rice wisely and well, and you have accomplished wonders with available resources and under the circumstances and conditions existing." Probably few among the faculty or alumni, then or later, fully understood the kind of restraints that had inhibited the full realization of Lovett's founding vision.

"You remarked in your address," Wiess continued, "that Rice Institute is passing through a period of transition. The transition is one based on the foundation you have laid and carrying forward the program which you would have liked to have undertaken if circumstances had allowed." That is, perhaps, the strongest confirmation of the degree to which financial and other restraints had tied Lovett's hands for almost two decades and required him to make unpleasant choices about the number of faculty and their rank and salaries, slowed the development of academic programs, and restricted enrollment growth. Now, on his way out, Lovett was obviously gratified that, in his words, a new day was dawning. Soon afterward, thinking retrospectively about the entire course of his own presidency as he wrote a congratulatory letter to the new president of the University of Texas, T. S. Painter, Lovett could say to him that "You have hard times ahead, yet, if my experience counts for anything, you have a very happy life before you." Lovett then vacated his office space on the fourth level atop the Sallyport and moved down a floor to smaller accommodations, and with his trusted secretary, Ann Wheeler (who had worked for him since 1919), provided for as long as he needed her, he began the personal transition to emeritus standing. Arrangements were also made to house Lovett's extensive book collection that he had maintained in his presidential office and in the long attic space of the administration building, books that he explained to Harry Hanszen in January 1946 had "been meat and drink to me, and now seem altogether necessary if I am to continue at work." He intended to remain intellectually active.

The university paused, on Sunday afternoon, May 12, 1946, for the unveiling of a formal portrait of the aging president emeritus. The board of trustees invited a veritable Who's Who of prominent Houstonians to witness this honoring of Lovett. "The history of the Rice Institute," the board proclaimed, "offers one of the most signal instances in educational annals of the effective translation of personal integrity, intelligence, and force into high action and achievement." The statement described how essential Lovett had been in shaping the institute to both fit the immediate needs of its locale and aspire to the loftiest conception of the university. The board acknowledged Lovett's academic training, his appreciation of "literary and historical culture," his "profound sense of the university as a corporate entity." "Beyond all this," the board so accurately understood, "he had concentration and continuity." The board went on to praise his character, his training at great American and European universities, his "happy marriage which bound him by ties of deepest affection and interest to the South," his exacting architectural taste, and his "sense of propriety and power of felicitous utterance which invested academic ceremonial with added dignity and significance." The board obviously had considered carefully Lovett's unequalled contribution to the shaping of the university, and the statement on this occasion continued to highlight his unique role. "Never losing sight of the best academic tradition, he sought patiently and deliberately to adapt this precious heritage to the needs of this place and time." In its summarizing and concluding sentence, the board ended with a resolution "that we extend to Edgar Odell Lovett our unbounded thanks and gratitude for the execution of a great task boldly undertaken and faithfully performed in the fullness of his wisdom and loyalty."

But the trustees still depended upon Dr. Lovett for leadership and advice, especially regarding such a high-profile ceremonial occasion as the official inauguration of President Houston, which was scheduled for Thursday, April 10, 1947. The board on July 17, 1946, reported that it had received a letter from Houston suggesting the outlines of such an event to be held later that year or in the spring of the following year. The board then asked Lovett to present to them at their next meeting his suggestions for the program and a list of people who might be appointed to an inaugural committee to "assist him and the Board in planning and carrying out an inaugural celebration," which would be the first on the Rice campus, for there had been no formal inauguration of Lovett in 1908. The inaugural ceremony took place in the courtyard of the chemistry building, with an invitation-only dinner held the next night at the Rice Hotel. Lovett presided at the ceremonies, which began at 11:00 a.m. Following the singing by the choir of Trinity Episcopal Church of "Veni Creator Spiritus," which has been sung at every Rice commencement, and the invocation by Bishop A. Frank Smith of the Methodist Episcopal Church, Lovett opened the event with an eloquent "Address of Welcome," after which Karl Taylor Compton, president of the Massachusetts Institute of Technology, gave the morning's formal address. Then President Houston, after an introduction by Harry C. Wiess, gave brief remarks; and, just before Bishop Smith's benediction, the choir and the entire audience joined together in singing "America."

The assembly of faculty, university administrators, board members, distinguished guests, and delegates from other universities and learned societies adjourned afterward to the dining hall of the university, after which Lee A. DuBridge, president of the California Institute of Technology, presented an address. At the evening dinner the next night at the Rice Hotel there were addresses by Dr. Dixon Wecter of the Huntington Library, a brief welcome to the visitors by Jesse Jones, and informal closing remarks by Houston.

It was in total a grand occasion, the tone of which had been set by Lovett's opening remarks. Beginning with a quotation from England's poet laureate, John Masefield, "The days that make us happy make us wise," Lovett remarked that "By that criterion, the Rice Institute has waxed mightily in wisdom in these latter days. To this consummation many moving circumstances have contributed. Some of them, for example, are manifested in the courage, imagination, understanding, and resourcefulness of a new Board of Trustees, in the stature, vision, zeal, and leadership of the new President, and in the further exaltation of hope and joy induced by subsequent benefactions of immediate availability and most generous dimensions." That aura of optimism Lovett projected onto the audience and by extension onto the entire enterprise of the university.

One final major honor came to President emeritus Lovett that fall. On December 4, 1947, in a ceremony attended by all seven trustees who stood just to the left of the Sallyport on the east front of the administration building, the board formally renamed the ornate building (which had always been the architectural logo of the Rice Institute) Lovett Hall. The following inscription was incised into the marble:

> In grateful homage to the clear vision
> unfaltering zeal and beneficial labors of
> Edgar Odell Lovett
> First President of the Rice Institute

Beneath these words came, in Greek, "Exegit Monumentum Aere Perennius," which translates "He has built a monument more lasting than bronze." Almost ten years later, after Lovett had died, President

Houston recalled that when he had shown this proposed inscription
to Lovett, Lovett had replied "that it seemed quite appropriate since
he had always tried to build, in the Institute, a monument to William
Marsh Rice. That modesty was characteristic," Houston reminded his
listeners, "but I think we all agree that the Rice Institute is a monument, as well, to Edgar Odell Lovett, a monument which will outlive
the bricks and mortar."

Lifted from Dr. Lovett's shoulders now were the administrative
chores of the presidency, but he still came to his office nearly every day
to read and often to receive visits from the older faculty, now friends
of many years. On certain key occasions he was still asked to give remarks. No doubt Lovett was pleased in April 1947 to be able to give the
dedicatory address at the opening of Fondren Library, a signal event in
the history of the university. "A library is a great deal more than a
storehouse of marvels, ancient and modern. It is a powerhouse of ideas
and ideals." Lovett often quoted the past and drew from the past, but
his thinking was always addressed to the present and future. "Today
the library is still a habitation of the spirit of man and the home of his
soul." Never a materialist but always a man of religious conviction,
Lovett felt this needed to be said in the midst of the emerging Atomic
Age. "It is a house of hope because everyone has deep within him a desire for perfection, and deep in his heart the hope of attaining at least
some degree of it. That desire has moved men and women to devote la-
borious nights and days to the single-minded pursuit of knowledge." In
addition, "A library is a haven for the renewal of life and the recovery
of reality." The library is not an escape from this world but preparation
for engagement with it, and toward that end the library "is a house
of light . . . the white light of honesty and integrity . . . that searches
impartially all statements, both of fact and of theory." The library was
integral both to the life of the university and to the life of free men if
they would remain free.

The immediate post–World War II years were years of angst for
many Americans, worried about the longtime future of civilization, indeed mankind, in the age of the atomic bomb and increasing Cold War
tensions. On this matter too Lovett showed the serenity he had often
exemplified when dealing with the problems facing his beloved insti-

tute. Replying to a worried correspondent in March of 1948, Lovett wrote that "Whenever disturbed about the way the world may seem to be going, we have followed a simple rule. We count up the good people we know whom we would trust to the end of the world. And always we begin wondering and always we end up marveling how many they are." Lovett's words revealed much about his character and spiritual grounding in the seventh decade of his life.

> Thus time after time in troubled times we have recovered faith and equanimity, regained courage and resolution, renewed energy and diligence, and from the fine example of our friends we have recaptured some of their honesty and candor, something of their fidelity and hope, something of their sincerity and joy. But above and beyond all this, in these present days it is on the good men and women we have known, still here or gone before, that we base our belief in the survival of Christian civilization in an orderly and well ordered universe under the dispensations of divine Providence and the unconquerable mind of man.

This attitude had been a constant in his life. At another of those special occasions for which Lovett was called upon, the naming of a new residential hall on March 26, 1950, for Harry C. Wiess, who had died in August 1948, Lovett's words in tribute to Wiess could in truth have served wonderfully well for Lovett himself. On this occasion Lovett quoted "a great poet" to the effect that "'He is the happiest of men who can make the end of his life closely agree with the beginning.' That happiness was granted to Harry Carothers Wiess." And we could add, also to Edgar Odell Lovett.

For almost three decades Lovett had circumscribed his social life to the extent his administrative duties had allowed. He did not attend the dinner parties that played such an important role in the lives of most faculty. Although he began each day with breakfast, for decades he had skipped lunch and only occasionally had an afternoon coffee. Every evening he returned to his suite in the Plaza Hotel, sat by his wife's bed in his rocking chair, and, holding her hand tenderly, talked about the day's events. Later, as she ate her dinner from a bed tray, he dined with her on a little table placed beside her bed, always referring to her as "my dear." Afterward he usually read to her for a while. Still later he read for himself—biographies, memoirs, belles lettres, classical literature in translation, often finding illustrations he would use in his own addresses. Sitting at his worktable with his pen in his right hand, a cigar in the left—but he never smoked in Mrs. Lovett's room—he wrote letters and speeches in his tiny, neat script.

By now Mrs. Lovett's arthritis had not only locked her legs but bent her fingers toward her palms. Almost every evening her physician, Dr. Fred Lummis (now a member of the Rice board), stopped in to see her briefly on his way home on nearby Yoakum Boulevard. Her pain was such that she employed a small canopy to keep the weight of the bed covers from pressing on her, and her grandchildren, whom she loved dearly, were not allowed to get up on the bed with her because the resulting movement of her body was simply too painful. One grandchild recalls hearing her cry out in agony. But her grandchildren never remember her complaining. She stayed interested in events, read or was read to (grandchildren remembered, in addition to books, that she continued to enjoy the *Illustrated London News* and *Blackwood's Magazine*), and she and Dr. Lovett never lost their sense of humor together. She enjoyed giving the grandchildren books; every St. Patrick's Day she had Mrs. Kleinfelder decorate the apartment in green; and at Christmas she had put up a large paper sculpture of beautiful church, at the foot of which were a number of shoes—ranging in size from the smallest grandchild's to "Father Lovett's"—filled with nuts for the reindeer of St. Nicholas. She told the children that Santa Claus was just fine for the United States, but for England and Germany St. Nicholas was the bearer of gifts. Until the very end she was daily raised up to the side of the bed, had her hair fixed and otherwise made presentable, and was moved for a while to a comfortable chair in her adjoining sitting room. One of her granddaughters recalls poignantly that sometime during the Christmas holidays of 1951 "Mother Lovett" had said, with a sense of resignation and finality, "It's been so long, it's been oh so long." Two weeks later, on Monday morning, January 14, 1952, after a short stay at Hermann Hospital across the street from the university, Mary Ellen Hale Lovett died at the age of seventy-six. Her body lay in state until Wednesday at the home of her daughter, Adelaide (Mrs. Walter Browne Baker), at 3665 Willowick Road, after which she was interred at Glenwood Cemetery, Houston's park-like burial ground laid out on handsomely treed, rolling hills just north of Buffalo Bayou overlooking the city's growing skyline. Her honorary pallbearers were the "trustees emeritus, trustees and governors, the faculty and officers of all students organizations of Rice Institute." Ironically, most of the younger faculty and none of the students had ever seen Mrs. Lovett. Her movement had been drastically limited for more than two decades before her death. Dr. Lovett's reserved nature meant that most students had been unaware of her long illness.

One can hardly imagine how lonely Dr. Lovett must have been after her death. Multiple tragedies had brought them even closer together. His living space in the Plaza Hotel was consolidated: he gave up the bedroom on the northern exposure that had been Mrs. Lovett's, as well as her small sitting room and the apartment of her nurse, Mrs. Kleinfelder. Mrs. Kleinfelder, who had taken care of Mrs. Lovett for years, stayed in his employ to cook and care for him, but she now moved to a small apartment on the south side adjacent to Dr. Lovett's bedroom and sitting room with its large table-desk, at which he would sit to read or write letters and look out over the art museum and toward Hermann Park and the zoo. (To the end of her life Mrs. Kleinfelder was included in all family gatherings.) He was in his early eighties now, obviously slowed by age, though he continued to come to his office for several hours most days—a daughter-in-law brought him after first having taken her children to school. Those who climbed to his office would find him sitting at his desk, surrounded by books, willing to talk—while often fumbling to light his corncob pipe—about "his experiences with many leading personalities of the past and present, including President Wilson, General Pershing, President Lowell of Harvard, Angell of Yale, etc." Sometime in these last years he was contacted by a woman whom he had known more than sixty years before at Bethany College. According to Lovett's grandchildren, they had dated then but she had in the end rejected him because she did not think he would be successful. Many years later, reading about the death of his wife, this "Miss Ella," herself a widow, contacted Lovett and they began a telephone relationship in which these two elderly people, having shared a collegiate experience together more than six decades before, enjoyed talking together. Dr. Lovett even took his first airplane trip to journey to Florida to visit her briefly. Such December-December relationships are common in today's retirement home communities—especially among those who have enjoyed long, loving relationships with their original spouses—and they grow out of deep loneliness and a desire to connect once again with persons from similar generations. Nothing came of these long telephone conversations—she turned out to be bitter about her life choices when they met in Florida—but earlier the phone calls must have added some pleasure to long evenings alone in the suite at the Plaza Hotel that was filled with such powerful memories. Luckily he enjoyed playing solitaire all his life, from those many tiresome train trips to these final years at the Plaza.

Nothing could have gratified Dr. Lovett more than a letter he received in April 1954 from Harold W. Dodds, president of Princeton University. The letter informed Lovett that the board of trustees of Princeton had "by unanimous vote instructed" Dodds to invite Lovett to attend the 1954 commencement exercises in June to receive an honorary doctor of laws degree. Accompanied by his daughter and son-in-law, Mr. and Mrs. Walter Browne Baker, and his elder son, H. Malcolm Lovett, the family group arrived in the lovely university town together. Also receiving honorary degrees that overcast day in the courtyard of Nassau Hall were Governor (and presidential candidate) Adlai S. Stevenson and President Nathan M. Pusey of Harvard. The commendation reminded Dr. Lovett of his life journey from the storied grounds of Princeton to the educational frontier of Texas:

> Edgar Odell Lovett: First president of the Rice Institute. A pioneer educator. A Princeton professor who took an open space of Texas and turned it into a campus. He attracted a first-rate faculty and quickly brought the Rice Institute to the front rank of American universities. He made it proudly, and we hope, pardonably, Princetonian: in the classical tradition, dedicated to liberal arts and sciences, by the honor system, with integrity of architecture. Even Texans are not indignant that he is not indigenous. He has put Princeton deep in the heart of Texas.

The changes that had been promised by the board of trustees in the decade after World War II gradually came to pass. Lovett watched with gratification as the campus grew: first the library, which for the first time blocked the western horizon from Lovett's window view in the now Lovett Hall, quickly followed by an office building named Anderson Hall and an engineering building named Abercrombie Hall, along with a president's house and a new gymnasium called Autry Court. In 1950 came a magnificent, 72,000-seat football stadium. The graduate student population grew, tripling by 1950 and almost doubling again by the late 1950s, and even though the undergraduate population did not grow much, since fewer were now from Houston, the need for additional housing on campus became critical. The board of trustees, in considering how to meet the housing crisis, began to examine how other leading American universities arranged their undergraduate residential system, but the board made this inquiry with Lovett's 1912 invocation of the residential college system in mind. By 1954 a decision had been made, and shortly construction began on additional facilities to the original men's dormitories (and soon a generous grant from the Houston Endowment—based on funds originally given by Jesse Jones—allowed construction of Rice's first on-campus housing for women). This new residential construction followed the recommendations of a special faculty-student-alumni committee that had called at last for the creation of a series of five residential colleges at Rice, to be named after benefactors and former trustees: James A. Baker College, Will Rice College, Harry C. Hanszen College, Harry C. Wiess College, and Mary Gibbs Jones College—she was the wife of Jesse Jones—all of which opened to students in 1957. At that time a new student center was being completed, along with Hamman Hall with its auditorium, and two laboratories, the M. D. Anderson Biological Laboratories and the Keith-Wiess Geological Laboratories. By 1957 Edgar Odell Lovett could count more than a dozen major new buildings and the new or expanded facilities that allowed the creation of five residential colleges. Moreover, faculty numbers had doubled since the beginning of World War II. In his mid-eighties now, Lovett knew that his days were numbered, but he could take enormous pride in what had been accomplished. He could not know the very significant enhancement yet to come, though he might have imagined it based on the foundation established and the vision still held forth by his 1912 address, "The Meaning of the New Institution." His words on that occasion about there being "no upper limit to its educational endeavor" would be the foundational philosophy for the university for decades yet to come.

On July 31, 1957, Dr. Lovett suffered a small stroke and fell in his apartment at the Plaza Hotel. He was subsequently moved to Hermann Hospital; he was conscious, and visitors recall him lying flat on his back, eyes closed, but able to respond to questions and comments, with a slight pause before his answers. To his older son Dr. Lovett said that he sensed death coming, as though the sea was coming in over him. At 3:55 on the morning of Monday, August 13, Dr. Lovett died, apparently of complications from pneumonia, in the eighty-sixth year of his life. His body lay in state at the home of his daughter, Mrs. Walter Browne Baker, who had often served as his hostess at Rice events after the incapacitation of Mrs. Lovett, from Wednesday noon to the time of his funeral services at 10:00 a.m. on Thursday at Palmer Memorial Episcopal Church, across the street from the university. He was buried in Glenwood Cemetery beside his wife of almost fifty-five years. Once again they were together.

His death made the front pages of the Houston newspapers, and both the *Houston Post* and the *Houston Chronicle* printed warmly appreciative editorials. The *Houston Chronicle* remembered him as possessing a "soft voice and courtly manners" and called him a "prototype of the learned educator, yet he never lost the common touch." The *Houston Post* described him as "not a man to seek the limelight. He was innately shy, but he had a warm spirit, a great understanding of his fellow man, and a fine sense of humor." Both noted what a loss to the community his death meant. Because Dr. Lovett died during the summer months, Rice students and faculty made their response known later, after classes had started. The *Thresher* acknowledged his unparalleled contribution to the university, and a memorial service, with President Houston presiding, was held on Sunday, September 29, in what is now called the Kyle Morrow Room of Fondren Library. After an invocation by the Reverend Stanley Smith of Palmer Memorial Episcopal Church, who had officiated at Dr. Lovett's funeral, J. Newton Rayzor, an alumnus and trustee, read a resolution that the board of trustees had adopted just four days previously. This resolution, as one would expect, extolled Lovett's steadfast contribution to the Rice Institute, but it spoke most movingly of his personal qualities: "We shall always remember his personal charm, his fine sense of classical humor, his ability to meet those of lesser attainments with quieting ease, and his graciousness and pleasant words for all. He will forever remain in our memory a rare combination of the dignified scholar and superb gentleman." (Lovett in an address to the freshman class in 1942 had spoken to them of the virtues of kindliness. "I know of no investment that costs less and pays larger dividends than this quality of gentleness and courtesy," inadvertently describing two of his own essential characteristics.) The board then stated that as it continued to oversee the university, "let us hope and pray that this great citadel of learning, as Edgar Odell Lovett planned and dreamed, will always hold a position in the front rank and move onward and upward to higher ground, with the torch of genuine intellectual endeavor illuminating its path."

Following the board resolution, Judge Phil Peden presented a brief "Tribute from the Alumni." Peden like so many others remarked on Lovett's legendary dignity, but he also praised the way he "lived his full, rich life" and said that for so many students, the image of him walking to and from campus daily was "as indelibly etched in our minds as the outline of the Sallyport." Then Professor Tsanoff, who had joined the faculty in 1914 and been a close friend of Lovett's for more than forty years, gave a heartfelt "Tribute from the Faculty." Tsanoff too, although he acknowledged Lovett's academic training and his formative role in shaping the university, focused on what he called the "personal qualities of his character." Those who knew him only at the twilight of his life had no firsthand acquaintance with the luminosity of spirit and charisma that, in the opening years of the university, allowed Lovett to persuade scholars to cast their lot with him in his adventurous educational experiment on the Texas prairie, and it was the nature of that early Lovett that Tsanoff recalled. Above all, there was a steadiness about his personality that made him enormously effective as a university administrator.

> He was deliberate in reaching conclusions, and was particularly reluctant to form an unfavorable judgment of another person, be he professor or student. He resisted impetuous action and could not be moved easily by an emotional appeal. But his mind recognized the imperative power of sound reasoning, and he would change his view or decision if good evidence or logic demanded it. To his occasional acquaintances Dr. Lovett sometimes appeared serious-minded, and we do not recall

any frivolous lapses in his manner. But he had a real sense of humor, to which he would give apt expression at a suitable time.

And perhaps most of all, Lovett "had a sort of timeless contemplation of Rice." As President Houston implied in his concluding remarks, just before Reverend Smith pronounced the benediction, the Rice Institute and Lovett were synonymous. Today, a half century after his death, his name is still revered on campus. The primary administration building bears his name, as does a residential college, and there is a professorship in mathematics in his honor. His words are quoted constantly by anyone advocating enhancement of the university. In spirit and in memory, Edgar Odell Lovett is still the shaping influence on the university he did more than anyone else to create and present to posterity.

# ACKNOWLEDGMENTS

So many people have helped me over the years that I hardly know where to begin, and since this book for more than a decade simmered on the back burner while more urgent projects demanded my attention, many who assisted me probably despaired of ever seeing a finished product. The amazingly competent staff of the *Journal of Southern History* have always facilitated everything I do, so I must begin by thanking such present and former staff members as Evelyn Thomas Nolen, Patricia Dunn Burgess, Julia Shivers, Patricia Bellis Bixel, Scott Marler, Bethany L. Johnson, Randal L. Hall, and a long list of part-time editors and graduate assistants simply too numerous to mention. My colleagues in the history department have made Rice a very congenial environment, and three deans of humanities, Allen Matusow, Judith Brown, and Gale Stokes, fully supported my research and writing over the years. Every historian owes an immense debt of gratitude to a lengthening list of archivists and librarians. Fondren Library has always been a most helpful, researcher-friendly institution, and I appreciate the attention and competence of its reference, interlibrary loan, and acquisitions staff. The succession of skilled archivists in Fondren's Woodson Research Center, which houses the archives, manuscripts, and rare books, have without exception been marvelously helpful, going out of their way to accommodate my needs and answer my questions. Nancy Boothe, Kinga Perzynska, and Lee Pecht as successive heads of special collections have been invaluable to me, as have other staff members such as Joan Ferry, Philip Montgomery, Amanda York Focke, and Lisa Moellering.

Jeanne Cobb as the head of archives and special collections, T. W. Phillips Memorial Library, Bethany College, did everything possible to make my research there fruitful, as did Ben Primer of the Firestone Library at Princeton University and Daniel J. Linke of the Seeley G. Mudd

Manuscript Library at Princeton. David and Carol Brown were wonderful hosts in Princeton. Lynn Niedermeier of the university archives at Western Kentucky University in Bowling Green helped me track down information about West Kentucky College. Anja Becker of the University of Leipzig generously shared her research on Edgar Odell Lovett and other American students at Leipzig with me, and Christin Rettke of the University of Leipzig proved to be a most resourceful research assistant. Thanks also to Professor Hartmut Keil at the University of Leipzig for making my stay in Leipzig so pleasant and productive. Robert and Kathy Moore also did much to help my wife and me adjust to life in Leipzig. Tim Noakes of Special Collections, Alderman Library, at the University of Virginia uncovered Lovett's academic record for me. Vesta Lee Gordon was indispensable as a research assistant in the Alderman Library special collections, helping me once again as she had almost forty years ago when I was a graduate student at Virginia.

Kate Kirkland shared information with me concerning Mike Hogg, the University of Texas, and Lovett. Matthew Penney's seminar paper on how World War II impacted the Rice Institute proved helpful, as indeed did his dissertation. Thomas R. Williams has helped me understand Lovett's astronomical education. Albert Van Helden translated from Dutch the book chapter written by Hugo de Vries describing his participation in Rice's opening ceremonies. James M. Lomax, M.D., has helped me to understand Mary Hale Lovett's illness and how it possibly affected both Dr. Lovett and their son Lawrence Alexander Lovett. Informal conversations over many years with many persons in the Rice community have informed my view of both Dr. Lovett and the early days of the Rice Institute. I hesitate to mention some names in fear that I will leave out others, but the following have been unusually helpful: Ed Oppenheimer, Helen Saba Worden, Bridget and Al Jensen, Catherine C. Hannah, S. W. Higginbotham, and Ray Watkin Hoagland Strange. Others have helped by reading the manuscript or otherwise sharing their knowledge of educational history. Melissa F. Kean very carefully read the book at every stage of its preparation, and I also value the readings and suggestions offered by Nancy Boles, Joseph W. Cox, Michele Gillespie, Randal L. Hall, James M. Lomax, Ipek Martinez, Clarence Mohr, and George Rupp. Conversations with

George Rupp, Malcolm Gillis, and David Leebron, successive presidents of Rice University, have helped me understand something of the life of a university president.

It has been a pleasure to work with the staff of LSU Press, from Alisa A. Plant, with whom I first discussed the project, to Lee Campbell Sioles, the managing editor, who has guided the manuscript along, to copyeditor Maria E. denBoer, designer Tammi L. deGeneres, and indexer Linda Webster. All in all, the folks at LSU Press have made what can be a tedious and frustrating project as pleasant as possible.

Friends and associates in the Rice Historical Society, especially its founder, Karen Rogers, have collectively taught me much about the university's history and given me a ready audience upon whom to try out my ideas. The Lovett family, by preserving Dr. and Mrs. Lovett's personal papers and giving me untrammeled access to them, by generously discussing their memories with me, and by allowing me total freedom of expression, made this biography possible.

# NOTE ON SOURCES

SINCE I MATRICULATED AS AN UNDERGRADUATE at Rice University in 1961, I have been interested in the history of the institution and in its founding president. Over the decades I have read and collected materials, discussed the university's early days with older alums, and given many lectures on the topic as well as taught two special undergraduate seminars on the history of the university. Over a decade ago I began to focus somewhat more exclusively on a biographical study of Edgar Odell Lovett, the result of which is the present volume. Because I hope to reach a general audience, particularly alumni and friends of the university, and did not want to burden the text with the inordinate number of footnotes that would have been required to reflect accurately the research behind many statements and characterizations, I chose—I trust not foolishly—to forgo footnotes entirely and let this note on sources and the bibliography indicate the evidence on which my work is based. But I do intend that the book also be useful to a scholarly audience, so I have consciously discussed Lovett and the university he shaped in the larger context of the history of American higher education. I will suggest in what follows some of the readings that helped me understand the history of Rice more broadly. I hope that the story I tell is illuminating to all those interested in educational history, and I believe that the importance of what Lovett attempted and accomplished is best comprehended by placing him in this national context.

I have interviewed a range of persons who I thought could provide different perspectives on Lovett and the university. Isaac Sanders, for example, came to Rice as a student in 1912 and subsequently helped Lovett prepare for publication the three volumes commemorating the opening; I interviewed Sanders in 1991 when he was a hundred years old. H. Malcolm Lovett was President Lovett's son, who obviously had valuable material to relate. In addition, I interviewed five of Lovett's grandchildren. Others interviewed include faculty who served under him and students who came to know him in a variety of ways. Each person interviewed understood that I was working on a biography, and I explained to each that I would not quote any of them verbatim. Except for a formal videotaped interview with H. Malcolm Lovett, I did not record these interviews. Rather, I took detailed notes, and I have not used material from any one interview (except for minute details) unless I had other interviews or other kinds of sources to back it up. For example, in reconstructing how Dr. and Mrs. Lovett lived in their apartment in the Plaza Hotel, I have developed a composite portrait based on extensive interviews with five living grandchildren. And my interviews with former faculty and students were used to help understand campus attitudes toward Dr. Lovett and the sense of what faculty/student life was like at the time. In addition to the formal interviews listed in the bibliography, I have informally discussed these topics with dozens of alumni and early faculty over the past several decades.

I have also read every issue of the student newspaper, the *Thresher,* and every edition of the yearbook, the *Campanile,* as well as more ephemeral publications, such as the humor magazine, the *Rice Owl.* While I was looking specifically for references to Lovett, I was simultaneously learning everything I could about every aspect of the history of the university. And of course I had recourse to the annual Rice catalogues, various pamphlets, and the newspaper files of the *Houston Post* and *Houston Chronicle.* To help recover the educational experiences of Lovett, I made extensive use of the archives and other resources of Bethany College, the University of Virginia, and the University of Leipzig. At Bethany College, for example, I was able to examine the college catalogues to study the curriculum Lovett followed, I read about him in the college literary magazine and therein read several of his addresses, including his address as class valedictorian, and the archives had a range of printed materials that helped me understand the history of the college as it existed then. Similarly, I read books on the history of the University of Virginia, used the university catalogue and archives to determine which courses Lovett took, and found several letters from Lovett to one of his professors, Ormond Stone, that described some of his experiences in Germany (Papers of Ormond Stone, MSS 100,

Special Collections, University of Virginia Library). The archives of the University of Leipzig do not contain any correspondence from Lovett, but they allowed me to see what courses he took, his grades, and the written comments of his professors and to determine where he lived each semester. A range of books in the library there revealed what the city was like in the 1890s, and simply walking around the city—as I did Bethany, West Virginia, and Charlottesville—provided insight.

The Seeley G. Mudd Manuscript Library at Princeton University contains the records of that university, and there are scattered references to Lovett in the faculty minutes, the minutes of the school of science faculty, and the minutes of the trustees (I quote two excerpts from the minutes of the trustees, volume 8, March 10, 1898, and June 13, 1898). The Mudd Library also contains runs of the alumni magazine, the university catalogues, and other such printed material, and these items assisted me in discovering what Lovett taught, where he lived, and the range of his duties as an active faculty member. The Firestone Library at Princeton has on microfilm a complete run of the student newspaper, the *Daily Princetonian*. Random correspondence was found in two other repositories: several letters (March 17, 1913; November 19, 1913; and November 11, 1916) from the first professor of physics at Rice, H. A. Wilson, are located in the papers of the eminent physicist Owen W. Richardson at the Harry Ransom Humanities Research Center at the University of Texas; and there is one letter from Lovett to Leipzig chemist Wilhelm Ostwald regarding his proposed lecture at the Rice opening that appears in the Ostwald Correspondence at the Berlin-Brandenburg Academy of Sciences.

The overwhelming majority of quotations from archival sources are based on research in the Woodson Research Center (WRC) of Rice University. The papers consulted are listed in the bibliography. Many of the collections utilized reveal by their name why they were useful—for example, the records of the Houston Philosophical Society or the papers of various faculty or board members. Several of the collections, however, were extraordinarily useful. I was allowed complete access to the minutes of the Rice board of trustees from 1891 to 1957, and these include detailed discussions of budget, faculty hires, and key decisions in the life of the university. The minutes of the faculty, 1914–1957, while interesting, proved not to be as useful as I had imagined, in part because the issues discussed were often covered in the board minutes, the various papers of Lovett himself, the issues of the *Thresher,* and so on. Of extraordinary value were the voluminous papers of Lovett and his family.

The Lovett papers are arranged in three separate collections. The President Edgar Odell Lovett Papers, 1912–1945, contain thousands of items—letters, memorandums, notes, and the like—that reflect the official presidential duties of Lovett, with the papers actually beginning in 1907, when he was first contacted by Rice officials. These sixty-two boxes of materials contain official correspondence, Lovett speeches, material relating to all the departments, and detailed information on the round-the-world trip and the opening ceremonies—this collection of official papers is remarkably complete. The President Edgar Odell Lovett Personal Papers, 1871–1957, sixteen boxes, contain extensive correspondence regarding practically every aspect of his life, from his education to his early days at Princeton to communications with other scholars and academicians on a number of subjects. Here are receipts, notes, mathematical papers, a copy of his Leipzig dissertation, notes on various projects (like a proposed observatory for Princeton in the southern hemisphere), and personal correspondence with hundreds of persons. There are also copies of speeches and papers given by Lovett in several capacities. I found of particular use the Edgar Odell Lovett and Mary Ellen Hale Lovett Family Papers, 1849–1979, which were recently deposited in the library. These sixty-three boxes contain an amazing range of materials—the Lovetts seemed to keep everything— and they are indispensable for every aspect of the Lovett's personal life, especially the wonderful correspondence between Dr. and Mrs. Lovett, material from their trip around the world including photographs and postcards, scrapbooks, honorary degrees—just an amazing range of materials. There are varying restrictions on the several Lovett papers; permission to publish material from them must be obtained from the Woodson Research Center, and permission to research the family papers has to be obtained in advance. There are also close restrictions on the Baker Family Papers and the Board of Trustees Minutes; for this last collection, written permission from the board must be obtained.

Rice officials and the Lovett family have accorded me complete free-dom to read and use these papers without restraint of any kind. With-out the extraordinary generosity and trust of both these university offi-cials and the Lovett family, this project could not have been completed. There are detailed descriptions of the three Lovett collections online, accessible through the WRC of Fondren Library, and any interested scholar should consult these guides carefully before going to the WRC. Most of the Lovett correspondence comes from these three collections unless I indicate in the text that a letter came from another source—for example, Lovett's annual welcoming letter published in the *Thresher*.

There is an extensive bibliography on the history of higher education. I have found the following general works most useful: Roger L. Geiger, *To Advance Knowledge: The Growth of American Research Universi-ties, 1900–1940* (1986), Frederick Rudolf, *The American College and University: A History* (1990), Laurence R. Veysey, *The Emergence of the American University* (1965), and especially John R. Thelin, *A His-tory of American Higher Education* (2004). For a broader context, see Willis Rudy, *The Universities of Europe, 1100–1914* (1994). The bibli-ography lists books and articles of a more specialized nature.

Background information on Lovett's education at Bethany, Virginia, and Leipzig is provided by William Kirk Woolery, *Bethany Years: The History of Old Bethany from Her Founding Years through a Cen-tury of Trial and Triumph* (1941), Philip Alexander Bruce, *History of the University of Virginia, 1819–1919* (5 vols., 1920–1922), and Anja Becker, "For the Sake of Old Leipzig Days: Academic Networks of American Students at a German University, 1781–1914" (2006). For the early history of the Rice Institute, see Andrew Forest Muir, *Wil-liam Marsh Rice and His Institute: A Biographical Study,* edited by Sylvia Stallings Morris (1972), and Fredericka Meiners, *A History of Rice University: The Institute Years, 1907–1963* (1982). For Princeton as Lovett found it, see Don Oberdofer, *Princeton University: The First 250 Years* (1995) and James Axtell, *The Making of Princeton: From Woodrow Wilson to the Present* (2006). Woodrow Wilson's formative role at Princeton I found very usefully described in both Arthur W. Link's *Wilson: The Road to the White House* (1947) and Arthur Wal-worth, *Woodrow Wilson* (1958).

The great majority of information for the bulk of the book comes from the archives of Rice University and relevant printed university materials. When important to place events at Rice in a larger national context—for example, the Great Depression and World War II—I have obviously used a wide range of standard sources. Less well known might be such books as Carol S. Gruber's *Mars and Minerva: World War I and the Uses of the Higher Learning in America* (1975) and Robert K. Murray's *Red Scare: A Study in National Hysteria, 1919–1920* (1955). For several issues I found helpful background information in Richard Hofstadter and Walter P. Metzger, *The Development of Academic Freedom in the United States* (1955). Three model histories of southern universities helped me understand something of the regional situation the Rice Institute found itself in: Paul K. Conkin, *Gone With the Ivy: A Biography of Vanderbilt University* (1985), Thomas G. Dyer, *The University of Georgia: A Bicentennial History, 1785–1985* (1985), and Clarence L. Mohr and Joseph E. Gordon, *Tulane: The Emergence of a Modern University, 1945–1980* (2001). Edgar Odell Lovett's 1912 opening address that so articulated his vision of the university, "The Meaning of the New Institution," was first printed in the *Rice Institute Pamphlet* for April 1915, though it has been reprinted. However, the chief evidentiary basis of this academic biography is the correspondence and addresses of Lovett found in rich profusion in the WRC.

# BIBLIOGRAPHY

## INTERVIEWS

Baker, Lovett
Brown, Katherine Tsanoff
Chapman, Alan
Drew, Katherine Fischer
Heaps, Neal B. and Billye C.
Hudspeth, C. M. (Hank) and Demeris
Lovett, Edgar Odell, II
Lovett, H. Malcolm
Lovett, Malcolm
McLean, Mary Hale
Pfeiffer, Paul
Randall, Eliza Lovett
Sanders, Isaac
Wischmeyer, Carl Riehl

## ARCHIVES

*Berlin-Brandenburg Academy of Sciences*
Wilhelm Ostwald Correspondence

*Bethany College Archives:*
Miscellaneous records

*Princeton University Library, Seeley G. Mudd Manuscript Library*
Faculty Minutes
Minutes of the School of Science Faculty
Minutes of the Trustees of Princeton

*Rice University, Fondren Library, Woodson Research Center*
Baker Family Papers
Captain James A. Baker Family Papers

Thomas Lindsey Blayney Papers
Floyd Seyward Lear Papers
Edwin L. Lunn Diary
Houston Philosophical Society Records
Julian Sorell Huxley Papers
Juliette Huxley Papers
President Edgar Odell Lovett Papers, 1912–1945
President Edgar Odell Lovett Personal Papers, 1871–1957
Edgar Odell Lovett and Mary Ellen Hale Lovett Family Papers, 1849–1979
W. M. Rice Institute Papers
Rice University Board of Trustees Minutes, 1891–1957
Rice University Faculty Meeting Minutes, 1914–1957
E. V. Stevenson Letter
William Ward Watkin Papers
George C. Wheeler Correspondence, Scrapbook, . . . 1915–1957
George G. Williams Papers
Harold A. Wilson Papers

*University of Leipzig*
Miscellaneous records

*University of Texas, Harry Ransom Humanities Research Center*
Owen W. Richardson Collection

*University of Virginia Library, Special Collections*
Papers of Ormond Stone


ARTICLES AND BOOKS
Axtell, James. *The Making of Princeton: From Woodrow Wilson to the Present.* Princeton, 2006.
Becker, Anja. "How Daring She Was! The 'Female American Colony' at Leipzig University, 1877–1914." In Anke Ortlepp and Christoph Ribbat, eds., *Taking Up Space: New Approaches to American History.* Trier, 2004.
———. "US-American Students in Leipzig and Their Struggle with the German Tongue, 1827 to 1909." In Hartmut Keil, ed., *Transatlantic Cultural Contexts: Essays in Honor of Eberhard Brüning.* Tübingen, 2005.

————. "For the Sake of Old Leipzig Days: Academic Networks of American Students at a German University, 1781–1914." Ph.D. dissertation, University of Leipzig, 2006.

Beckert, Herbert, and Horst Schumann, eds. *100 Jahre Mathematisches Seminar der Karl-Marx-Universität at Leipzig*. Berlin, 1981.

Biehn, Kirsten Jacobson. "Improving Mankind: Philanthropic Foundations and the Development of American University Research Between the World Wars." Ph.D. dissertation, Rice University, 2006.

Billings, Theo M. "The Museum of Fine Arts, Houston: A Social History." Ph.D. dissertation, University of Houston, 1994.

Blecher, Jens. "Vom Promotionsprivleg zum Promotionsrecht: Das Leipziger Promotionsrecht Zwischen 1409 und 1945 als konstitutives und prägendes Element der akademischen Selbstverwaltung." Ph.D. dissertation, Martin-Luther-Universität Halle-Wittenberg, 2006.

Bledstein, Burton J. *The Culture of Professionalism: The Middle Class and the Development of Higher Education in America*. New York, 1976.

Boles, John B. *A University So Conceived: A Brief History of Rice*. Houston, 1991; 3rd ed., 2006.

————, ed. *Edgar Odell Lovett and the Creation of Rice University*. Houston, 2000.

Bruce, Philip Alexander. *History of the University of Virginia, 1819–1919: The Lengthened Shadow of One Man*. 5 vols. New York, 1920–1922.

Carlson, Elof Axel. *Genes, Radiation, and Society: The Life and Work of H. J. Muller*. Ithaca, 1981.

Conkin, Paul K. *Gone With the Ivy: A Biography of Vanderbilt University*. Knoxville, 1985.

Cram, Ralph Adams. *My Life in Architecture*. Boston, 1936.

Cutlip, Scott M. *Fund Raising in the United States: Its Role in America's Philanthropy*. New Brunswick, NJ, 1965.

Dennis, Michael. "Reforming the 'Academical Village': Edwin A. Alderman and the University of Virginia, 1904–1915." *Virginia Magazine of History and Biography* 105 (Winter 1997): 53–86.

————. *Lessons in Progress: State Universities and Progressivism in the New South, 1880–1920*. Urbana and Chicago, 2001.

DeVorkin, David H. *Henry Norris Russell, Dean of American Astronomers*. Princeton, 2000.

Dyer, Thomas G. "Higher Education in the South Since the Civil War: Historiographical Issues and Trends." In Walter J. Fraser, Jr., R. Frank Saunders, Jr., and Jon L. Wakelyn, eds., *The Web of Southern Social Relations: Women, Family, and Education*. Athens, Ga., 1985. Pp. 127–145.

———. *The University of Georgia: A Bicentennial History, 1785–1985*. Athens, Ga., 1985.

Fox, Stephen. *The General Plan of the William M. Rice Institute and Its Architectural Development*. Houston, 1980.

———. *The Museum of Fine Arts, Houston: An Architectural History, 1924–1986*. Houston, 1992.

———. *Rice University: An Architectural Tour*. New York, 2001.

Freeman, J. H. *The People of Baker Botts*. Houston, 1992.

Fritzsche, Bernd. "Sophus Lie: A Sketch of his Life and Work." *Journal of Lie Theory* 9 (1999): 1–25.

Frost, Dan R. *Thinking Confederates: Academia and the Idea of Progress in the New South*. Knoxville, 2000.

Geiger, Roger L. "After the Emergence: Voluntary Support and the Building of American Research Universities." *History of Education Quarterly* 25 (1985): 369–381.

———. *To Advance Knowledge: The Growth of American Research Universities, 1900–1940*. New York, 1986.

Goodenow, Ronald K., and Arthur O. White, eds. *Education and the Rise of the New South*. Boston, 1981.

Gordon, Lynn D. *Gender and Higher Education in the Progressive Era*. New Haven, 1990.

Gould, Lewis L. "The University [of Texas] Becomes Politicized: The War with Jim Ferguson, 1915–1919." *Southwestern Historical Quarterly* 86 (October 1982): 255–276.

Gruber, Carol S. *Mars and Minerva: World War I and the Uses of the Higher Learning in America*. Baton Rouge, 1975.

Hall, Randal L. *William Louis Poteat: A Leader of the Progressive-Era South*. Lexington, Ky., 2000.

Haskins, Charles Homer. *The Rise of Universities*. New York, 1923.

Hofstadter, Richard, and Walter P. Metzger. *The Development of Academic Freedom in the United States*. New York, 1955.

Horowitz, Helen Lefkowitz. *Campus Life: Undergraduate Cultures from the End of the Eighteenth Century to the Present*. New York, 1987.

Huxley, Julian. *Memories*. 2 vols. London, 1970, 1973.

———. "Texas and Academe." *Cornhill Magazine* 45 (July 1918): 53–65.

Hyman, Harold. "William Marsh Rice's Credit Ratings, 1846–1866." *Houston Review* 6 (1984): 91–96.

Johnson, Clyde Sanfred. *Fraternities in Our Colleges*. New York, 1972.

Kean, Melissa Fitzpatrick. " 'At a Most Uncomfortable Speed': The Desegregation of the South's Private Universities, 1945–1964." Ph.D. dissertation, Rice University, 2000.

Kirkland, Kate Sayen. "Envisioning a Progressive City: Hogg Family Philanthropy and the Urban Ideal in Houston, Texas, 1910–1975." Ph.D. dissertation, Rice University, 2004.

Leslie, W. Bruce. *Gentlemen and Scholars: College and Community in the "Age of the University," 1865–1917*. Pennsylvania State University, 1992.

Levine, David O. *The American College and the Culture of Aspiration, 1915–1940*. Ithaca, 1986.

Link, Arthur S. *Wilson: The Road to the White House*. Princeton, 1947.

———, et al., eds. *The Papers of Woodrow Wilson*. 69 vols. Princeton, 1966–1994.

Lipartito, Kenneth, and Joseph Pratt. *Baker & Botts in the Development of Modern Houston*. Austin, 1991.

Lovett, Edgar Odell. "The Meaning of the New Institution." *Rice Institute Pamphlet* (April 1915), 45–132. (It also appeared in *The Book of the Opening of the Rice Institute*, 3 vols. [Houston, 1915], I, pp. 132–219.) Reprinted in Boles, ed., *Edgar Odell Lovett and the Creation of Rice University*, pp. 52–136.

MacIver, Robert M. *Academic Freedom in Our Time*. New York, 1955.

McCandless, Amy Thompson. *The Past in the Present: Women's Higher Education in the Twentieth-Century American South*. Tuscaloosa, 1999.

Meiners, Fredericka. *A History of Rice University: The Institute Years, 1907–1963*. Houston, 1982.

*Memorial Book of the Sesquicentennial Celebration of the Founding of the College of New Jersey and of the Ceremonies Inaugurating Princeton University*. New York, 1898.

Mims, Edwin. *Chancellor Kirkland of Vanderbilt*. Nashville, 1940.

Mohr, Clarence L., and Joseph E. Gordon. *Tulane: The Emergence of a Modern University, 1945–1980*. Baton Rouge, 2001.

Morrey, Charles B. "Griffith Conrad Evans: May 11, 1887–December 8, 1973." *National Academy of Sciences, Biographical Memoirs*. Washington, D.C., 1983. Vol. 54, pp. 127–155.

Murray, Robert K. *Red Scare: A Study in National Hysteria, 1919–1920.* Minneapolis, 1955.

Nelson, Adam R. "The Emergence of the American University: An International Perspective." *History of Education Quarterly* 45 (Fall 2005): 427–438.

Nevins, Allan. "The (Happy?) Relations of Public and Private Universities." In S. W. Higginbotham, ed., *Man, Science, Learning and Education.* Chicago, 1963. Pp. 149–159.

Nicholson, Patrick J. *William Ward Watkin and the Rice Institute.* Houston, 1991.

Oberdorfer, Don. *Princeton University: The First 250 Years.* Princeton, 1995.

Oleson, Alexandra, and John Voss, eds. *The Organization of Knowledge in Modern America, 1860–1920.* Baltimore, 1979.

Parshall, Karen Hunger, and David E. Rowe. *The Emergence of the American Mathematical Research Community, 1876–1900: J. J. Sylvester, Felix Klein, and E. H. Moore.* Princeton and London, 1991.

Penney, Matthew T. "'Instruments of National Purpose': World War II and Southern Higher Education: Four Texas Universities as a Case Study." Ph.D. dissertation, Rice University, 2007.

Reuben, Julie A. *The Making of the Modern University: Intellectual Transformation and the Marginalization of Morality.* Chicago, 1996.

Rhinehart, Raymond P. *Princeton University: An Architectural Tour.* New York, 1999.

Rice Historical Society, *Cornerstone,* 1995– .

*Rice Institute Announcements,* 1912–1948.

*Rice Institute Pamphlet,* vols. 1–47 (1915–1972).

*Rice Owl,* 1922–1946.

*Rice Thresher,* 1916–1947.

Rider, Robin. "An Opportune Time: Griffith C. Evans and Mathematics at Berkeley." In Peter Duran et al., eds., *A Century of Mathematics in America—Part II.* Providence, 1989. Pp. 283–302.

Rudolph, Frederick. *The American College and University: A History.* Introductory essay and supplemental bibliography by John R. Thelin. Athens, Ga., 1990.

Rudy, Willis. *The Universities of Europe, 1100–1914.* Rutherford, NJ, 1984.

Shand-Tucci, Douglass. *Ralph Adams Cram. An Architect's Four Quests: Medieval, Modernist, American, Ecumenical.* Amherst and Boston, 2005.

Slosson, Edwin E. *Great American Universities.* New York, 1910.

Steffens, Lincoln. *The Autobiography of Lincoln Steffens.* New York, 1931.

Storp, Richard J. *The Beginnings of Graduate Education in America.* Chicago, 1953.

[Strom, Steven]. "Cotton and Profits Across the Border: William Marsh Rice in Mexico, 1863–1865." *Houston Review* 8 (1986): 89–96.

Stubhaug, Arild. *The Mathematician Sophus Lie: It Was the Audacity of My Thinking.* Trans. from the Norwegian by Richard H. Daly. Berlin, Heidelberg, and New York, 2002.

Thelin, John R. *Games Colleges Play: Scandal and Reform in Intercollegiate Athletics.* Baltimore and London, 1994.

———. *A History of American Higher Education.* Baltimore and London, 2004.

Tucci, Douglass Shand. *Ralph Adams Cram: American Medievalist.* Boston, 1975.

Veysey, Laurence R. *The Emergence of the American University.* Chicago, 1965.

Walworth, Arthur. *Woodrow Wilson.* New York, 1958.

Watterson, John Sayle. *College Football: History, Spectacle, Controversy.* Baltimore, 2000.

Woolery, William Kirk. *Bethany Years: The History of Old Bethany from her Founding Years through a Century of Trial and Triumph.* Huntington, WV, 1941.

# INDEX